Warp Speed, Time Travel, Big Data, and More

About the Authors

Paul C. Zikopoulos, B.A., M.B.A., is the Director of Technical Professionals for IBM Software Group's Information Management division and additionally leads the World Wide Competitive Database and Big Data SWAT teams. Paul is an award-winning writer and speaker with more than 18 years of experience in Information Management. Paul has written more than 350 magazine articles and 15 books, including *Understanding Big Data: Analytics for Enterprise Class Hadoop and Streaming Data, DB2 pureScale: Risk Free Agile Scaling, Break Free with DB2 9.7: A Tour of Cost Features, DB2 Fundamentals Certification for Dummies, DB2 for Dummies*, among others. Paul is a DB2 Certified Advanced Technical Expert (DRDA and Clusters) and a DB2 Certified Solutions Expert (BI and DBA). In his spare time, he enjoys all sorts of sporting activities, including running with his dog, Chachi; avoiding punches in his MMA training; and trying to figure out the world according to Chloë, his daughter. You can reach him at: paulz_ibm@msn.com or follow him on Twitter @BigData_paulz.

George Baklarz, B. Math, M. Sc., Ph.D. Eng., has spent 28 years in IBM working on various aspects of database technology. From 1987 to 1991, he worked on SQL/DS as part of the product planning department, system test team, performance team, and application development group. In 1991, George was part of the team that helped moved the OS/2 ES database to Toronto to become part of the DB2 distributed family of products. Since that time, he has worked on vendor enablement, competitive analysis, product marketing, product planning, and technical sales support. George has a Doctorate in Computer Engineering (which took him only 15 years to get; the Engineering faculty didn't like the fact that he worked at IBM and believed that part-time students would never finish their degree if they had to work for a living). George is now the Program Director for DB2 Competitive Sales.

Matt Huras, B.A. Sc. (Comp. Eng.), M. Eng., is an IBM Distinguished Engineer and senior architect for DB2 on Linux, UNIX, and Windows. He focuses on the database kernel, which includes data management, index management, locking, concurrency, and other protocols. Matt has been with IBM for more than 25 years, and has a Bachelor of Applied Science from the University of

Waterloo, as well as a Masters of Engineering from the University of Toronto. Matt's most recent project at IBM was DB2 pureScale, a technology that is focused on delivering new levels of scalability and availability to distributed platforms.

Matthias Nicola, M. Sc., Ph.D. (Comp. Sci.), is a Senior Technical Staff Member for DB2 at IBM's Silicon Valley Research and Development lab. His focus is on XML, temporal data management, in-database analytics, performance and benchmarking, and emerging DB2 technologies. Matthias has published more than 45 articles on various database management topics, as well as a number of books. He's also a frequent speaker at DB2 conferences worldwide. Prior to joining IBM, Matthias worked on data warehousing at Informix.

Walid Rjaibi, B. Sc., M. Sc. (Comp. Sci.), CISSP, is an IBM Senior Technical Staff Member and a member of IBM's Security Architecture Board Steering Committee. He is the Chief Security Architect for DB2 for Linux, UNIX, and Windows, and he has direct technical and management oversight over its security architecture (identification, authentication, authorization, access control, auditing, and encryption), as well as design, development, and Common Criteria certification. Prior to his current role, Walid was a research staff member at the IBM Zurich Research Lab in Switzerland, where he established and led a new research program focused on database security and privacy; his research results from this tenure were the foundation for key security enhancements in DB2 on distributed platforms, for which he led the development efforts upon his return to the Toronto development lab. Some of Walid's key database security achievements include leading the research and development of label-based access control, role-based access control, trusted contexts, separation of duties, and fine-grained access control. His work has resulted in more than 20 patents and several publications in the proceedings of leading scientific conferences.

Dale McInnis, B.Sc., M. Eng., is a Senior Technical Staff Member at the IBM Toronto lab. He has a B.Sc. (Comp. Sci.) from the University of New Brunswick and a Masters of Engineering from the University of Toronto. Dale joined IBM in 1988 and has been working on the DB2 development team since 1992.

Dale's area of expertise includes DB2 for Linux, UNIX, and Windows kernel development, where he led teams that designed the current backup and recovery architecture and other key high availability and disaster recovery technologies. Dale is a popular speaker at the International DB2 Users Group (IDUG) conferences worldwide, as well as DB2 Regional user groups and IBM's Information On Demand (IOD) conference. His expertise in the DB2 availability area is well known in the Information Technology industry. Dale currently fills the role of DB2 Availability Architect at the IBM Toronto lab.

Leon Katsnelson, B. Sc., is an international award-winning speaker and the current Program Director for Big Data and Cloud. His primary responsibility is the enablement of the IBM Information Management portfolio on the Cloud. Working closely with industry-leading Cloud providers and development, Leon and his team help to ensure that IBM customers succeed with IBM products on the Cloud. Leon spent 19 years in DB2 development, working on application development and communication solutions, and is often referred to as the "Father of DB2 Connect" for his leading role in the creation and management of this very popular product.

BigDataUniversity.com is the brainchild of Leon's team. With more than 17,000 registered users in its first year of operation alone, this vendor-independent education portal helps people around the world to acquire database skills and Big Data technologies with its free "at your pace, at your place" resource center. Leon also led the team that launched DB2 Express-C, a free version of the IBM DB2 database, and he is the founder of the Toronto Hadoop Users Group (http://TorontoHUG.com). Leon is an author, prolific blogger (http://BigDataOnCloud.com), and an active participant in all facets of social media. He prefers to communicate in bursts of 140 characters on Twitter: @katsnelson.

Roman B. Melnyk (Technical Editor), B.A., M.A., Ph.D., is a senior member of the DB2 Information Development team. During more than 17 years at IBM, Roman has written numerous DB2 books, articles, and other related materials. Roman co-authored *DB2 Version 8: The Official Guide, DB2: The Complete Reference, DB2 Fundamentals Certification for Dummies,* and *DB2 for Dummies.*

Warp Speed, Time Travel, Big Data, and More

DB2 10 for Linux, UNIX, and Windows New Features

Paul Zikopoulos
George Baklarz
Matt Huras
Walid Rjaibi
Dale McInnis
Matthias Nicola
Leon Katsnelson

New York Chicago San Francisco
Lisbon London Madrid Mexico City
Milan New Delhi San Juan
Seoul Singapore Sydney Toronto

McGraw-Hill books are available at special quantity discounts to use as premiums and sales promotions, or for use in corporate training programs. To contact a representative, please e-mail us at bulksales@mcgraw-hill.com.

Warp Speed, Time Travel, Big Data, and More: DB2 10 for Linux, UNIX, and Windows New Features

1234567890   DOC DOC   1098765432

ISBN   978-0-07-180295-6
MHID   0-07-180295-9

Sponsoring Editor
Paul Carlstroem

Editorial Supervisor
Patty Mon

Project Manager
Emilia Thiuri, Fortuitous
Publishing Services

Acquisitions Coordinator
Ryan Willard

Copy Editor
Lisa Theobald

Proofreader
Paul Tyler

Production Supervisor
George Anderson

Composition
Fortuitous Publishing
Services

Illustration
Fortuitous Publishing
Services

Art Director, Cover
Jeff Weeks

To the people with whom I had the privilege to write this book, and who have shaped and influenced me during my many years at IBM. It's hard to imagine my professional or personal life without their mentorship, friendship, and interactions.

To my boss, Alyse Passarelli; because it's always good to thank your boss. Well, it's more than that, really. Alyse found a way to teach me things that I needed to know (she's teaching even when she doesn't know it), while allowing me the freedom to operate outside of the "typical" and feed the fire within.

Finally, to Chloë: I cherish the time we spend together. I cherish your need to laugh…loudly; your strong opinions and your decisiveness when you believe in your heart of hearts that something is true; your inability to go a minute without talking; your stubbornness when you ignore me and ski a diamond too fast for my comfort; and watching you smash a golf ball 108 yards to start your seventh year of life. I'm bewildered about where it all comes from, but it's been a freaking blast, kiddo!
—Paul Zikopoulos

As always, I'd like to thank Katrina for her continued support of my writing. She has shown remarkable patience over the years, even when I tell her that this will be my last book. She tells me that at last count, I have said that four times. My two sons support my writing as well, as long as it guarantees that they can call me for a cash advance. I also have to thank Tristan (cat), Ellie (dog), and Basil (dog-in-law) for staying up when everyone else told me I was too old to stay up past my bedtime. I suspect that the dog really just wanted to be let out into the yard, but I'll take that as support for my writing.
—George Baklarz

I'd like to dedicate this book to the amazing worldwide DB2 development team. It's an honor working with such a talented and dedicated team.
—Matt Huras

I would like to dedicate this book to my wife, Hue Phan, and our three children, Saif, Safa, and Haytham. It is their infinite love that gives me the strength and courage to tackle everyday life challenges while remaining sane. I would also like to dedicate this book to my parents, brothers, and sisters, whose love for me never ceased despite being an ocean away. I hope that they all find in this book an expression of my infinite love and deep gratitude.
—Walid Rjaibi

This book is dedicated to my wife, Vickie, and son, Austin, for their continuous availability and support.
—Dale McInnis

I'd like to thank the many talented people in the DB2 development organization who have implemented this exciting technology that we have the privilege of writing about. These engineers are not always in the spotlight with publications and presentations, but they are the true heroes behind DB2. Without their dedication, inventions, and teamwork, we wouldn't have this amazing new version of DB2!
—Matthias Nicola

The last time I wrote a book I promised my wife and daughters I would never do it again. To my wife, Natasha, and my daughters, Masha and Katya. Thank you for letting me go back on my word and for your unwavering support and understanding. You fill my life with meaning and everything that is good. To Paul Zikopoulos for persuading me to break my promise and for being a good friend. I'd also like to thank my mentor, Curt Cotner, for the wisdom and support that he has given me over the years.

Finally, I've been blessed with the opportunity to lead an amazing team. Our team is very much like a startup, only better. To Antonio Cangiano, Bradley Steinfeld, Henrique Zambon, Leons Petrazickis, Marius Butuc, Raul Chong, and Rav Ahuja: I'm grateful for having been on this journey with you, for everything that you have taught me, and for your putting up with my crazy ideas. You rock!
—Leon Katsnelson

CONTENTS AT A GLANCE

CONTENTS

FOREWORD

As I am writing this foreword, we have just kicked off our product launch of DB2 10 and are getting ready to release the product globally. As with my predecessors in this role, I have a long development history with DB2 starting in the mid 1990s. We have come a long way on this journey. One thing is clear: as data volumes continue to rise, the ability to gain insights quickly and effectively and make better business decisions based on these insights is becoming more critical to businesses and institutions worldwide. As these demands grow, your database management system is becoming even more critical.

DB2 10 is a major new release full of capabilities designed to bring significant value to our clients and partners while continuing to drive cost savings and performance and productivity gains, all while maintaining the industrial strengths that DB2 is known for around auditability, high availability, and security. To lower operational costs we have delivered capabilities for faster query response times, improved index management, enhanced compression with adaptive compression, multi-temperature data management, and real-time data warehousing.

Ease of development is strengthened further with PL/SQL compatibility enhancements, a NoSQL graph store, and row and column access control for security, and temporal capabilities. The DB2 value proposition is unparalleled in the industry. We continue to make it easier to move to DB2 while continuing to leverage business logic and skills from other database vendors. I continue to work with customers around the world who have moved to DB2 and gained tremendous value. We have extended our reliable industrial strengths through enhancements in DB2 pureScale, workload management, and HADR. Faster business decisions are realized through enhanced performance with improved data availability, auditability, and security.

DB2 10 is the result of a tremendous amount of innovation, dedication, and hard work from our global development, research, product management, marketing, technology ecosystem, and support teams. It is also the result of the involvement of hundreds of customers and partners who have been active and vocal participants in our Beta program; their ongoing efforts have helped us create an even better offering.

I would like to thank Paul, Walid, George, Matt, Matthias, Dale, and Leon for writing this book. They are a dedicated group who are committed to our clients and driving value with our products. Behind them is a truly amazing worldwide development team. I continue to be inspired by their commitment to excellence. They are an outstanding group whose dedication to our clients and to their fellow IBMers is unmatched.

These are exciting times filled with wonderful new opportunities to unleash the value of data. DB2 10 is ready and able to take on these new challenges.

Enjoy the book!

Judy Huber
Vice President, Distributed Data Servers and Data Warehousing
Director, IBM Canada Laboratory

ACKNOWLEDGMENTS

We want to thank the following people who, in one way or another, contributed more to this book than the amount of space that we have used to thank them: Curt Cotner, Jeff Jones, Conor O'Mahony, Linda Currie Post, Cindy Fung, William Kulju, Walter Alvey, Vivian Lee, David Kalmuk, Francis Wong, Bill Minor, Karen McCulloch, Paul Bird, John Hornibrook, Steve Pearson, Randy Horman, Steve Astorino, Rob Causley, Kayla Martell, David Sky, Dirk deRoos, Lynn Jonas, and Stan Musker.

We want to thank Roman Melnyk for taking time out of his busy schedule to be our technical editor; he makes us look smarter than we are.

We also want to thank our McGraw-Hill acquisitions and production team, especially Paul Carlstroem, Patty Mon, George Anderson, Emilia Thiuri, Howie Severson, Lisa Theobald, and Paul Tyler.

Finally, thanks to our "agent," Susan Visser. She works tirelessly to get all of our books to market. We couldn't do it without her, so we are volunteering George to pick up the bill for dinner when we celebrate getting this project off of our plates.

ABOUT THIS BOOK

The DB2 10 release is a significant one, though that shouldn't come as a surprise to anyone; DB2 has been raising the bar with every release that we can remember. We wrote this book with the intention of presenting to you, the reader, the features that we think are going to prove themselves most noteworthy in the DB2 10 release. With loads of new features and enhancements, there was a lot to pick from. This led to debates (sometimes name calling was involved) about what we would detail, what we would mention briefly, and what we would leave out. We hope that this book inspires thought and a thirst for more information about the features that we discuss, and that you'll leverage the rich IDUG community, BigDataUniversity.com, Developers' Domain, and other IBM resources and contacts to learn more.

You've got in front of you a captive conversation on the DB2 10 release; we hope that you enjoy reading this book as much as we enjoyed writing it!

Paul, George, Matt, Walid, Dale, Matthias, and Leon

How This Book Is Organized

We've organized this book into ten chapters that cover what we believe to be the key highlights and features in DB2 10.

Chapter 1 gives you the 101 on DB2 10: if you've only got 15 minutes, this is the chapter with the value proposition.

In Chapter 2, we show you how to use DB2 10 to get more out of your disks with yet another enhancement to our compression technology and management features that enable you to attach a business policy to the "temperature" of your data.

DB2 10 comes with a whole new policy-based security framework that provides row- and column-level access controls, and we explore these features in Chapter 3.

There's also some really cool "time travel" technology in DB2 10, providing you with turnkey facilities for DB2 10's native implementation of bitemporal tables; you can learn about this in Chapter 4.

Chapter 5 is the performance chapter; some of these enhancements are "in-your-face" performance improvements, such as parallel continuous data ingest or new join optimizations, and some are improvements that don't have the fanfare of other features, but you're really glad they are there (even if you don't know they are).

Chapter 6 highlights the key DB2 10 high availability and disaster recovery enhancements.

Chapter 7 gives you a taste of the Big Data world and how DB2 gets an injection of supporting features for this domain.

Every release of DB2 gets some serious consumability enhancements, and DB2 10 is no exception. In Chapter 8, we summarize those enhancements in a Top Ten list.

If you're an IT professional, you'd better know about Cloud computing; Chapter 9's objective is to highlight DB2's readiness for operation in the Cloud (even our beta program was run through the Cloud).

Finally, we suspect that after learning all about the value and capabilities of DB2 10, if you're not already a DB2 customer, you're going to want to learn more and perhaps move your applications from other database technologies onto the DB2 platform. Chapter 10 describes some of the new features that provide built-in run-time services for other database technologies such as Oracle. DB2 10 adds even more compatibility with and tolerance for proprietary Oracle applications running natively (not through emulation) in DB2.

1

If You've Got Only 15 Minutes: An Overview of DB2 10

In April 2012, IBM announced the release of DB2 Version 10 for Linux, UNIX, and Windows (DB2 10), a release that's packed full of innovative cost-saving and high-performance features. We're excited about the release of DB2 10, because it represents a lot of development investment in new technology that doesn't just SHARPen (provide Scalability, High Availability, Reliability, and Performance) DB2 for existing clients, but envelopes its feature set with governance and Big Data capabilities that push the superior DB2 value proposition even further.

This is the chapter to read if you've got only 15 minutes and want to know the "big ticket" items in DB2 10. If you don't read the rest of the book, you're going to miss a lot of great features that we can't cover here. Nevertheless, after reading this chapter, you'll be able to give the DB2 10 "elevator talk."

DB2 Gets Faster Still: Performance

DB2 10 is fast; it's faster than any previous release of DB2—but did you expect anything different? A lot of optimization work went into ensuring that DB2 10 is one of the world's most sophisticated database engines available today. DB2 10 takes intra-query parallelism to the next level by overhauling several of the key internal mechanisms that are used to control parallelism and concurrency, introducing new parallel algorithms, and externalizing new application controls.

High-speed continuous data ingestion (CDI) is a critical success factor for modern warehouse platforms, and DB2 10 delivers more capabilities in this area with its multithreaded INGEST utility that you can use to stream data from files in various data formats or pipes into DB2 tables. INGEST keeps tables ultra-available, because it doesn't lock the target table; rather, it uses row locking to minimize its impact on concurrent activities against the same table. CDI is especially useful in situations where new files containing data are arriving continuously, for example, from a continuous or trickle feed extract, transform, and load process. It just might be the case that the industry will rename ETL to ETI (extract, transform, and ingest) after seeing how beneficial this capability is!

One of the several significant advantages to the way that CDI is implemented in DB2 10 is that it's an SQL-based client-side utility. This means that the INGEST command is executed on a client machine, giving you complete flexibility as to where the data ingest processes are to be executed. You can kick it off from the coordinator database partition of a partitioned DB2 warehouse, from a server dedicated to data ingest, or from one of the servers that are involved in an ETL process. For example, if you have one of the IBM Big Data platform products, such as BigInsights (IBM InfoSphere BigInsights) or Streams (IBM InfoSphere Streams), generating data for import into a DB2 warehouse, you can invoke INGEST from servers that are part of a BigInsights or Streams cluster.

Another exciting new performance capability in DB2 10 is the new Workload Management Dispatcher, which provides DBAs with a fine-grained control mechanism to govern the assignment of CPU resources to the various classes of work in your database system. You can use this new feature to ensure that mission critical workloads get the CPU cycles they need, others don't take too much, and create a methodology by which to distribute excess CPU when some is left over after servicing required workloads.

There are all kinds of join optimizations in DB2 10, which includes a brand new Zigzag join operation and enhancements to Hash join techniques. Throw in DB2 10 enhancements to RUNSTATS, statistical views, index optimizations, code path optimizations, faster range partitioning ATTACH operations with optional bypass of SET INTEGRITY processing, CPU workload allocation controls, and more, and you've got a performance enhancing release that's ready for deployment. Moreover, the DB2 pureScale code base has been merged with DB2, thereby creating optimization choices for scale-up, scale-out, or both, and deployments for both data warehousing (typically done using the DB2 Database Partitioning Feature that's part of the IBM Smart Analytics System) and transactional processing (typically done using DB2 pureScale) with a single product.

One of the nice things about this release is that most of the optimization work is all automatic; you don't need to do anything to take advantage of it. We think that Wayne Kernochan from Infostructure Associates really summed up the value that DB2 10 provides when he said this after the beta program: "Analysts typically say, your mileage may vary. In the experience of this analyst, the DB2 10 database software appears to deliver excellent additional mileage that one can depend on. Infostructure Associates strongly recommends that IT buyers consider DB2 10 in their near-term buying plans."

To ensure that we were on the right track with DB2 10, we had Thomas Kalb (CEO of ITGAIN GmbH, a database consulting company) ask his team to use their "Easy Benchmarks" tool to test some DB2 10 performance features such as synchronous and asynchronous I/O performance. Their findings? "We measured DB2 10 to be three times faster than DB2 9.7.5. We also noticed significant improvements in the read-ahead I/O workloads. Finally, our measurements of the Transaction benchmarks showed improvement in writing the logs."

The lead DBA for Coca Cola Bottling Company's SAP implementation, Andrew Juarez, notes, "We've also seen the time it takes to process queries decrease dramatically. The performance improvements in DB2 10 have improved the average response time of our SAP online and background transactions anywhere from 30 to 60 percent. In an extreme case, we have seen one of the standard SAP programs go from 30-plus hours down to 2 hours, a 93 percent increase in performance." We hear stories like this all the time when clients underpin their SAP solutions with DB2 because it's built for SAP and runs in "SAP mode." A university client of ours had a nickname for one of their jobs, "Coffee Break"; they had to rename it after running it on DB2.

In this book, you'll find that we often remind you that *your mileage may vary* when we talk about some of the features and our experiences (it makes the lawyers happy), but there are improvements here that'll be apparent the moment you upgrade, and the performance envelope is one of them.

Storage Optimization

The DB2 feature that first delivered row compression was dubbed the *Storage Optimization Feature* for good reason; it's not just a single compression algorithm that's been put in place. There's a roadmap, and there's lots of road still left to drive (although we're not allowed to share those details with you right now). Storage optimization is really important, because it doesn't just help tame rising storage costs; it slashes the electrical footprint that's associated with storing more data, it optimizes the I/O pipe and memory buffers, which leads to better performance, it puts to work idle I/O waits in the CPU, and a lot more.

DB2 has a rich set of features that make it the leader in compression: XML compression, inline large object (LOB) compression, index compression, table compression (DB2 10 adds yet another technique), temporary table compression, backup compression, log archive compression (also new in DB2 10), NULL and DEFAULT value compression, and more.

One of the more notable features in DB2 10 is a new table compression algorithm that optimizes storage at the page level, called *adaptive compression*. Adaptive compression, combined with the compression capabilities that were delivered in DB2 9 and its associated point releases, has our customers achieving sevenfold table compression, and we have personally worked with some clients in the DB2 10 beta program who were delighted to find tenfold compression rates for their largest tables (warehouse or OLTP tables—it works with *both* types of workloads). Adaptive compression works with the familiar static row compression, and it's implemented in an autonomic way. In other words, if you set a business policy that instructs DB2 to optimize storage for a table, DB2 can automatically use two kinds of table compression algorithms, XML XDA compression, temporary table compression, static row compression, and up to three different index compression algorithms just because you told DB2 that you want to optimize the footprint of your table! How cool is that?

Aside from being engineered to be effective, adaptive, and autonomic, DB2 adaptive compression was engineered to be online. You don't have to worry about taking the table offline with a REORG command to re-optimize the compression dictionary after major changes to the data.

DB2 10 also includes log archive compression, which also occurs online: One of our beta customers generates about 60 GB of log data a day and is

mandated to keep eight weeks of log files; our log archive compression gob-
bled up all 3.3 TB of this required log space and spat it out as a mere 825 GB
for the eight-week requirement; that's about a 75 percent compression ratio!

Coca Cola Bottling Company runs DB2 10, and they've really been im-
pressed by the compression results that they've seen. (Check out their video
at http://tinyurl.com/787enkb.) When they first migrated from Oracle to
DB2, they saw a 40 percent storage savings. When they got to DB2 9.7, they
found an extra 17 percent storage savings because of the new compression
techniques that were introduced in that release. In DB2 10, they've seen an
additional 20 percent savings, bringing the average compression savings for
their databases to a dramatic 77 percent. This level of savings doesn't include restrictions to INSERT/UPDATE/DELETE activity, which is the case
with many other vendors.

We love what Tom DeJuneas (the IT Infrastructure Manager at the Coca
Cola Bottling Company) said when he summed up the value of the DB2
platform, "We've saved more than a million dollars over the past four years
in licensing, maintenance, and storage costs by migrating from Oracle to
DB2. We've reinvested these savings into other business projects while
keeping our operating expenses flat. As a result, we don't have to pass rising costs on to consumers, which allows us to maintain our sales volumes
and market share."

As new and faster disk systems replace older ones, organizations haven't
had the flexibility to easily map their underlying infrastructure to business
needs and administratively have pretty much been forced to put all of their
data (even older, less accessed data) on expensive media. DB2 10 includes
a multitemperature storage framework that enables you to define storage
groups and to migrate your data to storage whose characteristics correlate
with the intended use for that data.

A rich set of online tools are available to "age" data seamlessly across
your storage tiers via a defined business policy, giving you a framework not
only to optimize performance, but reduce costs and match the temperature
of the business data to the infrastructure on which it is stored. Enhanced
workload management is included to govern workloads based on who is
accessing the data and what type of data they are accessing. For example,
"hot" data can be given higher priority access and a larger share of system
resources. Feng Wang (DBA, Jianlong Steel Group) notes, "The Workload

Manager enhancements give us a 10 percent performance improvement." Can you imagine simply tweaking some business rules and experiencing a 10 percent increase to your applications' throughput?

Time Travel Query with Bitemporal Data Management

Time Travel Query provides both system temporal and business temporal semantics support in DB2. (More technically savvy folks will know this as bitemporal data management.) Specifically, this capability keeps historical versions of your data rows so that you can query tables using the AS OF clause, which enables you to retrieve data as it existed at a specific point in time in the past, or to determine the validity of certain data in the future. Time Travel Query is going to become a critical feature because it provides traceability of data changes and backdated corrections. For example, a financial securities audit might require the specific book value of an asset class at some specific point in time, or shrink avoidance retail auditors might want to see specific product inventories on specific days.

Many organizations also require efficient ways to capture, query, and update *effective dates* or *validity periods* for their business. For example, consider a health insurance policy on which claims can be made months after an expense was incurred, yet the coverage is subject to change during the intervening period. In other cases, a client may ask for an estimation of covered expenses for a future claim based on their policy as it will exist in the future, which could be different than how it exists today.

The DB2 10 implementation of bitemporal tables is based on the ANSI/ISO SQL:2011 standard and enables you to manage both system time and business time within a database *without* all of the trigger logic and programming efforts of the past. (You can also manage time in the future with DB2's support for business time temporal tables.)

We think you're going to find loads of value in this feature and not just because it's freely available in every DB2 edition (including DB2 Express-C). Time Travel Query provides a very cost-effective means to address auditing and compliance issues. (We would still be making this statement even if it were a chargeable component of DB2.) It's also deeply integrated into the DB2 engine, which enables outstanding performance characteristics and seamless integration into other DB2 features and utilities; in other words, it's not a bolted-on piece of technology, it's part of DB2's DNA. Agility is a cornerstone of Time Travel Query and because it supports short and efficient SQL:2011 coding of complex temporal operations, it increases developer productivity and reduces the cost to implement and maintain time-aware applications. Finally, DB2's bitemporal capabilities help improve data consistency and quality across the enterprise. As a result, organizations can reduce risk and achieve greater business accuracy and agility.

In our tests, we were able to reduce the amount of code required to implement common temporal operations by 45-fold (as compared to our Java implementation) and 16-fold (as compared to our SQL procedure solution).

Ivo Grodtke, a manager of IT training and a data management specialist at LIS.TEC GmbH, took this new feature for a test drive and noted, "Temporal tables greatly simplify the challenge of working with time-sensitive data or when historical data must be kept for audits." We think that you'll agree.

Database Lockdown

For a number of releases, DB2 has been hardening the database around the core values of any sound data security plan: the Principle of Least Privilege, Separation of Duties, and Defense in Depth. For example, the DB2 9 releases saw on-wire encryption and Secure Sockets Layer (SSL) for data transfer, a label-based access control (LBAC) multilevel security framework, database roles, the ability to assert identities and connect metadata with a trusted context, an official security administration (SECADM) role, and much more.

DB2 10 enhances the available set of security controls with row and column access control (RCAC) services in support of data-centric security. RCAC not only addresses the security issues inherent to non data-centric security models such as application security and views, but also significantly reduces the cost of effectively implementing and auditing database security policies.

Many of you are likely familiar with DB2's LBAC multilevel capability, which was introduced in DB2 9. The LBAC and RCAC security models are targeted for two different market segments (classified government spaces for LBAC and commercial customers for RCAC). The need for RCAC arose because a lot of work is required to classify data based on security classifications. Security classifications are the norm in government spaces; that is, every person and object is classified, thereby making LBAC a natural for these organizations. In the commercial sector, data is rarely classified, and companies are rarely willing to spend the energy and money to classify their data; therefore, RCAC (which comes from LBAC) is more suitable for them. (We'll note here, for clarification, that LBAC isn't just for government use, it's just a ubiquitous example where LBAC is often used. The kind of data you are storing ultimately drives the need for security classifications, and that can apply to any industry; for example, trade secrets or inventions are typically classified in such a manner.)

Without RCAC, you have to resort to programmatic security controls in your applications or create excessive amounts of view logic to implement what takes seconds to do with RCAC. RCAC also makes masking columns very simple, which is even a greater benefit to some. In the end, from a security perspective, DB2 10 gives you not only a rigorous and richly designed policy-based security framework that's free of charge, but it reduces the time that's needed to achieve this kind of lockdown compared to previous versions. Just ask Radu Parvu, a senior system analyst at Accenture, who concludes, "Row and Column Access Control significantly reduces the development costs of implementing access control in our application or reporting layers."

Big Data and the Cloud

It's hard to open a web page, attend a conference, or read your favorite IT subscription without hearing about Big Data. And although the term "Big Data" means different things to different people (we help to define it in Chapter 7), we'll note that it's not just the ubiquitous Hadoop engine. To tackle the challenge of Big Data, you need a Big Data platform that provides optimized engines for the analysis of data-in-motion and data-at-rest. It has to provide services for structured and unstructured analysis, deep analytics, SQL- and NoSQL-style approaches to problem solving, as well as integration and governance between both "worlds." IBM provides such a platform, and the DB2 technology is an engine within the IBM Big Data platform.

When you think about Big Data, XML often comes to mind—and DB2 delivered a truly native XML engine, called DB2 pureXML, in the DB2 9 release. It really caught the industry by storm, because, unlike its counterparts at the time, it was a genuinely pure and native XML framework: DB2 didn't shred the XML or stuff it into a LOB under the guise of a "native data type." In DB2 10, we extend the "first class" handling of some of the Big Data types with a triple graph store and support for import and export through the W3C Resource Description Framework (RDF).

A triplestore, as its name implies, is a database optimized for storing *triples*. A triple is a data entity that is composed of subject-predicate-object: for example, "Paul is 39" or "George knows Walid." A triplestore is optimized for the storage and retrieval of triples. Structuring data in RDF enables software programs to understand how disparate pieces of information fit together.

IBM Rational needed to manage a wide variety of data from different work teams to identify dependencies in its software development process; this made them quite interested in using NoSQL triples. Rational first implemented their graph store using an open source solution, but the Rational team soon encountered performance and availability issues. Specifically, they had to rely on an asynchronous indexer; as new triples were added, the indexing services slowed down during triple processing, and in some cases, they stopped and locked up the entire open source database. When the process was implemented on DB2 10, the IBM Rational team saw a substantial performance boost—up to four times faster!

Because the triplestore is implemented on top of DB2, many of the features within the DB2 engine can be used to provide reliability and scalability services to the triplestore. The NoSQL technology in DB2 opens up new opportunities for your organization to seize some of the benefits of a NoSQL approach. Specifically, organizations using DB2 can gain flexibility and the agility benefits of NoSQL deployment while retaining the ACID (atomic, consistent, isolated, and durable) properties, availability, and performance advantages of the DB2 relational database technology. Think about those DB2 enterprise-class attributes, such as compression, which allow organizations to minimize disk space—these are the kinds of attributes that open source projects typically don't provide (or provide with the level of sophistication found in the DB2 implementation). With the new triple graph store support in DB2 10, you don't have to lose the quality assurance of SQL or make expensive and risky architectural changes to gain NoSQL flexibility. Instead, use NoSQL APIs to extend DB2 and implement a paradigm that many of the NoSQL proponents are promoting.

DB2 has been CloudReady for a while, and it's ready for the Cloud when you are. There's a database pattern design template mechanism (used in the expert integrated IBM PureSystems technology), integration into IBM Workload Deployer (IWD), Cloud-friendly licensing, Separation of Concern technologies for multitenant databases, and much more.

High Availability

DB2 10 has a major enhancement to the High Availability Disaster Recovery (HADR) technology that's included in all of the paid-for DB2 editions. This technology provides a drop-dead simple turnkey HA and DR solution that's suitable for many database applications. In the past, an HADR cluster was limited to two entities: a primary and its associated standby. DB2 10 lets you have up to three standbys, enabling you to implement both HA and DR in a single solution. There's also a log delay that you can implement on a standby to provide a buffer zone for changes that are applied to your standby database; this adds a granular level of protection from human error. When HADR is combined with the DB2 Advanced Recovery Solutions toolkit, you get a strong framework for generating SQL UNDO, faster backups, simplified recovery, and a rich and flexible set of options for a simple yet sophisticated HA and DR protection-from-human-error framework.

In addition, DB2 10 delivers a number of backup and recovery (BAR) enhancements to the DB2 pureScale technology. For example, DB2 pureScale supports all of the existing table space–level recovery features in DB2, so you can use the same BAR plans for both single- and multipartition DB2 databases.

And a Lot More...

Because so much went into DB2 10, we seriously debated not writing this quick overview for fear of doing the release a disservice. For example, DB2 10 is DB2 CloudReady—it's been that way for a while—but we want to remind folks that DB2 includes various features that are key for bringing your database to the Cloud, including virtualization, multitenancy, Separation of Concerns, IBM Workload Deployer patterns that make setting up DB2 environments a snap, Cloud licensing, and much more.

There are many ease of use enhancements to be found in DB2 10, and as you delve into its feature set, it becomes more and more apparent that consumability is well grounded in all of the new technologies that IBM brings to market. Even more innovative value comes from the addition of some of the very capable Optim portfolio pieces into DB2 Advanced Enterprise Server Edition (DB2 AESE), additional Oracle compatibility, and more.

We couldn't possibly cover all of the value in DB2 10 in such a short chapter. Perhaps we should just say that by adhering to the design pillars of low operational costs, ease of development, and reliability, DB2 10 delivers a large number of enhancements to help save you time and money. The resulting improvements in productivity from both development and administrative perspectives support a new generation of applications operating in an increasingly complex and demanding business environment. Better yet, just read the rest of the book.

2

Get More Out of Your Disks: The Even More Storage-Optimized DB2

It's hard to find any major database vendor who is not concerned with compression technology. Stepping back, you might very well ask questions like, "Why do we need compression in the first place?" and "Why does it matter if that 1-TB drive for which I paid $500 a couple of years ago can now be had for $65?" It's true that the cost of storage has declined over the years as disk drive manufacturers continue to produce larger and denser drives. In theory, this means that it should be cheaper to store information. Compression is important, because, although we can store more data, corporations need to keep track of even more data for a variety of reasons:

- **Regulatory compliance** Up to seven years of data needs to be kept for governmental reporting.
- **Sales and marketing** Data is used to track consumer behavior and buying patterns over long periods of time.
- **Acquisitions** Additional data comes from companies that have been acquired.
- **Velocity** This concept represents the natural growth of data as the number of transactions increases.
- **Rich content** Video, audio, XML, and images are all becoming part of the transaction mix.

- **Social media** Big Data from nontraditional sources of information (such as blogs, forums, and Facebook) might need to be stored.

Now consider that all of this data needs to be stored, backed up, indexed, and disseminated among production, test, user acceptance, and other environments; the net result is enormous disk space requirements.

Although drives are increasing in size, the I/O throughput of traditional disk drives hasn't kept pace. Think about the three key performance characteristics that are associated with database workloads: CPU, memory, and disks. Since the 1980s, CPUs have seen at least 2000-fold increases in capability; memory and associated caches have grown more than 1000-fold; and disk densities have grown more than 10,000-fold. However, the average seek time and transfer rate of these disks over the same time period have grown only about 65-fold and 10-fold, respectively. If you can imagine your local city having to deliver all of its water through a garden hose, you've got a really good idea of the problem.

Now consider the introduction of solid-state drives (SSDs) in your environment, and you can see an evolving data placement challenge. If you were going to buy some brand new, expensive SSDs, why would you put data that is seldom used on those disks? The placement of data on a speed tier of disks in relation to its value or access patterns is referred to as *temperature controlled storage*. If you regard data as being "cold," "warm," or "hot," an underlying data management infrastructure that can map these data categories to disks of appropriate quality and speed is going to be an imperative. This is an enterprise storage optimization technique that has proven to be very effective.

For all of these reasons, multiple DB2 releases have been relentlessly focused on storage optimization techniques, including NULL and system default values, block indexes, various table and index compression techniques, temporary table compression, XML compression, inline large object (LOB) compression, backup compression, log compression, and multitemperature storage management, which are all part of the DB2 DNA.

DB2 Multitemperature Management

Organizations rely on data warehouses to store and process large volumes of data. Much of this data needs to reside on more expensive disks that provide the highest performance for critical business decision support systems.

It's been the practice of most DBAs to put all of the data on the same type of disk, even though the fastest response times are required for only a relatively small subset of the data. In fact, most of the data in a typical warehouse is used rather infrequently.

Temperature warehousing is meant to address this problem. The core principle of multitemperature data management is that the current usefulness of the data dictates the storage tier on which it resides. Usually, aging changes the temperature of data. A useful metaphor for this is a hot fashion trend. When data is new, everyone wants it, and you "wear it" all the time; then it becomes less intriguing, until, finally, it's tucked in the corner of your closest and barely gets worn.

Figure 2-1 shows an ideal mapping of disk technologies to the temperature of the data that they store.

In short, it makes sense to separate recent and frequently accessed (hot) data from older and inactive (cold) data by storing hot data on your fastest storage devices and cold data on your slowest storage devices. Priorities are usually based on frequency of access, acceptable access times as defined by a Service Level Agreement (SLA), data volatility, and your application requirements.

Customers often struggle with the question of how to optimize the performance of data warehouses without having to invest in SSD storage for the entire system. Another challenge is how to prioritize the execution of queries that access recent (hot) data: these are all challenges a multitemperature storage management infrastructure can help address.

Looking Back: Allocating Storage Prior to DB2 10

To understand temperature management, you need to have a basic understanding of how DB2 uses table spaces to map tables and related table objects to storage. DB2 has three kinds of table spaces:

Figure 2-1 *Data access patterns relate to data "temperature" and to the performance of the disks on which it is stored.*

- **System managed space (SMS)**   With an SMS table space, the file system manager allocates and manages the space where the table is stored. Storage space is *not* pre-allocated when the table space is created; it is allocated on demand.

- **Database managed space (DMS)**   With a DMS table space, the database manager controls the storage space, which is pre-allocated on the file system based on container definitions that you specify when you create the DMS table space.

- **Automatic storage table spaces**   With automatic storage table spaces, storage paths are used to manage storage automatically. As a database grows, the database manager creates containers across those storage paths and extends them or automatically creates new ones as needed. Automatic storage is the default storage allocation method for new databases created in DB2. We strongly recommend using this table space type for most of your data needs.

From an administrative perspective, SMS table spaces are the easiest to manage, but they do not optimize disk performance. DMS offers the greatest flexibility but requires a lot more administration on the part of the DBA. Automatic storage offers the ease of SMS administration with the benefit of using DMS containers "under the covers." Automatic storage has become a strategic direction for DB2 storage management, but it presents a number of challenges for temperature-based disk allocation. For example, all storage for automatic storage objects is allocated from a single storage group; therefore, allocating drives to a storage group does not guarantee that hot data will get the best performing disks. Figure 2-2 illustrates this problem.

In Figure 2-2, you can see that the table data is split across a number of date ranges (data partitions). The most recent quarter (2012Q1) is accessed most frequently (so we would consider this data hot), whereas the other quarters (2011Q4, 2011Q3, and so on) become colder as they age. However, all of these data partitions have their logical space allocated from a single storage pool, and this storage pool gets physical space from the storage paths that are attached to it. As you can see, a single storage group can't support multitemperature management, so some changes had to be made to DB2's underlying storage architecture.

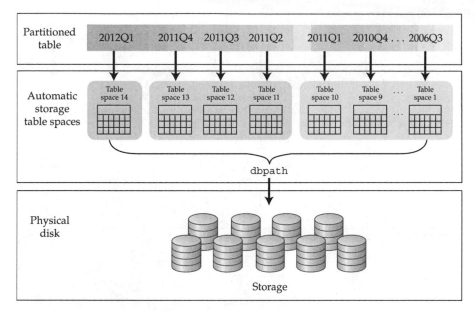

Figure 2-2 *Range partitioning with a single storage group*

Of course, you could map your table spaces directly to SSD containers. This was possible before the introduction of DB2 10 storage groups (you're going to learn about these in the next section), but that would require DBAs to manage the storage allocation for potentially hundreds of table spaces.

DB2 Storage Groups Change the Game

DB2 10 introduces a new concept known as *storage groups*. Storage groups create different classes of storage, in which frequently accessed (hot) data can be stored on faster storage tiers, and rarely accessed (cold) data can be stored on slower and less-expensive storage tiers. As hot data cools down and is accessed less frequently, DB2 10 enables you to move the data dynamically in a simple and efficient manner.

A storage group contains storage paths with similar characteristics. Some critical storage attributes you need to consider when creating or altering a storage group include available storage capacity, latency, data transfer rates, and the degree of RAID protection. Figure 2-3 illustrates how the architecture design in Figure 2-2 could be spread out over different storage groups with different disk performance characteristics.

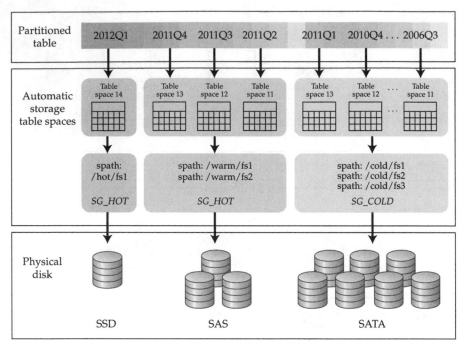

Figure 2-3 *Range partitioning with multiple storage groups.*

After you create a set of storage groups that map to the different classes of storage in your database system, you can assign automatic storage table spaces to those storage groups, based on which table spaces have hot or cold data.

To summarize, storage groups provide the following benefits:

- They add flexibility to the automatic storage model.

- They enable you to reassign a table space dynamically to a different storage group as the data or business requirements change.

- They allow you to assign different classes of storage to different storage groups. For example, hot data can be assigned to storage groups with faster devices, and warm or cold data can be assigned to slower devices.

- They make it easy to modify or move the storage that is used by table spaces.

Using Storage Groups

The default behavior in DB2 10 is to create all databases as AUTOMATIC STORAGE. For example, the following command creates a database on drives 'D:' and 'E:':

```
CREATE DATABASE production ON 'D:', 'E:'
```

The default storage group for the PRODUCTION database is IBMSTOGROUP (you'll find it in the SYSCAT.STOGROUPS catalog view) with its two associated storage paths: D: and E:. All of the catalog table spaces, including SYSCATSPACE, TEMPSPACE1, and USERSPACE1, are created in IBMSTOGROUP.

You can choose your own default storage group by using the DEFAULT keyword on the CREATE STOGROUP command, as follows:

```
CREATE STOGROUP hot_group on 'F:' SET AS DEFAULT
```

If you create a new default storage group on an existing database, it won't impact the tables that already exist. If existing table spaces need to be moved to the new storage group, you can use the ALTER TABLESPACE statement.

A storage group has a number of performance characteristics associated with it: overhead, device read rate, and data tag:

- **Overhead**   This attribute specifies the I/O controller overhead and the disk seek and latency time, in milliseconds.

- **Device read rate**   This attribute holds the device specification for the read transfer rate, in megabytes per second. The value is used to determine the cost of I/O during query optimization. If this value is not the same for all storage paths, it should be the average for all storage paths that belong to the same storage group.

- **Data tag**   This attribute specifies a tag on the data in a particular storage group, which the Workload Manager can use to determine the processing priority of database activities.

After a new storage group has been created, you can use the new USING STOGROUP clause on the CREATE TABLESPACE statement to place a table space into a specific storage group. For example,

```
CREATE TABLESPACE q1_2012 USING STOGROUP hot_group
```

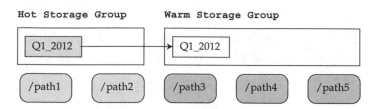

Figure 2-4   *Storage groups with different performance characteristics*

In this example, the Q1_2012 table space will inherit the data tag, transfer rate, and overhead from the storage group, unless these values are overridden on the CREATE TABLESPACE statement. For example,

```
CREATE TABLESPACE q1_2012 USING STOGROUP hot_group DATA TAG 5
```

The ALTER TABLESPACE statement has also been enhanced in DB2 10 to support the movement of table spaces to other storage groups. For example, let's assume that data in the Q1_2012 table space cools down and is no longer as important for queries; in this case, it's likely that you would want to move it to a storage pool with lower performance characteristics, as shown in Figure 2-4.

To move the cooling data in the Q1_2012 table space to a lower cost storage tier, the DBA could run the following ALTER TABLESPACE statement:

```
ALTER TABLESPACE q1_2012 USING STORGROUP warm_group
```

The ALTER TABLESPACE statement causes a background REBALANCE operation to occur on the table space. This operation is online, and therefore the table remains fully available during this process. You can monitor its progress by using the new MON_GET_REBALANCE_STATUS table function.

One nice thing to note here from an administrative perspective is that the target storage group layout doesn't have to be the same as the original storage group layout. The *only requirement* is that sufficient space exists in the storage group to accommodate the new table space.

After the ALTER TABLESPACE statement commits, containers are allocated on the new storage group's storage paths, existing containers residing in the old storage groups are marked as drop pending, and an implicit REBALANCE operation is initiated. This operation allocates containers on the new storage path and rebalances the data from the existing containers into the new containers. The number and size of the new containers depend on both the number of storage paths in the target storage group and the amount of free space on the new storage paths. Only after the entire table space has been moved to the new location will the original space be released and made available to other table spaces.

From a migration perspective, you can use the ALTER TABLESPACE statement to convert existing DMS table spaces to automatic storage table spaces.

Multitemperature Storage in Action: A Usage Scenario

In this section, we'll show you how storage groups can be defined in DB2 to enable multitemperature management of your data. Let's start with Figure 2-5, which illustrates the goal for this scenario: the final storage group layout for our data.

The storage paths /path1 through /path4 are defined by the storage administrator and should have performance characteristics that match their intended use. For example, let's assume that /path1 should be on SSD drives or on very high performance Serial Attached SCSI (SAS) drives. After the paths are available, the following commands create the storage groups:

```
CREATE STOGROUP HOTSG  ON '/path1' DATA TAG 1;
CREATE STOGROUP WARMSG ON '/path2', '/path3' DATA TAG 5;
CREATE STOGROUP COLDSG ON '/path4' DATA TAG 9;
```

The scenario includes four table spaces, one for each quarter of 2011. From a performance perspective, the last quarter is hot, the second and third quarters are warm, and the first quarter is cold. To support this access pattern,

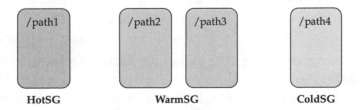

Figure 2-5 *The storage group layout we want for our database*

let's place each table space into the storage group that corresponds to the temperature of its data. For example,

```
CREATE TABLESPACE q1_2011 USING STOGROUP coldsg;
CREATE TABLESPACE q2_2011 USING STOGROUP warmsg;
CREATE TABLESPACE q3_2011 USING STOGROUP warmsg;
CREATE TABLESPACE q4_2011 USING STOGROUP hotsg;
```

With this set of table space definitions, we have guaranteed that table space Q4_2011 is placed into a storage group that will have the highest possible performance.

At some point in time, new data for Q1_2012 will be loaded into the database. To adjust the temperature of the older data, we can use the ALTER TABLESPACE statement to move the existing table spaces to slower storage. Specifically, Q4_2011 will move into the warm storage group, and Q2_2011 will move into the cold storage group:

```
ALTER TABLESPACE q4_2011 USING STOGROUP warmsg;
ALTER TABLESPACE q2_2011 USING STOGROUP coldsg;
```

Of course, the new table space will need to be created in the hot storage group using the following statement:

```
CREATE TABLESPACE q1_2012 USING STOGROUP hotsg;
```

Bringing It All Together: A Summary of Multitemperature Data Management in DB2 10

The use of automatic storage table spaces simplifies the management, backup, and restoration of a database by freeing the DBA from concerns about container allocation or any of the other complexities around DMS table spaces. With the introduction of DB2 10 storage groups, a DBA can implement multitemperature data management by using data temperature as the basis of a business policy-driven grouping criterion when spreading data across the storage subsystem.

The following list highlights some additional benefits of this feature:

- You can create storage groups that are backed up by different types of disks. This enables you to ensure that hot data is contained in SSDs or high-performance drives. As data ages, backups can be moved to a slower device in another storage group.

- You can age-synchronize your data from a scheduling and performance perspective, so that queries that need to access hot data can be prioritized through DB2 workload management. See Chapter 5 for more details.

- You can define a policy that determines appropriate storage for an automatic storage table space instead of having to rely on manual DMS table space definitions.

- You can easily modify or move the storage that is used by a table space.

Looking Back: A Quick Recap of Compression in Past DB2 Releases

Before we delve into the great new compression capabilities that are part of DB2 10, we thought it would be worthwhile to bring you up to speed on what's been done to address storage challenges that our customers faced in the past. In this section, we go a little deeper into the existing DB2 compression technology, because it's such a key piece of DB2 10. We also recommend that you read "Row Compression in DB2 9" (http://tinyurl.com/8xvehpb), "New Features in DB2 9.5 to Help Your Business Grow" (http://tinyurl.com/7neajo9), and "DB2 9.7: It All Adds Up" (http://tinyurl.com/6w9uydf), or visit the DB2 Information Center for all of the details.

DB2 Compression: An Anthology of Compression Techniques Across Previous Versions of DB2

Several forms of compression existed prior to DB2 9: *value compression, MDC block indexes,* and *backup compression.*

When value compression is enabled for a table, DB2 compresses the storage that is used for NULL values and system-defined defaults. That is, if a data row contains a NULL value or a system-defined default value, the associated column consumes no space for that value.

Multidimensional clustering (MDC) tables use block-based indexes that have the effect of compressing indexes by as much as 99 percent in many cases. This effect is accomplished by the use of efficient block ID pointers instead of traditional row ID pointers. For example, a block-level index whose row-level index equivalent consumes 220,000 index pages might consume only 72 index pages. This is an excellent form of compression that can improve query performance significantly. As a positive side effect, block-level index compression reduces index maintenance requirements during INSERT and DELETE operations, and the associated reductions in logging result in better performance.

Backup compression was also introduced before DB2 9; this feature enables the BACKUP utility to scan the data stream for repeating patterns and to apply compressions techniques to remove those repeating values from the data stream. The end result is a much smaller backup image.

The common issue with each of these forms of compression is that they do not compress the data pages on disk to a significant degree, nor do they pack more rows of data into the buffer pool for better memory utilization.

The Inflection Point: DB2 9.1 Row Compression

DB2 9.1 introduced a game-changing compression technology, originally referred to as *row compression,* which is based on a Lempel-Ziv (LZ) static dictionary-based compression algorithm (the same approach used with DB2 for z/OS). With row compression, repeating patterns within a table are replaced by 12-bit symbols, and the corresponding real data values are stored in an in-memory static dictionary. Customers saw highly significant benefits from this compression technique, with many tables experiencing up to 85 percent compression ratios. Of course, because row compression reduces the number of pages that are associated with a table, any utility operations (backup, statistics collection, and so on) against the table should run faster.

How Row Compression Works

To compress data rows, DB2 first scans the entire table for repeating patterns. DB2 looks for repeating column values and also looks across column boundaries for repeating patterns that span multiple columns. Finally, DB2 looks for repeating patterns in substrings of column values, making it one of the most sophisticated row compression techniques available today.

For example, consider the following EMPLOYEE table:

EMPLOYEE

NAME	DEPT	SALARY	CITY	STATE	ZIPCODE
Ellie	AZ1	32000	New York	NY	10038
Basil	AZ1	35000	New York	NY	10038

In the EMPLOYEE table, DB2 will obviously find the New York repeating pattern, because it's the same in each row; however, DB2 can actually discover and compress substrings of any column. For example, it could compress the New substring of New York, New Haven, New Orleans, and so on, and compress out just the 4-byte string, including the space. (DB2 will choose what to compress based on its cost-benefit estimation. For example, perhaps it would compress NEW and YORK as separate compression entries, because there are so many cities that prefix with NEW and other cities could contain the word YORK. All of this processing is fully automated by DB2.)

After DB2 is finished finding all of the repeating strings that it can handle, it builds a lookup dictionary of these strings. Each string is represented by a 12-bit symbol. DB2 replaces these strings with the corresponding 12-bit symbols and stores the rows in this compressed format. In this example, DB2 might decide that the 4-bytes associated with New (including the space) will be replaced with a single 12-bit symbol.

Now consider a row that contains a typical address including columns for CITY, STATE, and ZIPCODE. There's a high degree of correlation between these columns, so if they are placed next to each other within the table, DB2 will be able to replace all three column values with a single 12-bit symbol, as shown in Figure 2-6, which shows row compression techniques that include both substring and multicolumn compression.

In the figure, the string AZ1 followed by one character of the adjoining column (3) occurs in two rows, so DB2 might choose to compress the entire value (AZ1 3) out of the row and replace it with a 12-bit symbol. Similarly, the multicolumn string New York NY 10038 appears multiple times, so DB2 can replace this entire string with a single 12-bit symbol, too.

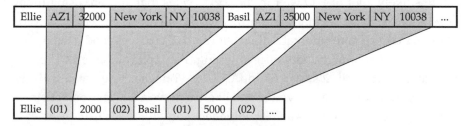

Figure 2-6 *Row-level compression patterns*

The generated compression dictionary is stored as part of the table being compressed and loaded into memory the first time that the table is referenced (it remains in memory until the database is deactivated or shut down), and when DB2 needs to expand a row or compress it, it refers to this dictionary.

A full spectrum of supported operations was a distinguishing feature of DB2 row compression when it was first introduced; basically, any method that you can use to get data into a DB2 database (INSERT, UPDATE, MERGE, IMPORT, and LOAD) is eligible for compression. The first iteration of the Storage Optimization feature proved to be much more effective at compression than other competing technologies at the time.

Storage Savings and Performance Results

Our tests (and, more importantly, what we've seen in our clients' production environments) have clearly shown the major benefits that row compression delivers to DB2 tables. For example, one of our SAP Business Information Warehouse (SAP BW) customer's compression resulted in savings between 67 to 82 percent reduction in space, depending on the table. Of course, compressing data tables also has the side benefit that backup images tend to be smaller and QA, test, and disaster recovery sites also consume less storage.

There's an old saying, that nothing comes for free, and people often ask us, "What is the cost of compression?" Well, it's CPU! There is nothing to hide here. If a row needs to be examined, DB2 must decompress the row into a memory-allocated work area, and this results in more CPU instructions, which *could* degrade performance (more on that in a bit). In one test on a completely CPU-bound server, our query workload degraded by 3 to 8 percent—a small tradeoff, considering that the largest tables compressed by 86 percent!

Now before you draw any conclusions, read this paragraph closely. There's likely a lot of I/O wait in the CPU cycles that you are using today (*especially* for business information [BI] workloads). We've seen this a lot: Those CPU cycles are automatically reallocated to compress and decompress the data, and you might not notice anything. Perhaps you have CPU cycles to spare; most of all, it's easy to add CPU to your machines, and with the money you save on storage, you're still likely to have a really strong business case. If compression creates a CPU bottleneck for you, that's usually an easy problem to solve, which isn't the case for I/O bottlenecks.

Now consider that with compression, fewer pages are needed to move the same amount of data from disk to the database engine, and you suddenly realize that not only are you saving on the storage that's required to host your data, but you've also got the effect of virtually widening the I/O pipe and optimizing memory. After all, if 1 TB of data now consumes 0.5 TB on disk, you can flow the same amount of data 50 percent faster (or double the amount of data in the same amount of time), and you can store 50 percent more of those pages in the database heap.

We've seen this performance effect firsthand: lots of cases where applications sped up by 35 percent or more, while the largest tables in the database were reduced in size by up to 85 percent! This is due to the fact that table scans and large range scans can complete more quickly as more rows are processed with each page read operation. In addition, more rows can be stored in the buffer pool, because DB2 keeps these rows compressed in memory, and this is going to drive up your buffer pool hit ratios. In fact, during one proof of concept that we ran, we measured four times more rows per data page compared to uncompressed data, which resulted in four times more rows residing in the same-sized buffer pool. These optimizations improved performance as a result of more efficient use of memory (effectively quadrupling the available memory on the server).

Now, "your results might vary," but we're confident that in most cases (especially for BI applications), you're going to come out on top, so try it out, measure the benefits, and go from there.

It Goes Autonomic: DB2 9.5 Compression

Although DB2 9 compression was a huge benefit for customers, it placed some administrative burden on the DBA. Existing tables required an ALTER TABLE operation (to enable it) followed by an INSPECT or an offline REORG command to build the compression dictionary.

DB2 9.5 introduced automatic dictionary creation (ADC) as an option for DBAs to enable compression without having to spend too much time administering the process of compressing tables. (Tables still need to be "nominated" for compression using an ALTER or CREATE statement with the COMPRESS YES option.) After a table reaches approximately 2 MB in size, autonomic compression kicks in to build the required compression dictionary. The dictionary building process starts after a transaction (INSERT, UPDATE,

MERGE, LOAD, IMPORT) completes and before the next one starts. Data that is already in the table is not compressed, but any subsequent transactions against the table are eligible for compression.

There are some considerations associated with automatic compression in DB2 9.5. DB2 automatic compression creates the compression dictionary based on 2 MB of data, rather than by sampling the entire table, as is the case in DB2 9. It's possible that such a compression dictionary doesn't have the optimal set of compression symbols, because not all of the table data was used. Our tests have shown single-digit compression degradation as a result of automatic compression (and our lawyers insist that we again remind you that "your results might vary"); however, we believe that loss of compression is easily outweighed by ease of administration.

Other Helpful DB2 9.5 Compression Features

DB2 9.5 expanded the set of compression-related SQL administrative routines, which made it easier to determine the potential benefits of compression on a table, rather than by using the INSPECT command, which was the only option available in DB2 9. For example, in DB2 9.5, the ADMIN_GET_TAB_COMPRESS_INFO function can be used to determine how much a table can be compressed:

```
SELECT COMPRESS_DICT_SIZE + EXPAND_DICT_SIZE AS DICTIONARY,
   PAGES_SAVED_PERCENT, BYTES_SAVED_PERCENT
     FROM TABLE (
       SYSPROC.ADMIN_GET_TAB_COMPRESS_INFO('GBAKLARZ', 'EMPMDC',
       'ESTIMATE')
       )


DICTIONARY              PAGES_SAVED_PERCENT BYTES_SAVED_PERCENT
-------------------- -------------------- --------------------
              64256                   34                   34
```

In DB2 9, the LOAD command compresses data according to a table's existing compression dictionary, but it can't create a new dictionary if one doesn't already exist. In DB2 9.5, the LOAD command was enhanced to better deal with compression dictionaries. New options enable you to specify whether a compression dictionary will automatically be created during the load operation (assuming that at least 2 MB of data is being loaded) or whether an existing dictionary will be replaced.

DB2 9.7: Compression Finds a Higher Gear

DB2 9.7 introduced a whack of additional compression capabilities, including index compression, temporary table compression, XML compression, inline LOB compression, and support for compressed replicated tables. In this section, we'll give you a brief overview of these key enhancements.

Index Compression

Sometimes the storage that is consumed by indexes can be as much or more than the storage that is consumed by the table data itself. Although tables can be compressed to as much as 20 to 30 percent of their original size with DB2 row compression, before DB2 9.7, indexes were not compressed.

Other technologies in the marketplace offered index compression, but they used their table compression algorithms to compress indexes. Because indexes are critical for efficient data retrieval, index compression overhead must be minimized to avoid degrading performance, but the techniques that are typically used for table compression don't fully optimize the storage footprint for indexes.

Not only did the new index compression algorithms in DB2 9.7 reduce physical disk space requirements, they also produced other benefits, such as reduced index page read requirements, which result in less I/O activity and faster access to records. DB2 9.7 index compression also yields a smaller number of index pages, which typically results in fewer index levels and leads to reduced leaf page access. Finally, buffer pool pages contain more index page entries, which reduce the number of times that the object needs to be read into memory. Simply, each object has different needs and requirements.

Hitting the Trifecta: Index Compression Optimizations

DB2's index compression is built from the ground up for consumability. For example, you can leverage a management-by-intent policy framework in which you define a business priority to optimize storage, and DB2 will compress the table and associated indexes automatically. (It will also compress temporary tables whenever it can—more on that in a bit.) What's more, DB2 will automatically choose the best combination among three index storage optimization techniques without DBA intervention—including the prefix! For example, with one popular database technology, the DBA has to monitor

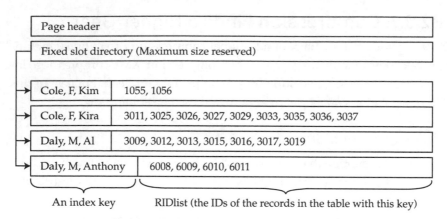

Figure 2-7   *Row-level compression patterns*

the prefix and then drop and re-create the index and its associated static prefix definition to compress the index. With DB2, it's all dynamic and automatic: nice!

DB2 9.7 index compression is unique in that it combines three different techniques for index optimization, as shown in Figure 2-7: row ID (RID) list compression, prefix compression, and the fixed header slot directory.

Index pointer (row ID or RID list) compression and index value (prefix) compression are the main components of index compression.

An index entry comprises a key value (data from the columns that define the index) and a list of row IDs that identify the rows on which this key can be found. A RID comprises a page number and slot number; the former points to the data page, and the latter points to the offset within that page where the row can be found. Rather than store the page and slot number for each row, delta offsets are stored after the first key value. RID list compression is most useful with non-unique indexes that have long RID lists. This technique can save 4 or more bytes per duplicate key value.

The second index compression algorithm is known as *prefix compression*. Index keys are stored on the leaf pages of an index in sequential order, which means that key values that are adjacent to each other on an index page have similar text strings.

For example, an index on two columns, LAST_NAME and FIRST_NAME, might look something like this:

```
BAKLARZ, GEORGE
BAKLARZ, GEOFF
ZIKOPOULOS, PAUL
ZIKOPOULOS, CHLOE
```

A number of key values share a common prefix. In this example, there are two patterns:

```
(1) BAKLARZ, GEO and (2) ZIKOPOULOS
```

Note that patterns are not limited to individual columns; in fact, they can cross column boundaries, which is something that's not supported by most competitors' offerings (their cross-column string must be contiguous from the beginning of the index key). Found patterns are stored in the header of the index page, and the original index value can then be compressed by using pointers to these patterns:

```
(1), RGE
(1), FF
(2), PAUL
(2), CHLOE
```

The best candidates for prefix compression are indexes that contain multiple columns and have character strings. Numeric columns can also be compressed, but in this case, the entire column value must be in the pattern.

As you might expect, a rich set of administrative functions and statistics is associated with index compression. For example, the SYSCAT.INDEXES catalog view has been updated with a COMPRESS column (values can be Y or N) as well as a PCTPAGESAVED (percent pages saved) column that represents the percentage of index pages that have been saved by using compression on a particular index.

The ADMIN_GET_INDEX_COMPRESS_INFO table function can be used to estimate the compression savings that you might achieve using index compression. This table function returns information about whether or not compression is enabled for an index, the current level of compression on the index, and the potential compression that is available to an index if it is not currently compressed. For example, the following query results show that index P1 and P2 can be compressed with a potential savings of 66 percent, but that index P3 is not a good candidate for compression (P3 is a unique numeric index).

```
SELECT INDNAME, COMPRESS_ATTR, INDEX_COMPRESSED, PCT_PAGES_SAVED
   FROM TABLE
     (SYSPROC.ADMIN_GET_INDEX_COMPRESS_INFO
       ('T','GBAKLARZ','PRODUCTS',NULL,NULL) )
INDNAME COMPRESS_ATTR INDEX_COMPRESSED PCT_PAGES_SAVED
------- ------------- ---------------- ---------------
P1      N             N                66
P2      N             N                66
P3      N             N                0
```

DB2 Even Compresses the Temp Stuff

Temporary tables are eligible for compression. For example, DB2 will create temporary tables to sort large result sets being returned by a query that is performing an aggregation or a query that contains an ORDER BY clause. DB2 will also store a partial query request in a temporary table as part of query processing. Temporary table compression is automatic, just like index compression.

Compressing Inline Large Objects

"Inlining" refers to the ability to place a column "within" a row on a page rather than having it spill into a separate storage area. In the same manner that most XML is stored in the XDA, DB2 LOBs are typically stored in different table spaces. With LOB inlining, you can tell DB2 to keep an object on the page as long as it doesn't exceed a certain size.

A number of benefits are associated with inline LOBs. DB2 LOBs are not placed into buffer pools, so repeated access to the same row increases I/O. In addition, if LOBs are placed into a separate LOB table space, each access to a LOB requires at least two I/Os: one to get the base page data and one to get the actual LOB. With LOB inlining, the LOB data is placed onto the page with the other column data, making the LOB data eligible for compression. Moreover, the data pages are placed into buffer pools so that access to frequently used LOBs will be improved. Finally, only a single I/O is required to access the page, rather than the two that are currently required to get to LOB data. After this data is inlined, DB2 sees it as part of the table and can leverage row compression.

This feature is very beneficial for some of the new applications that define LOBs as "bit buckets" to store data without the need for strict schemas (providing a NoSQL-like feel to a structured table). Inlining of LOB and XML data gives a performance boost to applications that deal with relatively small LOBs (or XML data) that can fit on the DB2 page. Anything greater than 32 KB (the largest DB2 page size, but remember that the data can be compressed) will need to be placed into a separate table space.

Going from Pure to Compressed: XML Compression

It's outside the scope of this chapter to explore the implementation aspects of pureXML technology, but we can assure you that the native capabilities that DB2 brings to the table with pureXML are head and shoulders above the rest. We recommend that you thoroughly understand the XML technology that you are considering, because lots of vendors use the word "native," but what they offer is not native at all—it involves shredding and LOB stuffing under the guise of "native" to get the job done.

As the title of this section implies, DB2 9.7 introduced the ability to compress XML data that is stored in the XML data area (XDA) using the same compression techniques that it uses for base tables (it could already inline compress XML, as of DB2 9.5, because inlined XML becomes part of the row format). XML column data is not stored on the same data page as the rest of the row but is stored in an XML-specific storage object known as the XDA. When a table is enabled for compression, any XML data that resides within the XDA area, as of DB2 9.7, is compressed. XML compression is similar to table compression in that DB2 will scan all of the XML data in the table and build a compression dictionary of the most common repeating patterns within that data. This compression dictionary is stored inside the XDA object, and repeating strings that are found in the XML data are replaced with 12-bit symbols pointing to the corresponding dictionary entries. A compressed table will end up with two separate compression dictionaries: one for the XDA-stored XML data and one for the rest of the table.

If you have tables with pureXML columns that were created prior to DB2 9.7, they will need to be re-created to take advantage of this new XML compression capability, because it's built on a new storage format for the XDA object.

As you'd expect, there are functions that give you information about both the potential and actual XML compression achieved; for example, the ADMINTABCOMPRESSINFO view or the ADMIN_GET_TAB_COMPRESS_ INFO_V97 table function gives information such as the current (or potential) compression ratio of the XML data that is stored in the XDA. In our experience, you're going to find that the compression savings are very significant; in fact, it's not uncommon to see numbers in the high 80 percent range because of the verbose nature of the XML format.

Replication of Compressed Tables

Prior to DB2 V9.7, the use of DATA CAPTURE CHANGES on a table was not compatible with the use of the COMPRESS YES clause for that table. In other words, replication was not supported with compressed tables. In DB2 9.7, DB2's log read interface was enhanced so that it can handle compressed records. DB2 can read a compressed log record and expand it prior to passing the record over to the replication CAPTURE program.

Looking Forward: What You Can Expect with Compression in DB2 10

DB2 10 finds yet another compression gear by implementing another transparent algorithm that improves compression ratios over time and minimizes the need for reorganization to optimize compression dictionaries. In short, DB2 10 makes compression even more effective and easier to use! For this reason, as of DB2 10, row compression (which is based on a table-wide compression dictionary) is referred to as *static compression*.

The Inspiration for Adaptive Compression

When we talked to our customers and scanned the marketplace for ideas on how to differentiate our leading compression technology even more, we focused on reducing compression maintenance and enhancing the compression algorithm to adapt to changes in data patterns. For example, if automatic compression was being used, the compression dictionary was built on a scan of no more than 2 MB of the table's data. Although automatic dictionary creation (ADC) was amazing from a manageability and table availability perspective, scanning such a small portion of the data didn't expose the best compression ratios that DB2 was capable of attaining. Of course, your results are going to vary, and in some scenarios it's worse, but we find that ADC produces compression ratios that are approximately less than 10 percent lower when compared with compression that is performed during a full REORG operation.

Another challenge is that over time, a static compression dictionary can become stale, because it doesn't change after it's built. For example, data that contains a lot of date fields will be less compressed over time because new dates are not in the compression dictionary, or perhaps a whole new set of customers from a new geography was loaded into the table. The only way to improve the efficiency of such a compression dictionary is to re-create the entire dictionary, which involves a table reorganization that effectively decompresses all of the table's data and then compresses it again with a new compression dictionary—a potentially time-consuming outage for many customers.

Another issue is that static dictionaries hold only a finite number of slots or entries for compression patterns. Although there might be many potential patterns, after the dictionary is full, no more patterns can be added. To offset this, DB2 performs pattern consolidation, as in one of the examples outlined in this chapter, but it still means that some compression-eligible data patterns won't be chosen and some data patterns could be overlooked because of their locality of reference. For example, if a data pattern is localized to a small group of pages rather than being distributed over the entire table, the static compression algorithm might miss it, because the algorithm focuses on data patterns that appear across the entire table. We've seen this behavior with time-dependent data, such as quarterly sales.

To reduce the need for data reorganization for optimal compression and to recognize more localized patterns, DB2 10 introduces *adaptive compression*. Adaptive compression works along with static compression to create page-level dictionaries (in fact, you can't have adaptive compression without static compression). Adaptive compression creates page-level dictionaries and compresses patterns within the page that are not part of the static dictionary.

There are numerous benefits of using adaptive compression. First, compression rates can be even higher (and are often considerably higher) when using adaptive compression on top of static table compression; our tests seem to yield compression improvements ranging from 30 to 60 percent better compression! From an availability and maintenance perspective, adaptive compression recognizes new data patterns and adapts to data skew over time, enabling you to leverage even more of the associated compression benefits *without* having to perform maintenance operations such as REORG. Finally, and perhaps most obviously, now that locally recurring patterns can be compressed (as opposed to table-wide patterns only), you're likely going to see significantly higher compression ratios when data contains locally recurring patterns.

Working with Adaptive Compression

Adaptive compression must always start with a static compression dictionary, generated by a classic REORG or the automatic compression associated with the COMPRESS YES table option, which contains patterns of frequently used data found across the entire table.

After a static dictionary is built, DB2 creates local page-level dictionaries. In the case of individual pages, some recurring patterns might not have been picked up by the static dictionary. This will also be the case as more data is added to the table, because new pages might contain data patterns that did not exist when the original static dictionary was created. Data that is stored as part of base data objects (for example, CHAR, VARCHAR, INTEGER, FLOAT, inline LOB, and inline XML data) can be compressed with both adaptive and classic row compression.

Adaptive compression places a small dictionary on the data page itself. In keeping with the theme of increased consumability and reduced administrative burden associated with new DB2 features, the adaptive compression algorithm automatically decides whether or not the compression savings outweigh the costs of storing the compression dictionary (just as it does with static compression). The actual process of creating a page dictionary is dependent on whether or not a "threshold" is met, because rebuilding a page dictionary for every data change operation would result in a very high amount of overhead. Instead, the algorithm checks to see how "stale" the dictionary is and updates the dictionary when it believes that higher savings can be achieved.

Let's assume, for example, that you have a flight school business called White Knuckle Airlines. Not even a month into your new venture, you've gotten so busy that you hire Paul. You assume that you'll grow even more and have lots of employees in due time, so you compress the EMPLOYEE table, which currently looks like the following:

EMPLOYEE

NAME	DEPT	EXTENSION	HIREDATE
Paul	YYZ	99999	2010-03-14
Jeffrey	YYZ	41256	2010-02-02

After enabling the table for compression on March 14, 2010, when Paul was hired, you run a REORG operation. DB2 finds some global patterns and builds the EMPLOYEE table's static compression dictionary, as shown here:

EMPLOYEE Table's Static Compression Dictionary

GLOBAL	PATTERN
1	YYZ
2	2010

If you were to look at an on-disk abstraction of the EMPLOYEE table at this point, it would show symbols for the data that was compressed:

EMPLOYEE

NAME	DEPT	EXTENSION	HIREDATE
Paul	[G1]	99999	[G2]-03-14
Jeffrey	[G1]	41256	[G2]-02-02

Toward the end of 2011, you hire George and Geoffrey, and now the EMPLOYEE table looks like the following:

EMPLOYEE

NAME	DEPT	EXTENSION	HIREDATE
George	YYZ	32000	2011-11-04
Geoffrey	YYZ	35000	2011-10-23
Paul	YYZ	99999	2010-03-14
Jeffrey	YYZ	41256	2010-02-02

The associated on-disk abstraction now looks like this:

EMPLOYEE

NAME	DEPT	EXTENSION	HIREDATE
George	[G1]	32000	2011-11-04
Geoffrey	[G1]	35000	2011-10-23

| Paul | [G1] | 99999 | [G2]-03-14 |
| Jeffrey | [G1] | 41256 | [G2]-02-02 |

Did you notice that only the department YYZ was compressed for George and Geoffrey and not the date? That's because this data existed in the static compression dictionary when the dictionary was created. In this scenario, because the dictionary wasn't updated, DB2 can't pick up new repeating patterns that surface after George is hired.

This is where the DB2 10 adaptive compression technology automatically kicks in to provide more compression without any administrative overhead. DB2 adaptive compression (as its name implies) can adapt to new data at the page level and therefore discovers new patterned data on November 4, 2011. It subsequently creates entries in the *local page-level* dictionary, as opposed to the table-wide dictionary, as shown here:

EMPLOYEE Table's Local Page-level Adaptive Compression Dictionary

LOCAL	PATTERN
1	Geo
2	ffrey, [G1]
3	000,2011

We want to note here that local patterns can include global symbols as part of the pattern. The local pattern L2 contains a local string, ffrey, followed by the global symbol [G1].

Rows on the page now contain symbols that represent both local patterns and global patterns, and the on-disk abstraction of this table now looks like the following:

EMPLOYEE

NAME	DEPT	EXTENSION	HIREDATE
[L1]rge	[G1]	32[L3--]	[--L3]-11-04
[L1] [L2--]	[--L2]	35[L3--]	[--L3]-10-23
Paul	[G1]	99999	[G2]-03-14
Je[L2--]	[--L2]	41256	[G2]-02-02

NOTE   *In this example, the notation* [L2--]   [--L2] *is used to represent a symbol that spans columns, with* [L2--] *representing the start of the symbol and* [--L2] *representing the end of the symbol.*

Did you notice that adding `Geoffrey` to the `EMPLOYEE` table created the `ffrey` pattern that could be applied to another data row (the row containing employee `Jeffrey`)? Moreover, that fact that both new employees were hired in the same year and have the same last three digits in their phone extensions created yet another opportunity for a cross-column pattern. Finally, the `Geo` pattern can be found in rows for existing employees, too.

Adaptive compression is automatically enabled for any new DB2 10 table when compression is enabled. For existing tables, adaptive compression must be explicitly enabled. When a page is almost full, a page-level dictionary is built, and the threshold for creating the dictionary is around 90 percent of the space used. When DB2 notices that less than about 70 percent of the data can take advantage of the page-level compression dictionary, the page might be compressed again following a subsequent data manipulation operation. As you'd expect, commonly recurring patterns in the original records are then replaced with bit symbols that can even contain static compression markers in the rows; quite simply, this means that you can use symbols from the table-wide dictionary to create larger local patterns.

After the page-level dictionary is built, DB2 compresses all of the existing records on the page. Any subsequent data change operation (`INSERT`, `UPDATE`, `MERGE`, `IMPORT`, `LOAD`, `REDISTRIBUTE`, `REORG`, or online table move) triggers adaptive compression on the impacted rows.

Enabling Adaptive Compression

DB2 10 introduces new syntax for creating adaptive compression tables. Before DB2 10, using the `COMPRESS YES` option on the `CREATE TABLE` statement enabled table compression:

```
CREATE TABLE … COMPRESS YES
```

To create tables with *static* compression in DB2 10, specify the `STATIC` clause:

```
CREATE TABLE … COMPRESS YES STATIC
```

If you omit the `STATIC` clause in DB2 10, the statement creates a table that uses *both* static and adaptive compression, which is equivalent to using the `CREATE TABLE … COMPRESS ADAPTIVE` statement. Remember that you can't create a table in DB2 10 that solely uses adaptive compression; adaptive compression requires that the table is also using static compression.

If a database is being migrated from a previous version of DB2, or an existing table was created with COMPRESS YES STATIC, adaptive compression can be turned on by using the ALTER TABLE ... COMPRESS YES ADAPTIVE statement. It's important to note that the process of turning on adaptive compression does not change the contents of the pages. Only a REORG operation causes DB2 to recompress the existing pages. For this reason, altering tables to use adaptive compression should be scheduled during a maintenance period.

To disable compression on a table, use the ALTER TABLE statement with the COMPRESS NO option. Rows that are subsequently added to the table will no longer be compressed; however, existing rows *will remain* compressed. To decompress the entire table after you turn off compression, you must REORG the table.

Estimating Compression

The ADMIN_GET_TAB_COMPRESS_INFO table function has been updated to include compression estimates for both static and adaptive compression. For example,

```
SELECT TABNAME, OBJECT_TYPE, PCTPAGESSAVED_STATIC,
   PCTPAGESSAVED_ADAPTIVE
 FROM
   TABLE(SYSPROC.ADMIN_GET_TAB_COMPRESS_INFO('GBAKLARZ','SUPPLIERS'));
TABNAME    OBJECT_TYPE PCTPAGESSAVED_STATIC PCTPAGESSAVED_ADAPTIVE
--------- ----------- -------------------- ----------------------
SUPPLIERS DATA                          59                     59
SUPPLIERS XML                           53                     53
```

> **NOTE**   *In DB2 10, the* ADMINTABCOMPRESSINFO *administrative view has been deprecated and should not be used.*

The "Your Results Might Vary" Section: Our Adaptive Compression Tests

We believe that you're going to realize significant benefits by using adaptive compression along with static compression. In Figure 2-8, you can see that by using only the powerful static compression technology that was first introduced in DB2 9, the total storage requirements for five of this client's biggest tables could be reduced from 54.1 GB to 21.2 GB. When DB2 10 adaptive

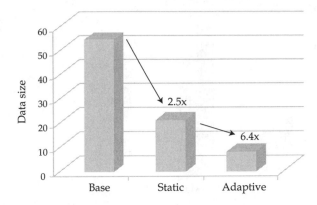

Figure 2-8   *The benefits of adaptive and static compression working together to optimize storage*

compression is added, the storage footprint is reduced to a mere 8.4 GB. This 6.4-fold reduction of storage results in better performance, improved memory utilization, smaller log files, smaller backup images, significantly less I/O overhead, and more.

Miscellaneous Space Enhancements

DB2 10 also introduces index space reclamation optimizations and log archive compression. Log archive compression can be enabled for the primary and secondary log archiving methods through two new database configuration parameters, LOGARCHCOMPR1 and LOGARCHCOMPR2. For example,

```
UPDATE DB CFG FOR SAMPLE USING LOGARCHCOMPR1 ON
```

Log archiving can result in substantial savings in disk space consumption; these savings are *very* dependent on the type of data being written to the logs. This is generally true for any type of compression (text fields tend to compress well). For example, Figure 2-9 demonstrates the log compression achieved on three different laboratory workloads. The OLTP workload has a large number of insert, updates, and deletes that take place. The DSS (Decision Support) workload is mostly reporting with some updates, and the ADC workload is similar to the OLTP workload except that it has adaptive compression enabled for most tables. Since the ADC database has compressed tables and indexes, the log records are already in a compressed state.

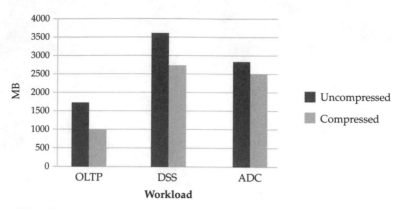

Figure 2-9 *Using log archive compression to add yet another layer of savings to your storage requirements*

Although the compression savings are small (about 20 percent), that still translates into almost 0.5 GB of saved disk space above and beyond what you had before. We've seen cases in which the savings were very significant.

As you might expect, log archive compression is fully automatic. The database manager automatically compresses log extents when they are moved from the active log path to the archive location. Upon retrieval into the active or overflow log paths (for example, during ROLLBACK and ROLLFORWARD operations) the database manager automatically expands the compressed log files.

DB2 10 also introduces an enhancement to the REORG INDEX command. This enhancement enables you to free extents (containing unused pages) from an index object back to the table space. These extents can exist anywhere within the object. For example, to clean up the pseudo-deleted keys and pseudo-empty pages in all of the indexes on the EMPLOYEE table while allowing other transactions to read and update the table, you could run the following command:

```
REORG INDEXES ALL FOR TABLE EMPLOYEE
   ALLOW WRITE ACCESS CLEANUP ONLY
```

To clean up the pseudo-empty pages in all of the indexes on the EMPLOYEE table while allowing other transactions to read and update the table, run the following command:

```
REORG INDEXES ALL FOR TABLE EMPLOYEE
    ALLOW WRITE ACCESS CLEANUP ONLY PAGES
```

When the CLEANUP option is used, a full reorganization is not done. The indexes are not rebuilt, and any pages that are freed up will be available for reuse by indexes that are defined on this table only.

The CLEANUP PAGES option searches for and frees committed pseudo-empty pages. A committed pseudo-empty page is a page whose keys are marked as deleted, and all of these deletions are known to be committed.

The CLEANUP ALL option frees committed pseudo-empty pages and removes committed pseudo-deleted keys from pages that are not pseudo-empty. This option also tries to merge adjacent leaf-pages if doing so will result in a merged leaf-page that has at least PCTFREE free space, where PCTFREE is the percent of free space that was defined for the index at index creation time. The default PCTFREE value is 10 percent. If two pages can be merged, one of the pages is freed.

Use of the CLEANUP option reduces the need to run a complete INDEX REORG when you want to reclaim wasted space.

Wrapping It Up

DB2 10 introduces a number of features and functions that help you manage your storage more effectively than ever before, and we believe that it does so better than any other offering in the industry. Some of the more notable value enhancing DB2 10 storage optimization features include:

- Adaptive compression, which can save an additional 30 to 60 percent of space over static compression and nearly eliminates the work that a DBA must do to maintain compression rates over time.

- Log archive compression, which can reduce the amount of log space that is taken up by transactional systems, and it's automatic!

- Storage groups that give you the ability to separate table spaces into different storage tiers and guarantee the type of disk performance that you expect from your workloads.

- A new REORG option to help to reclaim index space without the need for full index reorganization.

3

Lockdown: An Even More Secure DB2

Trusted information lies at the center of today's business transformations. But organizations are challenged to ensure that unauthorized users can't access confidential information unless they have a business need for it and potential hackers can't get at such data. Considering the high profile data breaches that have made their way to the front pages of blogs, magazines, and newspapers alike in the past few years, it seems that these challenges are becoming harder and harder to overcome. And although we were all raised not to believe everything we hear or read, even with the ever-growing focus on data security in recent years, studies tell us that companies aren't doing a good enough job of protecting their data (in many cases, *your* data). Study after study suggests that the database server is the ubiquitous culprit behind these escalating security breaches. In fact, in 2011 alone, the Verizon Data Breach Investigations Report (DBIR) shows that over 90 percent of breached records have resulted from compromised database servers.

Who's manning the front lines of data protection? Well, the DBAs, of course, and they need some help. It's a tough job and an enormous responsibility. To comply with various government regulations and industry standards from countries around the world, organizations need to implement procedures and methods to ensure that stored information is adequately protected. This means that DBAs are continually bombarded with an ever-increasing number of regulations. Whether it's Sarbanes-Oxley (SOX), Payment Card Industry Data Security Standard (PCI DSS), Health Insurance Portability and Accountability

Act (HIPAA), the Basel Accord's Basel II, or some other government regulation, the bottom line is that you need to comply—and the CIO, CSO, and even the CEO are all watching you! These regulations and standards stipulate that individuals are allowed access only to the subset of information that is needed to perform their jobs. For example, according to HIPAA, doctors are authorized to view the medical records of their own patients but not the records of another doctor's patients. Similarly, according to the PCI DSS, access to cardholder data, such as credit card numbers, must be restricted by the business's *need-to-know*. For information stored in relational databases, the ability to control data access at the row and column levels can help satisfy these requirements.

As if these regulations weren't enough, most enterprises put a disproportionate amount of their security investment and budget toward protecting offline data (backups), mobile devices, and end-user systems; however, the major point of compromise for breaches continues to be the online data found in the database server itself (according to the DBIR).

Today's DBAs need all the help they can get. The good news is that DB2 has a rich release-after-release history of delivering key features that contribute to the core principles of security: defense-in-depth, the principle of least privilege, and separation of duties. In the last few releases, we've introduced the security administrator (SECADM) role and provided trusted contexts, label-based access control (LBAC), secure sockets layer (SSL) for data-in-transit encryption, an encryption solution for data at rest, and more.

In this chapter, we'll explore yet another inflection point in DB2 security. We'll talk about the new finer-grained access control features in DB2 10, sometimes referred to as *row and column access control (RCAC)*, that allow you to hide rows from unauthorized users and to mask the value of columns for unauthorized users with a policy-driven security framework composed of row permissions and column masks alongside flexible policies that don't require upfront classification work.

Looking Back: Traditional RCAC Methods in DB2

In the past, three traditional methods have been used by DB2 DBAs to implement RCAC: database views, application-based security, and the DB2 LBAC feature first introduced in DB2 9.

The Database View Approach to Database Lockdown

If a DB2 DBA wanted to implement a form of RCAC with column masks using database views, the database developer first had to create either a single view that included all of the security rules affecting all of the users of the table, or create separate views for each user or group of users. Next, the database developer had to grant the appropriate privileges to these views and revoke access to the base table from all users and groups.

With this approach, if multiple views were created for different users or groups, you needed to ensure that the application contains logic to route user queries to appropriate views based on their identity, their group membership, or both. Finally, the database developer and the application architect had to rigorously test the solution.

This primitive database view approach can work well for granular security controls when the number of different restrictions you want to enforce is small or the intended restriction affects only large and easily identified groups of users. In other words, when the lockdown is "coarse," the use of views doesn't become overwhelming. If this isn't the case, however, a number of issues can arise. For example, view definitions might become complex if you try to pack all of the access restrictions into a single view. This complexity can strain system limits and can make maintenance of the view difficult.

Alternatively, you might consider defining a large number of simple views, each of which implements specific restrictions for a specific set of users; but then routing user requests to the correct view becomes an issue. Some DBAs might choose to grant access to the base table and bypass the views, but that violates the principle of least privilege, which stipulates that users or applications should not be granted more privileges than are needed to complete the task at hand; and don't forget, users with DATAACCESS authority still have full access to the data.

Because the methods that are outlined in the preceding paragraph come with overhead that inflates the cost of ownership, an alternative approach is to implement the security control mechanism within the application itself, thereby moving the mechanism farther away from the database.

The Application-Based Security Approach to Database Lockdown

With this approach, an application is programmed to fetch required data into its memory and to apply custom logic to filter the result set based on user identity and privileges. Alternatively, the application can be programmed to push down or append some or all of the filtering logic to the SQL so that some or all of that filtering logic can be executed by the database. Because this implementation is all programmed logic, it follows that the database development and application architecture teams need to be involved in testing. Although application-based security might initially seem attractive and less cumbersome than the database view approach, it also has several drawbacks.

First, the security policy is exposed to the application programmer's side of the business, which means that more people need to know and have access to the security policy. This strains the separation of duties principle of good data governance. Second, if you want to change the security policy, you have to reflect this change in the application. Now you need to align resources to evolve the security policy over time. This leads directly to the third drawback: Whenever you change an application, you introduce a certain amount of risk into the process; the probability of error makes additional code reviews necessary. Finally, with this approach, users with DATAACCESS privilege also have full access to the data.

Label-Based Access Control

If you choose to leverage DB2's very capable LBAC facility to protect each database table that requires protection, you'd have to follow a number of steps to implement this security mechanism. First, the database security administrator (a user with SECADM authority) would have to create the security label component and security policy objects that are needed to map the security requirements to security labels. Then the SECADM would have to create the associated security label objects needed for user access to the protected tables and grant labels and exemptions to the appropriate users. Finally, the SECADM would have to grant security labels and exemptions to appropriate users and test those grants with the application architect.

Although LBAC is a strong security model, it is rarely suitable for commercial applications, because it implements a set of rigid security rules for classified data: the *no read up rule* and the *no write down rule*. LBAC and multilevel security (MLS) are generally intended for intelligence and defense customers, which is where MLS originated.

Looking Forward: What You Can Expect with RCAC in DB2 10

Row permissions and column masks are two new database concepts introduced in DB2 10 that address the shortcomings of traditional RCAC methods outlined in the previous section. These new features act as a second layer of security that complements the table privileges security model available in prior releases of DB2.

One advantage of row permissions and column masks is that no database user is automatically exempted from them—not even users with the DATAACCESS authority. The ability to manage row permissions and column masks within a database is vested solely in a user with SECADM, thereby ensuring that users with DATAACCESS authority can no longer freely access all data in the database.

Another key advantage is that row permissions and column masks ensure that table data is protected regardless of how the SQL accesses the table, be it through an application, through ad hoc query tools, or through report generation tools.

Finally, and perhaps most significantly, row permissions and column masks require no application changes; RCAC is transparent to existing applications. This approach represents an important paradigm shift in the sense that data access security controls are no longer about *what is being asked*, but *who is asking for what*. That is, result sets for the same query change based on the context in which the query was submitted, no warnings or errors are returned to the application or end user, and no TRY/CATCH logic is required to handle data that violates the security policy. Note that application designers and DBAs need to know that database queries won't present all of the data in the table to the user unless the user (or group) was specifically granted permission to view that data.

Essentially, in DB2 10, the table privileges security model is first applied to determine whether a user is allowed to access the target table. If the user can access the table, row permissions are applied to determine what specific rows of the table the user can access. Column masks are then applied to determine whether the user sees an actual or masked value in a column. For example, row permissions ensure that if Dr. Jane Smith queries the PATIENTS table, she can see only rows that represent patients under her care. Other patients are nonexistent as far as she is concerned, because DB2's row permissions have filtered out the data. Similarly, a column mask defined on the PHONE_NUMBER column of that same table ensures that Dr. Smith sees phone numbers only for those patients who consented to share this information with her. The phone numbers for other patients are set to a NULL value or redacted according to the column mask definition. We'll cover how all of this works in more detail later in the chapter.

Working with DB2 RCACs

In this section, we discuss how RCAC can be defined on a table. A usage scenario illustrates how these concepts actually work.

Defining Row Permissions

A *row permission* is a database object that *expresses a row access control rule for a specific table*; it's basically an SQL search condition rule that describes what set of rows a user can access. SECADM authority is required to create, alter, or drop a row permission object using the CREATE PERMISSION, ALTER PERMISSION, or DROP PERMISSION SQL statement. For example, the following code creates a row permission rule that limits access to rows in the PAYROLL table to normal business hours:

```
CREATE PERMISSION payrollp ON payroll
 FOR ROWS WHERE CURRENT TIME BETWEEN '8:00' AND '17:00'
 ENFORCED FOR ALL ACCESS ENABLE;
```

The FOR ROWS WHERE search condition defines the actual row access control rule for the table; it specifies a condition that can be either true or false for a row of the table. Generally speaking, this search condition follows the same rules as a WHERE clause in a subselect. In this example, we've enabled the permission, and you can assume that DB2 will enforce it; you can also assume that if you specify DISABLE, the row permission would be defined but not enforced. Row permissions are dynamic; like a light switch, you can turn them on or off, and depending on their enforcement and associated rules, the same query will return different results. Specifically, for RCAC, there are two "light switches." The first switch turns row access control for a table on and off. If this table-level switch is turned off, no matter whether row permissions are enabled or disabled, they won't be enforced. The second switch is at the permission level as described in the preceding example.

Row permission definitions are recorded in the SYSCAT.CONTROLS catalog view. Depending on its definition, a row permission might have a dependency on one or more database objects (whose dependencies are also recorded there). For example, if the row permission refers to a user-defined function (UDF) in its FOR ROWS WHERE search condition, this dependency is recorded in the SYSCAT.CONTROLDEP catalog view.

Activating Row Access Control on a Table

A SECADM must *explicitly* activate row access control on a table for it to be enforced, using an extension to the ALTER TABLE statement. Here's an example: ALTER TABLE HR ACTIVATE ROW ACCESS CONTROL (use the DEACTIVATE ROW ACCESS CONTROL clause to explicitly deactivate the control). This operation is dynamic, and the table remains online during processing.

The activation of row access control on a table results in the automatic creation of a database-managed row permission that represents a false predicate ('1 = 0'). This particular row permission is stored in the SYSCAT.CONTROLS catalog view and can be easily recognized by its schema and name; its schema is the same as the schema of the table on which it is defined, and its name contains the prefix SYS_DEFAULT_ROW_PERMISSION.

The effect of this database-managed row permission (after access control is activated on a table) is that rows in the table are not accessible unless a row permission is defined and enabled that would allow for some, or all, of the rows in the table to be returned (depending on the criteria specified in the search condition). When more than one row permission is defined and enabled, a row access control search condition is derived by applying the logical OR operator to the search condition in each of these row permissions. This derived search condition acts as a filter on the table before any user-specified operations such as predicates, grouping, or ordering are processed.

The Application Context of Row Permissions

Row permissions that are defined on a table are applied when the table is accessed through the following SQL statements: SELECT, INSERT, UPDATE, DELETE, and MERGE.

Row Permissions and Your Data Manipulation Language (DML)   When a table for which row access control is activated is referenced in a SELECT statement, all enabled row permissions that were created for the table, including the database-managed row permissions, are implicitly applied by the DB2 database manager to control which rows in the table are accessible.

When you issue an INSERT statement against a table for which row access control is activated, the rules specified in all the enabled row permissions defined on that table determine whether the row can be inserted. A *conformant row* is a row that, after being inserted, can be retrieved by the same user; you can consider this row one that satisfies the rules implemented in the database. This behavior is identical to how an insert operation into a symmetric view works; you can't insert a row into such a table if you can't later retrieve that row.

An UPDATE statement follows the same logic as INSERT processing for row permissions: namely, you can't update a row that you are not authorized to select, and the row that is to be updated must be conformant (selectable by the update operation); this is similarly identical to update operations against a symmetric view.

The DELETE statement operates just like the UPDATE statement, except that the enabled row permissions in this case filter the set of rows that are to be deleted. Again, you can't delete rows that you can't retrieve.

Finally, the MERGE statement process is identical to the manner in which a MERGE statement operates, namely as a combined INSERT and UPDATE operation.

Defining Column Masks

A *column mask* is a database object that *expresses a column access control rule for a specific column in a specific table*. This access control rule is defined through a CASE expression that describes what users should see when they access the column. As you've likely figured out, SECADM authority is also required to create, alter, or drop a column mask object using the CREATE MASK, ALTER

MASK, or DROP MASK SQL statement. For example, the following creates a
column mask rule that limits access to the PAYROLL table's SALARY column
only to those users who belong to the HR role; a NULL value is returned for
users who are not members of the HR role.

```
CREATE MASK salarym ON payroll FOR COLUMN salary RETURN
 CASE WHEN verify_role_for_user(session_user, 'HR')= 1
   THEN salary
   ELSE NULL
 END
ENABLE;
```

The CASE expression represents the actual column access control rule that's
evaluated by the database security services. The resultant data type (including metadata such as its nullability and length attributes) must be identical
or promotable to that of the secured column. If your table is defined with
a user-defined type (UDT), the resultant data type of the CASE expression
must be the same UDT. For example, if a SECADM tried to define a column
mask that returns a NULL on a column that was defined as NOT NULL, the
database manager would surface an error that's returned during processing.

Column masks can also be dynamically enabled or disabled, yielding different query results depending on their enforcement and associated rules.
Column mask definitions are also recorded in the SYSCAT.CONTROLS catalog view. Depending on its definition, a column mask might have a dependency on one or more database objects (for example, a column mask might
refer to a UDF in its CASE expression); as you have likely guessed, this dependency is also recorded in the SYSCAT.CONTROLDEP catalog view.

When a column mask is evaluated, the database manager returns either
the actual or redacted value. The redacted value is defined by the SECADM
and can be a NULL value or whatever the SECADM chooses. When a column
is embedded in some expression (for example, an expression figuring out
average client net worth), the column mask is always applied *before* that expression. In other words, the expression will operate on the redacted value
if the user cannot see the actual value. Operations such as AVG would treat
NULL values as they do regularly. DB2 ensures that when you are defining
a mask, the result of that mask is compatible with the column definition.
For example, if the column is NOT NULL, the mask definition cannot return a
NULL as a redacted value.

Activating Column Access Control on a Table

A SECADM must *explicitly* activate column access control on a table for it to be enforced, using an extension to the ALTER TABLE statement. Here's an example: ALTER TABLE HR ACTIVATE COLUMN ACCESS CONTROL (use the DEACTIVATE COLUMN ACCESS CONTROL clause to explicitly deactivate the control).

The Application Context of Column Masks

Column masks that are defined on a table are applied when that table is accessed through a SELECT statement; and determine the values of the final result set that is returned to the requesting application. If a column with an associated column mask appears in the outermost SELECT list, the column mask is applied before the final result table is materialized to the application. If the column *does not* appear in the outermost SELECT list, *but* it participates in the final result table, the column mask is applied to the column in such a way that the masked value is included in the result table of the materialized table expression or view so that it can be used in the final result table. As a general rule of thumb, column masks are applied in the following contexts:

- The outermost SELECT clause, or clauses, of a SELECT or SELECT INTO statement, or if the column does not appear in the outermost SELECT list but participates in the final result table, the outermost SELECT clause or clauses of the corresponding materialized table expression or view where the column appears.

- The outermost SELECT clause, or clauses, of a SELECT FROM INSERT, SELECT FROM UPDATE, or SELECT FROM DELETE statement.

- The outermost SELECT clause or clauses that are used to derive the new values for an INSERT, UPDATE, or MERGE statement, or a SET transition-variable assignment statement. The same applies to a scalar-fullselect expression that appears in the outermost SELECT clause or clauses of the preceding statements, the right side of a SET host-variable assignment statement, the VALUES INTO statement, or the VALUES statement.

The application of column masks does not interfere with the operations of other clauses within the statement, such as WHERE, GROUP BY, HAVING, DISTINCT, and ORDER BY. The rows that are returned in the final result table remain the same, except that values in the resulting rows might be masked.

As such, if a masked column also appears in an ORDER BY clause, the order is based on the original column values, and the masked values in the final result table might not reflect that order. Similarly, the masked values might not reflect the uniqueness that is enforced by the DISTINCT clause.

Putting Row Permissions and Column Masks to Work

In this section, we'll fold the new granular DB2 10 security controls into a working scenario. Let's assume that a fictitious wealth management company called *GuaranteedReturns* (we told you it was fictitious) has a large customer base that spans many branches and that it uses DB2 10. GuaranteedReturns wants to take advantage of the new time-saving lockdown row permissions and column masks to help securely implement database policies that match the company's charter and fulfill members' privacy and security requirements.

For simplicity, let's assume that GuaranteedReturns has the following data access controls in its charter:

- Advisors can see only *their own* clients.
- Customer service representatives (CSRs) and telemarketers can see *all* clients.
- Whenever advisors, CSRs, or telemarketers access account information, they see a redacted account number; specifically, they can see the last four digits of the account number and the preceding digits are replaced by Xs. However, CSRs using the *CustomerKeeper* service application to update a client's account information can see the whole account. (This application leverages the ACTFUNCS.FUNCUPD routine to perform account activity.)

GuaranteedResults customer information is stored in the CUSTOMER table, and employee information is stored in the INTERNAL_INFO table. If you want to work through this example, run the following data definition language (DDL) to create these tables:

```
CREATE TABLE CUSTOMER (ACCOUNT VARCHAR(19), NAME VARCHAR(20),
    INCOME INTEGER, BRANCH CHAR(1));
CREATE TABLE INTERNAL_INFO (EMP_NAME VARCHAR(10), HOME_BRANCH CHAR(1));
```

Advisors, CSRs, and telemarketers all have business roles that include authorizations and permissions related to what they can do with customer data. These roles are defined by the business itself. GuaranteedReturns leverages the roles capability, introduced in DB2 9.5, to minimize the administrative burden of handling multiple users who share permissions in the database. Using this capability, GuaranteedReturns implemented database roles that match the business roles—namely, ADVISOR, CSR, and TELEMARKETER. Every role is able to view customer data, and therefore the SELECT privilege was granted to all of these roles.

The DBA created database roles for each business role at GuaranteedReturns and assigned employees to each database role using the following DDL:

```
CREATE ROLE advisor;
GRANT SELECT ON customer TO ROLE advisor;
GRANT ROLE advisor TO USER amy;

CREATE ROLE csr;
GRANT SELECT ON customer TO ROLE csr;

CREATE FUNCTION ACTFUNCS.FUNCUPD()
 RETURNS TABLE (ACCOUNT VARCHAR(19), NAME VARCHAR(20), INCOME INTEGER,
  BRANCH CHAR(1))
 LANGUAGE SQL
 MODIFIES SQL DATA
 NO EXTERNAL ACTION
DETERMINISTIC
RETURN SELECT * FROM customer;
GRANT EXECUTE ON PROCEDURE ACTFUNCS.FUNCUPD TO ROLE csr;
GRANT ROLE csr TO USER pat;

CREATE ROLE telemarketer;
GRANT SELECT ON customer TO ROLE telemarketer;
GRANT ROLE telemarketer TO USER haytham;
```

From this DDL, you can see that Amy is an Advisor at GuaranteedReturns, Pat is a CSR, and Haytham is a telemarketer.

Did you notice that the DBA granted EXECUTE privileges on the ACTFUNCS.FUNCUPD routine to the CSR role? This was done so that the CSR can see the entire account number if the account is being updated using the CustomerKeeper application, which leverages this routine for this specific purpose.

To populate the CUSTOMER and INTERNAL_INFO tables with data that you can use to work through the examples in the remainder of this chapter, issue the following commands:

```
INSERT INTO customer VALUES ('1111-2222-3333-4444', 'ALICE', 22000, 'A'),
  ('2222-3333-4444-5555', 'BOB', 71000, 'B'),
  ('3333-4444-5555-6666', 'CARL', 123000, 'B'),
  ('4444-5555-6666-7777', 'DAVID', 172000, 'C');
INSERT INTO INTERNAL_INFO VALUES ('AMY', 'A'), ('PAT', 'B'),
  ('HAYTHAM', 'C');
```

If you were to select all of the data from either table, the data would look like the following (note that you can see all of the data at this point because we've not yet applied any row restriction or column masking controls to the data):

CUSTOMER

ACCOUNT	NAME	INCOME	BRANCH
1111-2222-3333-4444	ALICE	22,000	A
2222-3333-4444-5555	BOB	71,000	B
3333-4444-5555-6666	CARL	123,000	B
4444-5555-6666-7777	DAVID	172,000	C

INTERNAL_INFO

EMP_ID	HOME_BRANCH
AMY	A
PAT	B
HAYTHAM	C

Now that we've defined the tables, data, and roles, we need to implement the business enforcements that ensure that people have access to data on a need-to-know basis, as outlined by the business charter.

Recall that one of the data access controls in the charter stipulates that advisors can see information only for their own clients. To implement this rule, a SECADM needs to create an associated row permission object using the CREATE PERMISSION statement, as shown next. (In our example, the SECADM leverages the VERIFY_ROLE_FOR_USER function to ensure that the user is a member of the ADVISOR role.)

```
CREATE PERMISSION advisor_row_ACCESS ON customer
  FOR ROWS WHERE
    VERIFY_ROLE_FOR_USER (USER, 'ADVISOR') = 1 AND
    BRANCH = (SELECT HOME_BRANCH FROM INTERNAL_INFO WHERE EMP_NAME =
    USER)
      ENFORCED FOR ALL ACCESS
ENABLE;
```

Another rule in the charter stipulates that CSRs and telemarketers can see all clients, so the SECADM implements this rule by creating another row permission object on the table using the following CREATE PERMISSION statement. (The VERIFY_ROLE_FOR_USER function is used again, but this time it ensures that the user is a member of the CSR or TELEMARKETER role.)

```
CREATE PERMISSION csr_row_access ON customer
  FOR ROWS WHERE
   VERIFY_ROLE_FOR_USER (USER, 'CSR') = 1 OR
   VERIFY_ROLE_FOR_USER (USER, 'TELEMARKETER') = 1
  ENFORCED FOR ALL ACCESS
ENABLE;
```

The third rule is different than the first two, because it defines restrictions on *column* data rather than row data. The third rule states that all roles will see redacted account numbers except when a CSR is using the CustomerKeeper application for the specific purpose of updating account details. To implement this rule, the SECADM creates a column mask object using the following CREATE MASK statement. This time, the VERIFY_ROLE_FOR_USER function is used to ensure that the non-redacted version of an account number is visible only to users with the CSR role, and that the FUNCUPD routine is being called from the CustomerKeeper application.

```
CREATE MASK csr_column_ACCESS ON customer
  FOR COLUMN account RETURN
   CASE WHEN (VERIFY_ROLE_FOR_USER(SESSION_USER, 'CSR')= 1
    AND ROUTINE_SPECIFIC_NAME = 'FUNCUPD'
    AND ROUTINE_SCHEMA = 'ACTFUNCS'
    AND ROUTINE_TYPE = 'F')
   THEN ACCOUNT
   ELSE 'xxxx-xxxx-xxxx-' || SUBSTR(ACCOUNT,13,4)
   END
ENABLE;
```

If you're following the examples in this chapter, you now have everything that you need to apply the data access controls defined in the charter to the database; you just have to "turn on the light switch" by altering the CUSTOMER table to activate both the row access and column access control rules. To activate the data access control rules, the SECADM executes a statement similar to the following example:

```
ALTER TABLE customer
 ACTIVATE ROW ACCESS CONTROL
 ACTIVATE COLUMN ACCESS CONTROL;
```

At this point, *any* SQL access to the CUSTOMER table (either direct or through an application) is subject to the rules that were specified in the previously defined permission or mask objects.

For example, if Amy's application issued a SELECT * FROM CUSTOMER statement, the result set would look like the following example:

CUSTOMER

ACCOUNT	NAME	INCOME	BRANCH
XXXX-XXXX-XXXX-4444	ALICE	22,000	A

Notice that Amy's application returns only the rows for clients at Branch A (which, according to the INTERNAL_INFO table, is where Amy works), and that a redaction mask has been applied to the ACCOUNT column.

When Haytham's telemarketing application issues *exactly* the same query, the results resemble the following output example:

CUSTOMER

ACCOUNT	NAME	INCOME	BRANCH
XXXX-XXXX-XXXX-4444	ALICE	22,000	A
XXXX-XXXX-XXXX-5555	BOB	71,000	B
XXXX-XXXX-XXXX-6666	CARL	123,000	B
XXXX-XXXX-XXXX-7777	DAVID	172,000	C

Notice that Haytham can see all of the rows in the table, but the ACCOUNT column is still masked. This is consistent with the charter's second rule, which specifies that CSRs and telemarketers can see data from all clients. The ACCOUNT column is still redacted, however, because the charter's third rule specifies that only CSRs using the CustomerKeeper application can see full account numbers. The column mask determines what should appear as an alternative value. In this example, the SECADM decided to show only the last four digits, but they could have chosen for DB2 to return NULL values instead (assuming the column definition allows NULL values). When defining a column mask, the SECADM explicitly defines what the representation of masked data should be.

When Pat, the CSR, uses the CustomerKeeper application to issue the *same* query, the following result set is returned:

CUSTOMER

ACCOUNT	NAME	INCOME	BRANCH
1111-2222-3333-4444	ALICE	22,000	A
2222-3333-4444-5555	BOB	71,000	B
3333-4444-5555-6666	CARL	123,000	B
4444-5555-6666-7777	DAVID	172,000	C

The CustomerKeeper application, which calls the FUNCUPD routine to update a client's account, returns a non-redacted version of the ACCOUNT column to Pat; and because he is a CSR, he is also entitled to look at the entire client list.

Any users who are not authorized by the row access control rules that are defined on the CUSTOMER table won't see any rows at all when they attempt to access this table. For example, if George's Procurement application issues the same query, the database returns an empty result set:

CUSTOMER

ACCOUNT	NAME	INCOME	BRANCH

The Inside Track: Our Hints and Tips to Get Going Fast

Because row permissions and column masks are new to DB2 10, we'll give you some advice on how to get going with this feature and how to implement these finer-grained security controls in your database environment.

Dependencies

Creating, altering, or dropping a table's row permissions or column masks, and activating (or deactivating) row or column access controls, invalidates any existing SQL packages or dynamically cached SQL statements. For this reason, we recommend that you avoid multiple invalidations of these objects by creating all of your row permissions and column masks *before* activating RCAC on the target table.

Even better, we recommend that you create, verify, and test the enforcement of row permissions and column masks on a test system first (yes, it seems like common sense, but you'd be surprised…), then use the nifty db2look tool to extract the row permission and column mask definitions from the test system, and finally apply those definitions to the production system when you know everything is working just the way you expect.

Performance

If we were sitting in a room with you and said that you could ask us any question you want, as long as you buy us a beer, the first question you'd likely ask is this: "What is the performance impact of activating row or column access controls on a table?" Our standard response to any such performance question is, "There is no easy answer to that question."

The performance impact of RCAC is going to depend on the row permissions and column masks that are associated with the table itself. For example, suppose you have a simple table named T1 and that you define a simple predicated row permission (a = 5) on that table. When you activate row access control on this table, any SELECT statement against T1 runs internally with the additional predicate (a = 5), and the performance of the query *could actually be better* because row access control is active.

But here is the very important point we want to leave you with when it comes to a discussion on using row permissions or columns masks in a question about performance: Asking "What is the performance impact?" is the *wrong* question! After all, if you're implementing these kinds of security controls (with or without RCAC), you are likely mandated to do so, or there is a value proposition to protecting data. So the real question you need to ask is, "What is the performance comparison of RCAC compared to using application-based security or a combination of views?" We've found that the performance of both approaches is very comparable since in both cases what ends up being executed is the statement and the security rules. In the application case, the rules are submitted by the application as part of the statement itself; in the case of DB2 10's RCAC, they are added transparently by DB2. We're pretty confident in what we stated at the beginning of this chapter: you are going to find this new DB2 10 feature very rewarding from a total cost of ownership perspective, and also because you'll be able to address the shortcomings of the non-native database approach.

If the predicate were a complex expression involving a number of UDFs, you would likely see a small performance hit. We'd love to give you a better answer, but, in general, any performance impact will depend on the specific row permissions or columns masks that are defined on the table.

You've likely concluded by now that you could potentially use a row permission *or* column mask to enforce the same security requirement. Here are a couple of tips that will help you to decide which method to use from a performance perspective.

When your queries involve a UDF as a predicate, DB2 ensures that the row permissions are evaluated before the UDF to avoid potential data leakage through that UDF. This means that the optimizer may be forced to select a query plan that is not optimal to avoid the potential for data leakage through the UDF. However, when the UDF is declared secure, the optimizer will always pick the optimal plan. Thus, a user with SECADM authority (or their delegate) should mark such functions secure if they are trusted.

Second, we recommend that you approach any objects used in a row permission search condition or in a column mask CASE expression (tables, indexes, functions, and so on) with the same best practices that you would follow for any healthy database. For example, use RUNSTATS regularly on tables that are referenced in an access control's CASE expression or search condition so that the statistics are up to date. Similarly, create appropriate indexes and run REORG operations against tables and their indexes as required.

Three-Tier Application Models

In the typical three-tier application model that dominates shop-and-buy web sites (among others), a generic user ID is typically used to access the database for all requests by all users. This is a longstanding problem in the database world, because whatever the security doctrine (principle of least privilege or separation of duties), this approach violates it. Using a generic ID creates challenges for database security implementations, because the database sees only a single generic ID for access control and auditing purposes.

The good news is that the DB2 9 point releases enhanced the security blanket that DB2 is able to drape over access to your data. In the same manner that role-based security helps with the new RCAC in DB2 10, the Trusted Context feature introduced in DB2 9.5 works hand-in-hand with this feature as well. For an effective database security implementation in a three-tier environment, *use row permissions with trusted context database objects*. This approach allows mid-tier applications to assert end-user identities to the database, so that a user's true identity is known for access control and auditing purposes. Trusted contexts are supported by IBM WebSphere Application Server and IBM Cognos software. In those environments, leveraging trusted contexts is simply a configuration setting on the application server side.

Another potential security issue in three-tier application models is data caching. Some mid-tier applications might cache a query result and reuse that result to service the same query in the future. Such caching is problematic when the user identity is not taken into account, because different users might not necessarily have access to the same information in the database. Even when user identity is taken into account, data caching could still be a problem if the query results cache is not kept synchronized with changes to row permissions and column masks in the database. Our advice? Carefully think through any data caching at the mid-tier layer when designing three-tier applications.

Wrapping It Up

Row permissions and column masks are potent database security features that address the shortcomings of traditional RCAC methods. Not only are they new in DB2 10, but they showcase a synergy with other previously added features (SECADM, roles, trusted context, and so on) to make DB2 one of the most secure databases in the industry. Row permissions and column masks are based on SQL expressions and therefore provide greater flexibility to fine-tune the security model. They're also transparent to applications and provide data-centric security that is managed solely by users with database security administrator authority (SECADM). Row permissions and column masks can be applied to meet the security and privacy requirements around regulatory compliance, multi-tenancy, database hosting, and data consolidation.

We'll leave you with a final recommendation. If the security of your database is important, row permissions and column masks should be at the top of your database security strategy. With DB2 10, more than any previous DB2 release, you'll be able to simplify your security strategy. You'll be able to protect data in motion and at rest, lock down the surface area configuration of your database, separate security duties from administrative duties, restrict privileges such that users and applications have the fewest privileges necessary to carry out the task at hand, and provide defense in depth features that will be the cornerstone to your database security strategy.

4

Time Traveling with DB2: Bitemporal Data Management for Ultimate Business Accuracy and Compliance

Traveling through time to observe the past or look into the future has always been a dream of mankind, because as humans we are inevitably stuck in the present. And yet, the passing of time is of critical importance to all of our endeavors. Time is the fundamental concept that enables us to observe change. Without time, there would be no change, no movement, and no increase or decrease of any business metric. As a consequence, organizations must track and capture time for the purpose of understanding and measuring change in their business. And although we all wish that we could look into the future, being able to travel forward in time based on the data that we have today is a benefit that is rather unique to our industry. DB2 10 makes this task easier and more cost-effective than ever before with the introduction of the *Time Travel Query feature*.

The Business Need for Temporal Data Management

Temporal data management is a discipline that manages and processes data in relation to time. Several business drivers demand temporal data management, and its appeal becomes apparent as time-related data management usage patterns show up in virtually all industries and organizations.

Some of the most critical business drivers for temporal data management are *compliance and auditing regulations*. The governance stipulations that we outlined in Chapter 3 typically require that chartered organizations keep a history of data changes so that one can go back in time to verify what information existed when. The marketplace sometimes refers to this as the *traceability* of data, and it's exceptionally important for audit purposes. For example, most financial companies are subject to rigorous compliance and auditing requirements and might need to answer questions such as these:

- On January 1, what was your expected total investment in asset class X for year end?

- What data was used when the price and risk of a given investment was assessed six weeks ago?

- Can you rerun the risk assessment based on the applicable past state of your data?

- Can you prove that all parts of your firm have been using the same data at the same point in time?

- Do you have full traceability of all data changes and retroactive data corrections?

Similar questions arise in other industries as well. Failure to retain an accurate and complete history of data can have dire consequences, such as loss of investments, fines for noncompliance, legal repercussions, and a damaged reputation.

Many organizations not only require traceability of data changes but also efficient ways to capture, query, and update *effective dates* or *validity periods* of their business. Examples of effective dates include the period of time for which a specific interest rate for a certain account is valid, the time during which a specific address for a given customer is valid, and the period during which a product is on sale at a discounted price. For example, if you decide *today* that a product will be on sale at a 20 percent discount *next week*, this is an update that will be effective in the future. Or, imagine an insurance policy for which the coverage amount, deductibles, and other terms and conditions may have changed at various points in time. When processing a claim involving a car accident, the insurance company must be able to determine the policy's terms in effect when the accident occurred.

Managing effective dates also requires efficient enforcement of temporal constraints. For example, if you've taken a variable-rate mortgage, the bank needs to ensure that only one interest rate is valid for a loan at any given point in time. Similarly, a reservation system must guarantee that no two guests book the same hotel room for overlapping periods of time.

In short, temporal data management enables companies to trace data changes, meet compliance requirements in a cost-effective manner, manage effective dates, and enforce temporal constraints. As a result, temporal data management helps organizations reduce business risk, increase data quality, and make more reliable decisions.

Looking Forward: Temporal Data Management in DB2 10

DB2 10 offers a rich set of temporal data management capabilities collectively known as *DB2 Time Travel Query*. DB2 Time Travel Query is a catchall for a number of related technologies that include temporal tables, temporal queries, temporal updates, and temporal constraints, along with other temporal functionality. All of these capabilities are available in all DB2 editions, so there are no licensing considerations when you want to use this feature.

The Benefits of Time Travel Query

If you wanted to implement some kind of time travel capability before DB2 10, you had to create triggers and complex application logic to trace data changes, manage effective dates, and enforce temporal constraints. If we had to include examples of how to implement temporal data management in previous versions of DB2 (or in databases that don't have temporal features), this book would need to have many more pages, so we decided to leave them out.

DB2 10 pretty much eliminates (the term our lawyers would like us to use is *minimizes*) such efforts through the introduction of temporal tables and support for temporal SQL operations based on the ANSI/ISO SQL:2011 standard. The latter is important because, unlike other solutions in the marketplace, DB2 Time Travel Query is standards-based. Without standardized and declarative SQL constructs for temporal operations, different applications or departments within an organization inevitably end up with different implementations of time-based data processing logic. This greatly dilutes economies of scale, inhibits code reuse, and creates needless risk exposure because of the high potential for error. A lack of standards and reusable logic makes it very challenging to ensure temporal data consistency across applications.

Through simple declarative SQL statements, you can instruct DB2 10 to maintain a history of database changes or track effective business dates automatically, eliminating the need for such logic to be hand-coded into triggers, stored procedures, or application code: this is a tremendous benefit. We conducted a study to quantify how much code you can actually save using the bitemporal table support in DB2 10. In that study's sample application, we implemented temporal update and delete operations for effective dates in the "old" and the "new" ways. The new way uses DB2's business time support and SQL:2011 statements, whereas the old way implements equivalent logic in stored procedures or in Java code. As you can see in Figure 4-1, we found that DB2 10 can reduce the amount of code required to implement

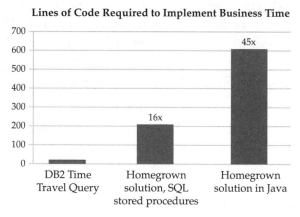

Figure 4-1   *An example of savings secured through the DB2 10 Time Travel Query feature instead of the "old" way of doing things*

such temporal logic by up to 45 times, which greatly reduces the cost for developing and maintaining temporal applications.

Did you know that DB2 10 for Linux, UNIX, and Windows *and* DB2 10 for z/OS are *the first database products in the industry* to provide temporal capabilities based on the ANSI/ISO SQL:2011 standard? The DB2 temporal features discussed in this chapter are deeply integrated into the database engine, which provides exceptional performance as well as seamless integration with all other database features.

Understanding System Time, Business Time, and Temporal Tables

The first step in fully leveraging DB2's temporal tables is to distinguish between system time and business time. *System time* refers to the time in the DB2 database at which INSERT, UPDATE, or DELETE statements are performed inside the database (since MERGE is really a combination of an INSERT and UPDATE operation, we won't explicitly call it out in this chapter). System time is also known as *transaction time*. In contrast, *business time* deals with the tracking of effective dates that reflect when certain information is valid in the "real world." Business time, also known as *valid time* or *effective time*, can be in the past, present, or future. If you choose to manage data along both dimensions of time—system time and business time—then it's appropriate to refer to DB2 Time Travel Query as *bitemporal* data management.

The temporal data management capabilities in DB2 are based on three types of temporal tables:

- **System-period temporal tables**   These tables manage data according to system time. DB2 keeps a history of rows that have been updated or deleted over time. Each row and its corresponding history are automatically assigned a pair of system timestamps. The new SQL standard constructs for temporal tables enable you to go "back in time" and to query the database from any chosen point in the past.

- **Application-period temporal tables**   These tables manage business time. Applications provide dates or timestamps to describe when the data in a given row was or will be valid in the real world. Again, new standardized SQL constructs enable applications to query, insert, update, or delete data from the past, present, or future.

- **Bitemporal tables** These tables manage both system time and business time. Bitemporal tables combine all of the capabilities of system-period and application-period temporal tables. This enables applications to manage the effective dates of their business data while DB2 keeps a full history of data changes. You can even query a bitemporal table along two axes of time.

DB2 10 is currently the only database that has implemented these temporal capabilities based on the SQL standard. In the remainder of this chapter, we tell you how to work with each of these types of temporal tables and provide detailed examples.

Recording and Accessing History with System Time

DB2's support for system time enables you to automatically track and manage multiple versions of your data. When you define a system-period temporal table, you're instructing DB2 to automatically capture changes to the state of your table and to save "old" rows in a history table—a separate table with the same structure as your current table. Whenever a row is updated or deleted, the "before image" of the affected row is inserted into this history table. Timestamps are automatically generated to produce an exact history of all INSERT, UPDATE, and DELETE operations that have taken place on the base table, and queries with temporal references to the base table cause DB2 to transparently access the history table when needed.

Creating a Table with System Time and Versioning

To create a system-period temporal table that leverages system time and versioning, you need to define a base table that stores the current data, create a matching history table for historical data, and then link both these tables by enabling versioning. Let's look at these three steps one by one. For example, to create a table called PRODUCT_ST that stores current data, enter the following data definition language (DDL):

```
CREATE TABLE product_st (
    id              INT PRIMARY KEY NOT NULL,
    name            VARCHAR(32),
    weight          INTEGER,
    price           DECIMAL(10,2),
    sys_start       TIMESTAMP(12) GENERATED ALWAYS AS ROW BEGIN NOT NULL,
    sys_end         TIMESTAMP(12) GENERATED ALWAYS AS ROW END NOT NULL,
    trans_id        TIMESTAMP(12) GENERATED ALWAYS AS TRANSACTION START ID
                                  IMPLICITLY HIDDEN,
  PERIOD SYSTEM_TIME (sys_start, sys_end) );
```

You can see that the PRODUCT_ST base table requires three TIMESTAMP(12) columns whose values are always generated automatically by DB2, as specified by the GENERATED ALWAYS AS clause. Two of these columns indicate the start (sys_start) and end (sys_end) points of the period during which the row is (or was) a current row in the database. The column names are arbitrary, so you can choose your own names. By using RESTRICT ON DROP, you avoid losing historical data when a system-period temporal table is dropped. The third timestamp column (trans_id) is a transaction identifier; it's used to identify which rows from multiple tables were modified by the same transaction. Note that you can define these timestamp columns using the IMPLICITLY HIDDEN clause so that they don't show up in the result set of a SELECT * statement run against the table.

The PERIOD SYSTEM_TIME clause in this example declares that the sys_start and sys_end columns form a system time period. Notice that this declaration is similar to how you declare a primary key or a constraint for a regular table.

Next, create the PRODUCT_ST_HISTORY table such that it has the *same columns* in the *same order* and with the *same data types* as the PRODUCT_ST base table. We recommend that you create this table using the LIKE clause, which is easier and less error prone, as shown here:

```
CREATE TABLE product_st_history LIKE product_st WITH RESTRICT ON DROP;
```

Finally, you need to alter the base table to enable versioning and identify its associated history table. You can add versioning to convert any existing table into a system-period temporal table using the ALTER TABLE statement. To enable versioning on the PRODUCT_ST table, enter the following command:

```
ALTER TABLE product_st ADD VERSIONING
    USE HISTORY TABLE product_st_history;
```

After you execute this statement, any update or delete activity on the PRODUCT_ST table will automatically write history rows in the associated PRODUCT_ST_HISTORY table. Similarly, if you add a column to a versioned table, the same column will be automatically added to the defined history table so that both tables are kept synchronized.

You might wonder why DB2 doesn't just store the current and history rows in the same table. That's because there are a number of critical advantages to having these rows in separate tables:

- The size of the base table remains the same, as it would be without history data. This ensures that the recording of the table's history does not impact the performance of critical operations, such as queries against current data, the insertion of new data, or the building of an index for current data.

- You can assign different physical storage characteristics for the base and history tables; for example, you can leverage an MDC table, range partitioning, compression, page size, or different buffer pool assignments.

- You can define different indexes, constraints, or access privileges for the base table and the history table, depending on your usage scenarios.

Inserting Data into a Table with System Time

Inserting data into a table with system time isn't any different from inserting data into an ordinary table. For example, imagine that on November 15, 2010, you needed to enter two new product records into the PRODUCT_ST table that we created in the previous section. You could use the following INSERT statement to accomplish this:

```
INSERT INTO product_st (id, name, weight, price)
 VALUES (1111, 'Astro-X', 22, 129), (1414, 'Mega-Y', 17, 69.95);
```

Note that this INSERT statement does not provide values for the system-period columns or the transaction ID column that we defined earlier, because these values are almost *always* provided by DB2. One exception to this rule is that the LOAD utility can override the generated columns and load existing timestamps—for example, from a previously exported table.

After running the INSERT statement, the PRODUCT_ST and PRODUCT_ST_HISTORY tables have the following data:

PRODUCT_ST

ID	NAME	WEIGHT	PRICE	SYS_START	SYS_END
1111	Astro-X	22	129	2010-11-15	9999-12-30
1414	Mega-Y	17	69.95	2010-11-15	9999-12-30

PRODUCT_ST_HISTORY

ID	NAME	WEIGHT	PRICE	SYS_START	SYS_END

Because we've not yet updated or deleted any rows in the PRODUCT_ST table, the PRODUCT_ST_HISTORY table is empty. Recall that when we created the PRODUCT_ST table's trans_id column, it was defined using the IMPLICITLY HIDDEN clause, which has the effect of hiding the column from SELECT * queries. The sys_start values in the PRODUCT_ST table reflect the point in time when the rows were inserted (November 15, 2010, in our example), and the sys_end values are set to December 30, 9999, to indicate that these rows have not expired—that is, the rows contain current data.

NOTE   To keep things simple, we're showing only the date portion of the rather long TIMESTAMP(12) data type values in this chapter's examples.

Updating and Deleting Data in a Table with System Time

When you update or delete current data, DB2 transparently and automatically inserts the old version of this data into the base table's associated history table. For example, assume that you entered the following UPDATE statement to change the price for product 1111 to 99.99 on January 31, 2011:

```
UPDATE product_st SET price = 99.99 WHERE id = 1111;
```

If you select the contents of the PRODUCT_ST and PRODUCT_ST_HISTORY tables after running the preceding UPDATE statement, the results look like the following sample output:

PRODUCT_ST

ID	NAME	WEIGHT	PRICE	SYS_START	SYS_END
1111	Astro-X	22	99.99	2011-01-31	9999-12-30
1414	Mega-Y	17	69.95	2010-11-15	9999-12-30

PRODUCT_ST_HISTORY

ID	NAME	WEIGHT	PRICE	SYS_START	SYS_END
1111	Astro-X	22	129	2010-11-15	2011-01-31

Notice that the single UPDATE statement changed the price of Astro-X to $99.99 (as expected) *and* automatically set the sys_start column to the point in time when the UPDATE transaction ran successfully. Also note that the old version of the row (where price=129) has been automatically inserted into the PRODUCT_ST_HISTORY table. The sys_end value for the history row is the timestamp of the UPDATE, because that's when this old version of the row "expired" and was no longer the current row.

Now imagine that the row for the product Mega-Y is deleted on March 31, 2012, with the following DELETE statement on the base table:

```
DELETE FROM product_st WHERE name = 'Mega-Y';
```

After running this DELETE statement, the PRODUCT_ST and PRODUCT_ST_HISTORY tables look like the following:

PRODUCT_ST

ID	NAME	WEIGHT	PRICE	SYS_START	SYS_END
1111	Astro-X	22	99.99	2011-01-31	9999-12-30

PRODUCT_ST_HISTORY

ID	NAME	WEIGHT	PRICE	SYS_START	SYS_END
1111	Astro-X	22	129	2010-11-15	2011-01-31
1414	Mega-Y	17	69.95	2010-11-15	2012-03-31

You can see that the effect of this DELETE operation removes the target Mega-Y row from the PRODUCT_ST table, inserts the row into the PRODUCT_ST_HISTORY table, and sets the value of the corresponding row in the PRODUCT_ST_HISTORY table to the timestamp associated with the successful completion of the DELETE operation that generated this history row.

Now that we've shown you a simple scenario for Time Travel Query, it should be obvious that you can continue to use UPDATE, MERGE, and DELETE statements as you normally would; the history of data changes are automatically recorded. We can't stress how important this is, because it means that application developers don't even have to know about the existence of the history table, which makes things easier and more secure.

Querying a Table with System Time

Querying a table with system time is simple because any queries for current data remain unchanged. It's nice to know that existing applications, routines, and database reports won't be impacted by adding DB2 10's versioning to your database tables.

For example, consider the following SELECT statement, which returns a single row because only the current data is requested. This implicitly means that only the base PRODUCT_ST table needs to be accessed by the database manager:

```
SELECT id, name, weight, price, sys_start, sys_end
 FROM product_st
 WHERE name = 'Astro-X';

1111   Astro-X   22   99.99   2011-01-31   9999-12-30
 1 record(s) selected.
```

You might be wondering how you would query historical data associated with the PRODUCT_ST table that's stored in PRODUCT_ST_HISTORY. Queries that "go back in time" reference only the current table and include a new and simple SQL clause to indicate at which point in time to look. For example, you can use the FOR SYSTEM_TIME AS OF clause to request data from the target table that was current on a particular date or timestamp. A query executed with this clause causes DB2 to transparently access the target table's history table and retrieve the matching history rows that *were* current at the time that is specified by the query. For example, the following query requests the Astro-X product attributes that were in effect on January 1, 2011:

```
SELECT id, name, weight, price, sys_start, sys_end
 FROM product_st FOR SYSTEM_TIME AS OF '2011-01-01'
 WHERE name = 'Astro-X';

1111   Astro-X   22   129   2010-11-15   2011-01-31
 1 record(s) selected.
```

DB2 10 lets you not only query data as of a specific *point in time* (as shown above), but it also gives you the option of requesting rows that were current in a certain *range of time* as well. DB2 10 lets you express time ranges in two ways:

- FOR SYSTEM_TIME FROM <value1> TO <value2>
  This clause specifies a range of time that starts at value1 and *extends up to but does not include* value2. It includes all points in time that are *greater than or equal to* value1 and *less than* value2. Such a range is called an *inclusive-exclusive* period, because the start point is included but the end point is excluded from the specified range.

- FOR SYSTEM_TIME BETWEEN <value1> AND <value2>
  This clause specifies an *inclusive-inclusive* period, which contains all points in time that are *greater than or equal to* value1 and *less than or equal to* value2. If you want your temporal search to include the end points of a specified range of time, this is the right clause to use.

Let's put a range clause to work with an example. Assume that you want a SELECT statement that returns all of the information about Astro-X that was current any time between January 1, 2011 and December 31, 2011 (inclusive). In the following SELECT statement, any rows whose system period overlaps with the time frame that is specified in the temporal query must be returned. DB2 automatically retrieves the relevant rows from both the current and the history table to produce a result set that satisfies the query:

```
SELECT id, name, weight, price, sys_start, sys_end
 FROM product_st FOR SYSTEM_TIME BETWEEN '2011-01-01' AND '2011-12-31'
 WHERE name = 'Astro-X';

1111    Astro-X    22    99.99    2011-01-31    9999-12-30
1111    Astro-X    22     129     2010-11-15    2011-01-31
   2 record(s) selected.
```

It's worth noting that the dates or timestamps that you use in the FOR SYSTEM_TIME AS OF clause don't necessarily have to be literal values; they can be parameter values, host variables, special registers, or expressions that evaluate to the DATE or TIMESTAMP data type. For example, the following query accepts a date or timestamp as a parameter and retrieves all rows that were current at some point between the specified time and "now" (which is represented by DB2's special register CURRENT_TIMESTAMP):

```
SELECT id, name, weight, price, sys_start, sys_end
 FROM product_st FOR SYSTEM_TIME BETWEEN ? AND CURRENT_TIMESTAMP
 WHERE name = 'Astro-X';
```

With these simple yet powerful standard SQL language features, it's easier than ever to implement temporal queries and travel back in time.

Tracking Effective Dates with Business Time

Business time involves tracking when certain business information is, was, or will be valid. For example, a credit card might have a promotional interest rate of 6 percent one month and 18 percent after the promotion expires; or your insurance policy could have different coverage for different times of the year (for example, when you've got your motorcycle on the road).

It's important to appreciate how business time is different from system time. System time produces a history of data changes with automatically generated timestamps that reflect when INSERT, UPDATE, or DELETE operations were performed inside a DB2 database. In contrast, business time represents your application's logical notion of time. That is, it reflects when information was, is, or will be effective (valid) in the real world. Business time by itself does not involve a history table, and the effective dates must be provided by the application.

To illustrate, consider the following two very different questions:

- Which product price was stored in the database on June 30? (system time)

- Which product price was effective in our business on June 30? (business time)

For example, if a product will be offered at a discounted price next week, the price change might get entered into the database today (system time) with an effective date of next week (business time). Similarly, a new insurance policy might get created and inserted into the database in May but backdated with an effective start date of April 15. In short, the business validity for a record is independent of when that record was or was not physically present in the database.

Creating a Table with Business Time

To create a table with business time, you need to have a pair of DATE or TIMESTAMP columns that describe the start and end points of the business validity of each record; although these columns can have arbitrary names, they must be declared using the BUSINESS_TIME period clause in the CREATE TABLE statement. This period declaration enables DB2 to enforce temporal constraints and to perform temporal UPDATE and DELETE operations for business time.

Let's go though a working example. To create an application-period temporal table that enables you to manage business time, run the following DDL:

```
CREATE TABLE product_bt (
    id          INT NOT NULL,
    name        VARCHAR(32),
    weight      INTEGER,
    price       DECIMAL(10,2),
    bus_start   DATE NOT NULL,
    bus_end     DATE NOT NULL,
  PERIOD BUSINESS_TIME (bus_start, bus_end),
  PRIMARY KEY(id, BUSINESS_TIME WITHOUT OVERLAPS) );
```

The primary key constraint in this CREATE TABLE statement uses the optional clause BUSINESS_TIME WITHOUT OVERLAPS. This clause is new in DB2 10 and enforces temporal uniqueness, that is, rows with duplicate ID values are allowed if the business time periods of these rows do not overlap. In other words, BUSINESS_TIME WITHOUT OVERLAPS means that for any given point in time there is at most one row that is effective (valid) for a given product. You can also use the ALTER TABLE statement to add a business time period to existing tables and, optionally, a BUSINESS_TIME WITHOUT OVERLAPS constraint.

Inserting Data into a Table with Business Time

Inserting rows into a table with business time is straightforward: simply provide appropriate values for the business time start and end columns. For example, run the following INSERT statement on the PRODUCT_BT table:

```
INSERT INTO product_bt VALUES
  (1111, 'Astro-X', 22, 129, '2012-01-01', '2012-06-15'),
  (1111, 'Astro-X', 22, 144, '2012-06-15', '2013-01-01'),
  (1414, 'Mega-Y', 17, 69.95,'2011-06-01', '9999-12-30');
```

At this point, the contents of the PRODUCT_BT table looks like the following table:

PRODUCT_BT

ID	NAME	WEIGHT	PRICE	BUS_START	BUS_END
1111	Astro-X	22	129	2012-01-01	2012-06-15
1111	Astro-X	22	144	2012-06-15	2013-01-01
1414	Mega-Y	17	69.95	2011-06-01	9999-12-30

The first row in the PRODUCT_BT table shows that Astro-X has a price of 129, which is in effect from January 1, 2012, until (but not including) June 15, 2012. From June 15, 2012, onward, the price of this product is 144, which is valid until (and including) December 31, 2012.

Look at the second row in this table. It's important that you understand that business time periods are *always* specified in an *inclusive-exclusive* manner. This means that the business start value indicates the first point in time at which the information in a row is valid (inclusive), and the business end value indicates the first point in time at which the information is no longer valid (exclusive). Managing valid periods in an inclusive-exclusive form makes it easy and efficient for applications to detect or avoid gaps between the valid periods of two rows. If the business end value of one row is identical to the business start value of another row, you know for sure that there is no gap between the valid periods of these two rows. This simple equality test works regardless of whether the business time columns are defined as DATE, TIMESTAMP(0), TIMESTAMP(6), or any other timestamp precision.

The third row in the PRODUCT_BT table indicates that the price of Mega-Y became effective on June 1, 2011, and remains valid until further notice. If there is no known business end date, we recommend that you use a very large value (such as 9999-12-30) to represent infinity.

Finally, because the PRODUCT_BT table tracks business time and not system time, it doesn't contain any information about when the rows were inserted, updated, or deleted.

Updating and Deleting Data in a Table with Business Time

You can still write traditional UPDATE statements for tables with business time periods. For example, if you need to change the weight information for Astro-X to 23, irrespective of time, you could run the following UPDATE statement and it will modify both rows in the PRODUCT_BT table that correspond to this product:

```
UPDATE product_bt SET weight = 23 WHERE id = 1111;
```

You can also use the FOR PORTION OF BUSINESS_TIME clause to restrict update or delete operations to a specific business time period. For example, let's assume that you want to increase the price of Astro-X to 155 for the months of November and December 2012 only. You can accomplish this with the following UPDATE statement:

```
UPDATE product_bt
  FOR PORTION OF BUSINESS_TIME FROM '2012-11-01' TO '2013-01-01'
SET price = 155
WHERE id = 1111;
```

If this UPDATE statement is executed against the PRODUCT_BT table in our working example, it would apply only to the second row that references the product Astro-X (the row whose business period overlaps with the period that the UPDATE seeks to modify). Because the portion of business time that's being updated in this UPDATE statement (November 1 to January 1) only partially overlaps with the existing period (June 15 to January 1), DB2 automatically performs a *row split*, as shown in Figure 4-2.

As Figure 4-2 shows, the UPDATE operation produces one row with a period from June 15 to November 1 during which the old price of 144 still applies, and another row with the new price of 155 that is valid from November 1, 2012, to January 1, 2013.

At this point, the PRODUCT_BT table looks like the following (we've shaded the cells that we want you to notice):

PRODUCT_BT

ID	NAME	WEIGHT	PRICE	BUS_START	BUS_END
1111	Astro-X	22	129	2012-01-01	2012-06-15
1111	Astro-X	22	144	2012-06-15	2012-11-01
1111	Astro-X	22	155	2012-11-01	2013-01-01
1414	Mega-Y	17	69.95	2011-06-01	9999-12-30

You can see that such row splits are nontrivial operations, because existing rows must be modified and one or more new rows might need to be generated, depending on how the existing dates in the table relate to the

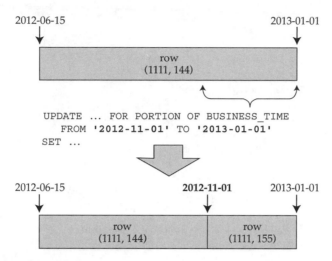

Figure 4-2 *Row split caused by an* UPDATE FOR PORTION OF BUSINESS_TIME
operation

dates that are specified in the FOR PORTION OF BUSINESS_TIME clause of
the UPDATE statement. Luckily, the new SQL syntax makes this very easy for
the application developer and leaves the difficult part for DB2 to figure out.

Similarly to an UPDATE operation, if you want to *delete* data from a table
with business time periods, you can restrict the DELETE operation to a specific range of time by specifying the FOR PORTION OF BUSINESS_TIME
clause. If the row to be deleted holds data that isn't fully contained within
the specified time range, DB2 will automatically preserve the row's data for
the unaffected time period.

Let's use an example to illustrate these concepts. Assume that the Mega-Y
product will be unavailable during the month of October 2013 and therefore
must be deleted for this period of time. The following DELETE statement
implements this business requirement:

```
DELETE FROM product_bt
  FOR PORTION OF BUSINESS_TIME FROM '2013-10-01' TO '2013-11-01'
WHERE id = 1414;
```

When DB2 processes this DELETE statement, it can't simply remove
the row for product 1414; it has to retain one row to reflect the time *before*
October 1, 2013, (when the product was available) and another row to represent the time from November 1, 2013, onward (when the product becomes

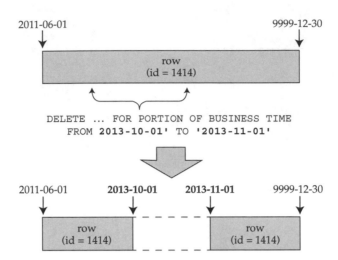

Figure 4-3   *Row split caused by a* DELETE FOR PORTION OF BUSINESS_TIME *operation*

available again). In this case, DB2 has to perform a row split operation with automatic adjustment of business dates, as shown in Figure 4-3.

At this point in our working example, the PRODUCT_BT table looks like the following:

PRODUCT_BT

ID	NAME	WEIGHT	PRICE	BUS_START	BUS_END
1111	Astro-X	22	129	2012-01-01	2012-06-15
1111	Astro-X	22	144	2012-06-15	2012-11-01
1111	Astro-X	22	155	2012-11-01	2013-01-01
1414	Mega-Y	17	69.95	2011-06-01	2013-10-01
1414	Mega-Y	17	69.95	2013-11-01	9999-12-30

Querying a Table with Business Time

The new FOR BUSINESS_TIME clause in SQL SELECT statements makes it simple to query a table with business time, because it lets you easily formulate temporal queries that look at past, current, and future business conditions. Of course, you can still run regular SELECT statements (for non-temporal queries) against a table with business time, and DB2 processing of such queries remains unchanged from what you know today. To demonstrate the power, flexibility, and simplicity of querying a table with business time, let's work through a couple of examples.

First, use the following SELECT statement to run a simple non-temporal query that requests information about the product Astro-X:

```
SELECT id, name, weight, price, bus_start, bus_end
 FROM product_bt WHERE name = 'Astro-X';

1111    Astro-X    22     129     2012-01-01    2012-06-15
1111    Astro-X    22     144     2012-06-15    2012-11-01
1111    Astro-X    22     155     2012-11-01    2013-01-01
   3 record(s) selected.
```

As you can see, this query returns all of the information about the product *regardless* of business time. Remember, with business time, there's no distinction between current data and history data—and also no history table—which only exists with system time. In fact, in this example, all of the rows in the PRODUCT_BT table are considered current, because they reflect our current knowledge about this business in the past, present, and future.

If you want to obtain data that has business validity at a specific point in time, just use the FOR BUSINESS_TIME AS OF clause when you reference the table in your query. For example, the following query retrieves the information about product Astro-X that is effective on June 25, 2012:

```
SELECT id, name, weight, price, bus_start, bus_end
 FROM product_bt FOR BUSINESS_TIME AS OF '2012-06-25'
 WHERE name = 'Astro-X';

1111    Astro-X    22     144     2012-06-15    2012-11-01
   1 record(s) selected.
```

This time, only the second row in the PRODUCT_BT table is returned, because that row's period contains the point in business time that we specified in the query. If we had specified FOR BUSINESS_TIME AS OF '2013-01-01', the result set would have been empty.

Although the PRODUCT_BT table contains a row that describes the product Astro-X from November 1, 2012, to January 1, 2013, the inclusive-exclusive nature of the periods implies that January 1, 2013, isn't part of the validity period. Therefore, the PRODUCT_BT table doesn't contain any information for Astro-X that's effective on January 1, 2013.

DB2 10 lets you not only query data for a specific *point* in business time, but also request the information that is valid during a certain *range* of business time. The keywords FROM and TO specify the desired range as an *inclusive-exclusive* period, whereas the keywords BETWEEN and AND specify this range as an *inclusive-inclusive* period, so that the end point of the range is included in the search.

For example, the following SELECT statement retrieves all information about Astro-X that is valid between October 1, 2012, and October 1, 2013, inclusively.

```
SELECT id, name, weight, price, bus_start, bus_end
 FROM product_bt FOR BUSINESS_TIME BETWEEN '2012-10-01' AND '2013-10-01'
 WHERE name = 'Astro-X';

1111    Astro-X    22    144    2012-06-15    2012-11-01
1111    Astro-X    22    155    2012-11-01    2013-01-01
 2 record(s) selected.
```

Note that any row whose business time period *overlaps* with the time frame that is specified in the temporal query must be returned, which means that some rows in such a result set might only partially match the requested range in the query.

As you can see by the examples in this section, DB2 10's exploitation of the new SQL language standard makes it easier than ever to implement business time travel to the past, present, or future.

Bitemporal Tables: Working with System Time and Business Time

Many organizations have to manage business time periods and retain a full history of all data changes and corrections simultaneously. This creates a need to manage data along two time dimensions: business time and system time. To manage business and system time simultaneously, DB2 10 provides *bitemporal data management*.

For example, only bitemporal data management can answer business questions such as "On January 1, what was our expected volume of loans for year-end?" In this question, "On January 1" refers to system time, because it considers data that was recorded and current in the database for the month of January. The "for year-end" part of the question refers to a future point in business time. In essence, bitemporal data management provides comprehensive information about *what* is known and *when* it is known.

Creating a Bitemporal Table

Creating a bitemporal table is easy: just define a table that has both system and business time periods. To work with the examples in this section, create a PRODUCT_BITEMP table using the following three DDL statements:

```
CREATE TABLE product_bitemp (
    id          INT NOT NULL,
    name        VARCHAR(32),
    weight      INTEGER,
    price       DECIMAL(10,2),
    bus_start   DATE NOT NULL,
    bus_end     DATE NOT NULL,
    sys_start   TIMESTAMP(12) GENERATED ALWAYS AS ROW BEGIN NOT NULL,
    sys_end     TIMESTAMP(12) GENERATED ALWAYS AS ROW END NOT NULL,
    trans_id    TIMESTAMP(12) GENERATED ALWAYS AS TRANSACTION START ID
                    IMPLICITLY HIDDEN,
    PERIOD SYSTEM_TIME (sys_start, sys_end),
    PERIOD BUSINESS_TIME (bus_start, bus_end),
    PRIMARY KEY(id, BUSINESS_TIME WITHOUT OVERLAPS) );

CREATE TABLE product_bitemp_history
    LIKE product_bitemp WITH RESTRICT ON DROP;

ALTER TABLE product_bitemp
 ADD VERSIONING USE HISTORY TABLE product_bitemp_history;
```

This DDL creates a bitemporal table with a BUSINESS_TIME period based on the bus_start and bus_end columns and a SYSTEM_TIME period that's defined by the sys_start and sys_end columns.

As you know, system time requires a history table to track changes, and the history table has to have the *same columns* in the *same order* and with the *same data types* as the base table. That's why we recommended that you create this table using the LIKE clause earlier in this chapter. Finally, alter the base table to enable versioning, and identify the history table for this bitemporal table.

Now that you've created a bitemporal table, you can insert, update, delete, and query rows in this table using the system time and business time concepts and syntax that we described earlier.

Inserting, Updating, and Deleting Data in a Bitemporal Table

Let's illustrate how to insert, update, and delete data in a bitemporal table using a scenario in which a product manager (PM) keeps product information in the PRODUCT_BITEMP table that we defined in the previous section. On November 15, 2011, this PM creates a record for the new Astro-X product that includes its name, weight, and a price of 129 that's set to go into effect on January 1, 2012, and remain valid for the entire year:

```
INSERT INTO product_bitemp (id,name,weight,price,bus_start,bus_end)
VALUES(1111, 'Astro-X', 22, 129, '2012-01-01', '2013-01-01');
```

On March 27, 2012, the PM decides to run a summer promotion and reduces the price of Astro-X to 99.95 for the months of June and July. His product planning application submits the following UPDATE to DB2:

```
UPDATE product_bitemp
  FOR PORTION OF BUSINESS_TIME FROM '2012-06-01' TO '2012-08-01'
SET price = 99.95
WHERE id = 1111;
```

After these statements run successfully, the PRODUCT_BITEMP and PRODUCT_BITEMP_HISTORY tables look like the following. To keep things simple, we're showing only the date portions of the sys_start and sys_end timestamps:

PRODUCT_BITEMP

ID	NAME	WEIGHT	PRICE	BUS_START	BUS_END	SYS_START	SYS_END
1111	Astro-X	22	129	2012-01-01	2012-06-01	2012-03-27	9999-12-30
1111	Astro-X	22	99.95	2012-06-01	2012-08-01	2012-03-27	9999-12-30
1111	Astro-X	22	129	2012-08-01	2013-01-01	2012-03-27	9999-12-30

PRODUCT_BITEMP_HISTORY

ID	NAME	WEIGHT	PRICE	BUS_START	BUS_END	SYS_START	SYS_END
1111	Astro-X	22	129	2012-01-01	2013-01-01	2011-11-15	2012-03-27

You can see that the PRODUCT_BITEMP_HISTORY table contains the old version of the updated row, which reflects the state of the data *before* the

UPDATE statement was executed. The current data in the PRODUCT_BITEMP table now consists of three rows, because the update caused a three-way row split. The first row reflects the information that is valid before June 1, 2012; the second row holds the updated information for the June and July summer price promotion; and the third row represents the data that is effective from August 1 onward. All three rows have a sys_start value equal to 2012-03-27, which is when the UPDATE transaction was successfully executed.

If subsequent delete or update operations cause additional row splits, the old versions of the affected rows are saved in the associated PRODUCT_BITEMP_HISTORY table and the row-split operations are performed on the PRODUCT_BITEMP table. As a result, any changes to the effective dates in the past, present, or future are recorded in the PRODUCT_BITEMP's history table.

Querying a Bitemporal Table

To query a bitemporal table, write a regular SELECT statement and optionally include one or both of the following clauses in your query:

- **FOR SYSTEM_TIME** Retrieves data that was present in DB2 at a specific time

- **FOR BUSINESS_TIME** Retrieves data that was valid at a certain time

For example, consider a sales manager who wants to ask the following question: On March 15, 2012, what was the intended product price for June? The sales manager could easily get the answer to this question by running the following bitemporal query against the PRODUCT_BITEMP table:

```
SELECT id, price, bus_start, bus_end, sys_start, sys_end
  FROM product_bitemp FOR SYSTEM_TIME  AS OF '2012-03-15'
                      FOR BUSINESS_TIME FROM '2012-06-01' TO '2012-07-01'
  WHERE name = 'Astro-X';

1111    129    2012-01-01    2013-01-01    2011-11-15    2012-03-27

1 record(s) selected.
```

When DB2 evaluates this query, it looks at the intersection of the specified system time and business time to retrieve the relevant records. There's no need to reference the history table, because DB2 accesses it transparently, if needed, when working with bitemporal tables. This makes sense, because bitemporal tables are simply tables that are defined with both system and business time.

The DB2 Time Machine: Autopilot for Time Travel Queries

No time machine would be complete without an autopilot. If you have existing applications or SQL scripts that you want to run against a specific point in system time or business time, it can be a lot of work to add FOR SYSTEM_TIME and FOR BUSINESS_TIME clauses to all of your queries. New DB2 special registers enable you to pick a specific point in system time (or business time) and run your applications or SQL scripts against that specified time without having to modify existing queries. We like to refer to this as *autopilot* mode for time travel query. Autopilot for time travel query is implemented through a pair of DB2 special registers that set a database session to specific points in time. The CURRENT TEMPORAL SYSTEM_TIME special register sets a database session to a chosen point in system time, and the CURRENT TEMPORAL BUSINESS_TIME special register sets a database session to a chosen point in business time.

Using Autopilot for System Time

If an application wants to see historical data that was current at, say, 10:00 a.m. on January 1, 2008, it can issue the following SET statement to specify the session's system time:

```
SET CURRENT TEMPORAL SYSTEM_TIME = '2008-01-01 10:00:00';
```

Subsequently, any queries against system-period temporal tables or bitemporal tables that are performed in the same session will see data as of 10:00 a.m. on January 1, 2008. All queries in the session are internally rewritten to use the clause FOR SYSTEM_TIME AS OF '2008-01-01 10:00:00'. DB2 performs this rewrite automatically for you, so you don't need to change your SQL statements in any way.

Similarly, you could issue the following SET statement to look at data from one month ago:

```
SET CURRENT TEMPORAL SYSTEM_TIME = CURRENT_DATE - 1 MONTH;
```

To disable the autopilot mode, so that queries see only the most current data in system-period temporal tables, set the special register back to NULL (which is the default value):

```
SET CURRENT TEMPORAL SYSTEM_TIME = NULL;
```

When the CURRENT TEMPORAL SYSTEM_TIME register is set to a value other than NULL, any data manipulation language (DML) operation (INSERT, UPDATE, or MERGE) against a system-period temporal or bitemporal table will return an error. You simply can't go back in time and change history (though at times we all wish we could).

Using Autopilot for Business Time

When you access tables with business time, you can set the CURRENT TEMPORAL BUSINESS_TIME special register so that any table activity sees the data that is valid at a specific point in business time. For example, consider the following register setting:

```
SET CURRENT TEMPORAL BUSINESS_TIME = '2014-06-01';
```

With this setting, any queries against tables with business time are automatically rewritten to use the clause FOR BUSINESS_TIME AS OF '2014-06-01' and select data that's valid on June 1, 2014.

If you update or delete rows in a table with business time while this register is set, the UPDATE or DELETE statement affects only rows that are valid on June 1, 2014—that is, DB2 automatically adds a WHERE clause to the DELETE or UPDATE statement to target rows whose business time period overlaps with the time that was set in the special register. Note that the special register does *not* add a FOR PORTION OF BUSINESS_TIME clause to a DELETE or UPDATE statement and, therefore, setting the special register does not cause any row splits.

To disable autopilot for business time, set the special register to NULL.

Usage Guidelines for the Autopilot

You can set both special registers at the same time, which can be useful if you query bitemporal tables or if you access a mix of system-period temporal tables and application-period temporal tables.

For either time dimension (system or business time), you must not apply two time constraints simultaneously. This means that you can either set the system time special register to a non-NULL value, or use a FOR SYSTEM_TIME clause in your SQL queries, but not both at the same time. The same applies to business time. If you execute queries that contain a FOR BUSINESS_TIME clause, the CURRENT TEMPORAL BUSINESS_TIME register must be set to NULL.

You can choose whether or not applications or stored procedures respect the temporal special register settings. New bind options and routine options enable you to make this choice; find more details in the DB2 Information Center.

The Inside Track: Our Hints and Tips to Get Going Fast

DB2 10's temporal support has been designed to enable easy migration of existing database tables to the new temporal capabilities. In this section, we'll give you some hints and tips to get started with Time Travel Query from a migration standpoint.

We expect two very common migration scenarios:

- Convert an existing table without suitable timestamp columns into a temporal table.

- Convert an existing table with timestamp columns and values into a temporal table.

Migrating a Table Without Timestamp Columns

Let's say you have an existing table (whose DDL is shown next) that doesn't have any TIMESTAMP columns, and you want to turn this table into a temporal table with a system time or business time period.

```
CREATE TABLE product_to_temporal (id INT PRIMARY KEY NOT NULL,
  name VARCHAR(32), weight INTEGER);
```

The following statements convert this table into a system-period temporal table. The ALTER TABLE statement adds the required timestamp columns and declares the SYSTEM_TIME period. The other two statements create the corresponding history table and enable versioning, which you've learned about in this chapter.

```
ALTER TABLE product_to_temporal
   ADD COLUMN sys_start TIMESTAMP(12) NOT NULL GENERATED AS ROW BEGIN
   ADD COLUMN sys_end TIMESTAMP(12) NOT NULL GENERATED AS ROW END
   ADD COLUMN trans_id TIMESTAMP(12) GENERATED AS TRANSACTION START ID
   ADD PERIOD SYSTEM_TIME (sys_start, sys_end);

CREATE TABLE product_to_temporal_history LIKE product_to_temporal
 WITH RESTRICT ON DROP;

ALTER TABLE product_to_temporal
 ADD VERSIONING USE HISTORY TABLE product_to_temporal_history;
```

When you add timestamp columns for a system time period to an existing table, DB2 doesn't know when the existing rows in the table were originally inserted and what their `sys_start` values should be. Therefore, all existing rows initially get the `sys_start` value of `0001-01-01`, which is January 1, 0001. If you prefer to use the current time as the system start time for all existing rows, export and reload all rows *before* you enable versioning:

```
EXPORT TO prod.del OF DEL SELECT * FROM product_to_temporal;

LOAD FROM prod.del OF DEL MODIFIED BY PERIODIGNORE
 REPLACE INTO product_to_temporal;

ALTER TABLE product_to_temporal
 ADD VERSIONING USE HISTORY TABLE product_history_to_temporal;
```

The `PERIODIGNORE` modifier in the `LOAD` command instructs DB2 to ignore the timestamps in the exported data and to generate new timestamps during the load operation. In other situations, you might find it helpful to use the `PERIODOVERRIDE` modifier; this modifier enables you to load existing timestamps into the system time columns instead of generating new timestamps during the load operation.

Migrating an existing table to an application-period temporal table (or a bitemporal table) is very similar but uses a slightly different `ALTER TABLE` statement to add business time columns and a `BUSINESS_TIME` period. You can use regular `UPDATE` statements to update the new business time columns with suitable values for existing rows in the table.

Migrating a Table with Timestamp Columns

Now let's assume that you have an existing table with timestamp columns. These timestamp columns might have been populated by an application or by database triggers. You might also have a corresponding history table that you have maintained with triggers to keep a record of deleted and updated rows, because you didn't have the facilities that are now available in DB2 10.

Let's assume that your table with a TIMESTAMP column was defined by the following DDL and that you want to convert this table into a system-period temporal table:

```
CREATE TABLE product_nontemporal_timestamp (
  id       INT PRIMARY KEY NOT NULL,
  name     VARCHAR(32),
  weight   INTEGER,
  price    DECIMAL(10,2),
  sys_start TIMESTAMP(6) NOT NULL,
  sys_end   TIMESTAMP(6) NOT NULL);
```

One important thing to note about this table is that the existing timestamp columns are of type TIMESTAMP(6). This data type needs to be altered, because, as you learned earlier in this chapter, a system time period requires TIMESTAMP(12) values. This requirement can be satisfied by issuing the following ALTER TABLE statement that also adds the mandatory transaction ID column:

```
ALTER TABLE product_nontemporal_timestamp
 ALTER COLUMN sys_start SET DATA TYPE TIMESTAMP(12)
 ALTER COLUMN sys_end   SET DATA TYPE TIMESTAMP(12)
 ADD COLUMN trans_start TIMESTAMP(12) GENERATED AS TRANSACTION START ID;
```

Next, you need to convert the sys_start and sys_end columns into generated columns that are automatically populated upon INSERT, UPDATE, or DELETE operations. The same ALTER TABLE statement can also declare the required SYSTEM_TIME period:

```
ALTER TABLE product_nontemporal_timestamp
  ALTER COLUMN sys_start SET GENERATED AS ROW BEGIN
  ALTER COLUMN sys_end   SET GENERATED AS ROW END
  ADD PERIOD SYSTEM_TIME (sys_start, sys_end);
```

After these alterations, you can create a history table and enable versioning as you've done throughout this chapter. Alternatively, if you have an existing history table, you can modify it so that it has the same column names and types as the altered PRODUCT_NONTEMPORAL_TIMESTAMP table. Afterward, you can enable versioning of this table using your existing history table.

Wrapping It Up

The temporal data management capabilities in DB2 10 provide simple yet sophisticated capabilities for managing multiple versions of your data and tracking valid business dates. Based on the temporal features in the SQL:2011 standard, DB2 10 enables database professionals to work with temporal data in an efficient manner, saving considerable time and effort in comparison to hard-coding temporal logic into triggers, routines, or homegrown applications. The deep integration of bitemporal data processing logic into the DB2 engine reduces the cost of developing and maintaining temporal applications, while simultaneously improving their performance. The bitemporal capabilities of DB2 provide companies with a cost-effective means to achieve exceptional data quality and regulatory compliance, which in turn enables them to reduce risk and increase operational efficiency.

The following comment about this feature, from Craig Baumunk, principal, BitemporalData.com, speaks volumes: "The use of standardized SQL syntax for temporal operations and the integration deep into the database engine make DB2 a leader in second-generation Bitemporal data management."

We believe that the temporal and bitemporal capabilities in DB2 10 are quite different from anything else that is available in today's database market because of the way it has been implemented. For example, DB2 10 is the first database system that supports system time and business time according to the new SQL:2011 standard. With these capabilities, DB2 10 enables bitemporal data management with exception performance and flexibility.

Finally, as you get started with Time Travel Query, make sure that you keep up to date with this feature's best practices (www.ibm.com/ developerworks/data/bestpractices/db2luw/) and with a visit to the discussion forum that is dedicated to this amazing DB2 10 feature (http:// tinyurl.com/bw27uj5).

5

The (Yet Again) Even Faster DB2

We want to note explicitly here that every release of DB2 includes a whack of performance enhancing features; we feel sorry for some of our developers whose performance enhancing heroics make DB2 run faster and faster every release, yet their work seldom gets the spotlight, a name, fanfare, and so on. We're not going to cover all of the fine-tuning nip-and-tuck work that went into DB2 10 to make it the fastest DB2 database ever, but you can assume a lot more went into features that push the DB2 10 performance envelope than what we cover in this chapter.

The Not-so-Little Engine that Could: Scaling Your Workloads with DB2 10

Over the years, DB2 has earned a strong reputation for its ability to scale as workload demands and the number of users increase. This reputation is based on a powerful database engine whose comprehensive scaling features enable it to optimize workloads by *scaling up* and *scaling out* applications, as shown in Figure 5-1.

On the left, you can see how DB2 *scales up*, utilizing a single host computer with autonomic exploitation of multicore parallelism across different concurrent database requests and within single queries. When you scale up a workload within a single host computer (or virtual partition, such as a logical partition [LPAR] or VMware session—in this chapter, we'll assume that

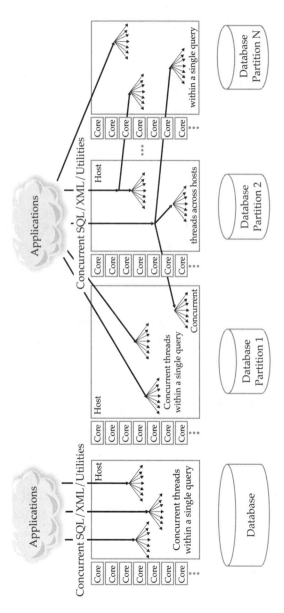

Figure 5-1   *DB2's scale-up and scale-out capabilities*

they are all the same thing), you effectively add more processor cores and memory to the engine. These new computing resources are subsequently allocated across concurrent transactions (even within a single SQL query) using DB2's powerful *intra-partition parallelism*.

On the right of the figure, you can see how DB2 *scales out* across multiple host computers (again, these could be virtualization sessions) by partitioning the database and exploiting multiple cores in multiple hosts across concurrent database requests (this parallelism approach also works for single queries). The workload is spread across multiple database partitions, which have their own processor cores and memory, and DB2 utilizes resources across concurrent transactions using *inter-partition parallelism*.

There has been a long-standing debate about scale-up and scale-out technologies; the truth is that DB2 has been a leader in both for a very long time. Scale out is effective for business intelligence–like workloads using a shared nothing architecture: the hosts each have their own resources. We've seen a number of vendors jump on this scaling approach in recent years, but it's been part of DB2 for over two decades.

What's interesting about the shared nothing scale-out approach is that it's part of the architectural boasting of the Hadoop Big Data craze, and all of those value propositions have been part of DB2 for a long time. That's not to say that you can use DB2 for all of your Big Data needs—since Big Data encompasses use cases involving unstructured data, schemaless data, and more—but DB2 is definitely an engine for some of your Big Data problems. Although DB2 has some really cool applicable characteristics (pureXML and the new multiple graph store in DB2 10, for example), we're making the point here that DB2 has been a leader in spreading workloads across independent computing clusters for a very long time. It's also evident from multiple transactional benchmark wins over the last decade, and more, that DB2 is terrific at leveraging host compute resources to scale workloads. Finally, DB2 can mix both inter- and intra-partition parallelism (scale up and scale out) to fuel a whopping scalability boost for your workloads.

DB2 10 enhances its scaling repertoire with significant enhancements for intra-partition parallelism and the "folding in" of DB2 pureScale technology (another scale-out option that provides exceptional transaction-based scalability and availability characteristics) into the code base. In this section, we look at both of these DB2 10 scalability enhancements in detail.

Intra-partition Parallelism "Reloaded"

Multicore parallelism continues to be a significant industry trend; in fact, even in the home computer and tablet markets, CPUs with multiple processing cores are ubiquitous. When we talk about multicore servers, we are referring to machines whose motherboards have one or more CPU sockets with CPU chips that allow for multiple processing cores, each of which is capable of running multiple concurrent hardware threads. The addition of multiple cores implies more threads, and today's servers are characterized by the ability to run 256 or more threads in a single address space! For example, the most powerful IBM POWER7 servers available at the time that this book was written can dispatch more than 1000 threads! DB2 has been engineered to exploit his kind of capability and was rearchitected from a process-based model to a threaded model in DB2 9.5.

All this talk about multicore servers can sometimes cause confusion, because when folks say that they have a four-way server, is that a single quad core CPU, or is it four sockets with multiple cores? For this reason, we recommend that you explicitly mention the number of cores when you have a reference architecture discussion; this way, everyone is on the same page, which is especially important when it comes to licensing discussions.

IBM recognized the beginnings of this trend many years ago when it developed DB2's initial intra-partition parallelism capabilities. DB2 10 takes intra-query parallelism to the next level by overhauling several of the key internal mechanisms that are used to control parallelism and concurrency, introducing new parallel algorithms, as well as introducing new external application controls that we'll discuss in this section. The nice thing about these features (and we hope that you are spotting a key trend here) is that they are all autonomic; you don't need to do anything to take advantage of them.

One of the most common causes of suboptimal scaling revolves around row filtering during query execution, which causes a work imbalance between subagents. For example, let's assume that during the processing of a nested loop join, DB2 might use eight subagent threads to execute the join in parallel (with each subagent responsible for scanning a fixed portion of the inner table) and then compare the result against the outer table rows.

Now consider the case in which the query's join predicates are such that after row filtering, only one subagent is left with rows to compare. In this case, all but one of the subagents will have no work to do, and this join will execute no more quickly than if intra-partition parallelism were not used at all! To address this condition, DB2 10 introduces a new REBAL operator (it stands for rebalance). When DB2 uses this operator in a query's access plan that includes a join, DB2 automatically rebalances rows across all eight subagents to spread that work around and drive more parallelism. We've seen this feature dramatically speed up query execution; in this example, there could be as much as an eight-fold improvement in performance!

Another DB2 10 feature that supports strong performance through multicore parallelism is the ability to perform scans on partitioned indexes in parallel. A *partitioned index* is an index that comprises a set of individual indexes, one for each data partition in a range-partitioned table. Before DB2 10, a scan on a partitioned index couldn't be executed in parallel by the host computer's subagent threads. This all changes in DB2 10, because partitioned index scans can now be executed in parallel! This is a really big deal: A parallel scan on a partitioned index is divided into ranges of records based on index key values and the number of key entries for each key value. Each subagent is assigned a range of records in the first qualifying index partition, and each subagent is assigned a new range when it has completed work on its current range. Index partitions are scanned sequentially, with subagents potentially moving on to the next index partition, as necessary, at any point in time, without waiting for other subagents. Only those subsets of index partitions that are relevant to the query (based on data partition elimination analysis) are scanned. As you might expect, this single improvement alone could improve query performance by several factors, particularly if you have a significant number of partitioned index scans in your workload.

Other multicore performance enhancements in DB2 10 include more efficient parallelization techniques during query execution through various algorithm improvements, subagent contention reduction techniques in GROUP BY processing, sort processing, hash join processing, and prefetching.

We are at that point in the chapter where we are supposed to tell you that "your results are going to vary." Although it's nearly impossible to provide a definitive performance statement that applies to all workloads, we can say with confidence that in our internal pre-GA DB2 10 lab tests, we saw *very* significant improvements in query performance. We mean three-fold overall improvements in some cases, particularly in environments with a high number of concurrent hardware threads (12 or more).

New DB2 10 Parallelism Controls

Before we leave the topic of intra-partition parallelism, we want to mention some of the new parallelism controls in DB2 10.

Application Control   DB2 10 introduces a built-in stored procedure that enables an application to turn intra-partition parallelism ON or OFF at the transaction boundary, regardless of the current setting for the INTRA_PARALLEL database manager configuration (dbm cfg) parameter. (We should point out that this routine takes effect on the next transaction boundary if there are no open WITH HOLD cursors.)

Using this procedure, you can easily enable intra-partition parallelism for applications that can benefit from it, or disable this feature for applications (such as lightweight OLTP applications) that typically won't benefit from it, thereby avoiding a small overhead. For example, if you want to run a report on a DB2 database for which intra-partition parallelism is disabled (INTRA_PARALLEL=OFF), you could issue the CALL SYSPROC.ADMIN_SET_INTRA_PARALLEL('YES') statement to enable intra-partition parallelism specifically for this workload, even though the feature is turned off for other workloads.

Workload Control   DB2 10 also introduces a workload-level attribute named MAXIMUM DEGREE that enables you to set an upper limit on the degree of intra-partition parallelism that will be used for any database work being mapped to that workload. For example, issuing the ALTER WORKLOAD reports MAXIMUM DEGREE 4 statement limits each query in the REPORTS workload to four parallel subagents. This level of intra-partition parallelism control can be very useful if you don't have access to the actual application code that is generating the workload.

The MAXIMUM DEGREE workload attribute can also be used to enable intra-partition parallelism regardless of the current setting for the INTRA_PARALLEL dbm cfg parameter.

DB2 pureScale Folded into DB2 for Ultimate Scale Out

DB2 pureScale is an exciting distributed DB2 scale-out technology that provides *application transparent* scaling to over 100 servers, while simultaneously delivering exceptional levels of availability. The DB2 pureScale technology was first available as a pureScale-only release called DB2 9.8 (if you weren't using this technology, you didn't move from DB2 9.7 to DB2 9.8). In DB2 10, this technology merges with the DB2 code base and is offered as an add-on to select DB2 editions.

Although DB2 pureScale is relatively new technology for distributed servers, its fundamental design principles are far from new. In fact, DB2 pureScale is based on IBM's proven DB2 for z/OS Parallel Sysplex architecture, which is widely regarded (even by a major competitor's CEO) as the industry "gold standard" for maintaining availability and meeting the most demanding scalability needs for mission-critical applications.

Figure 5-2 shows the data sharing approach that's used by the DB2 pureScale technology. As you can see, an application can connect to any host computer (known as a *member* in the DB2 pureScale nomenclature) to process its transactions. Within that member, intra-partition parallelism can be used to speed up query execution. Connections, by default, are automatically and transparently distributed across members to balance workload demands across all of the host computers that make up the cluster; this balancing can

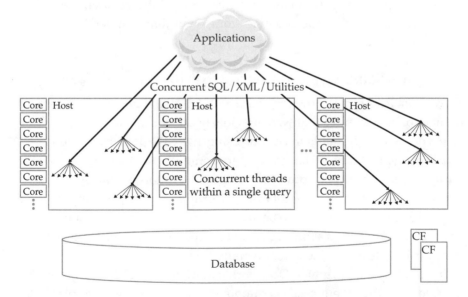

Figure 5-2   *Highly available application transparent scale out with DB2 pureScale.*

occur at the transaction or connection boundary level. The Cluster Caching Facility (CF) aids in providing global buffer coherency and global locking. (We should note that both the host computer and the CF in Figure 5-2 could be virtualized sessions, such as a logical partition [LPAR].)

We like to refer to the CF as "secret sauce"; it's unique to IBM's shared data solutions, and it gives the DB2 pureScale feature its marketplace advantages, namely scalability and true transparent application scaling. (We say "true" here because if you delve beneath the marketing veneer of some vendor's transparent scaling claims, you'll find it's just that, marketing.) Pervasive redundancy provides extreme availability across the cluster, and if any member or CF fails, another member or CF very quickly takes over its workload.

In a DB2 pureScale environment such as the one shown in Figure 5-2, each host computer has equal access to the database. This enables applications to connect to any of the cluster's host computers to access the database. IBM's unique CF technology is used to provide global locking and buffer management. Redundant components (for example, hosts and CFs) provide exceptional availability characteristics.

We can't possibly discuss all of the details that you need to understand all there is to know about the DB2 pureScale technology here. For this reason, we recommend that you download a free copy of the book entitled "DB2 pureScale: Risk Free Agile Scaling" from www.ibm.com/software/data/education/bookstore.

New pureScale Capabilities in DB2 10

Aside from a merging of the code base with DB2, DB2 pureScale users get a number of new features that were previously unavailable to them.

If you're already familiar with or using the DB2 pureScale technology, you'll be happy to hear that range partitioning is now supported. Range partitioning enables you to divide a large table into several separate data partitions. This results in significant performance improvements, because only relevant partitions need to be accessed during query processing. Range partitioning also brings about significant availability improvements through data partition-level maintenance operations.

In addition, the integrated DB2 Workload Manager (DB2 WLM) can now be used in a DB2 10 pureScale environment to manage and control the different classes of work that run on such a cluster. Support for DB2 WLM is comprehensive and includes all of the capabilities that are available for DB2 WLM on non-pureScale databases, including new features such as the DB2 WLM Dispatcher service that is discussed elsewhere in this chapter.

DB2 10 enhances the support for interconnected DB2 pureScale clusters with its extended support for Remote Direct Memory Access (RDMA) over Converged 10 GB Ethernet (RDMA over Converged Ethernet, or RoCE) networks, now including selected POWER7 and Red Hat Enterprise Linux (RHEL) 6.1 platforms. This provides another alternative to the existing InfiniBand interconnect support offered on these platforms.

From a backup and recovery (BAR) perspective, DBAs will be pleased to know that they can now use table space–level BAR operations in a DB2 pure-Scale environment. Support for this feature gives you finer grained control over BAR operations and should help you to plan and implement mean time to repair (MTTR) guidelines for your business. We talk about these enhancements in Chapter 6.

Other enhancements include new ways to monitor the CF, new diagnostic capabilities, and a new CURRENT MEMBER special register.

Table Partitioning Enhancements

Table partitioning (also known as *range partitioning*) is a very popular DB2 technique, first introduced in DB2 9, that provides faster query execution and simplified table management. Tables that are partitioned by range store the ranges in separate table objects called *data partitions*. Queries can avoid reading entire partitions if their predicates specify no data from those partitions. From an administrative point of view, the ease with which you can attach or detach (without logging) ranges of data that match the business taxonomy makes range-partitioned tables a key piece of most DBA reference architectures. Range-partitioned tables give you data partition-level granularity for management activities such as reorganization, which can be done on a partition basis, thereby improving your database's availability and performance characteristics.

DB2 10 packs some major improvements for table partitioning when it comes to attaching new ranges of data, which is often referred to as *data roll-in*. In DB2 10, data roll-in can be conducted online while users are querying the table. Range-partitioned tables also get a roll-in performance boost in DB2 10 through the SET INTEGRITY...IMMEDIATE UNCHECKED statement.

ATTACH Goes Online to Boost Table Availability During Data Roll-in Operations

The typical way of getting new data into a range-partitioned table is to *attach* it. For example, let's assume you've got a SALES table that is partitioned by month to support the roll-in (attach) and roll-out (detach) of monthly sales data. In such a scenario, DBAs typically implement what's called a *rolling range*: when the current month ends, you add its sales data to your SALES table while data from the oldest month drops off. In this scenario, a DBA typically first loads data into a separate staging table (in our example, STAGINGTABLE is defined with the same schema as the target table) and then attaches the staging table to the target table (in this case, the SALES table). The following code shows an example of this scenario:

```
LOAD FROM lastmonthsales.del OF DEL REPLACE INTO stagingtable;
ALTER TABLE sales ATTACH PARTITION sales_2012_07
   STARTING('2012-07-01') ENDING('2012-07-31')
   FROM stagingtable;
COMMIT;
```

We've kept this example simple by omitting the SET INTEGRITY step, because we're going to come back to it later in this section to help illustrate some of the other table-partitioning enhancements in DB2 10.

One of the drawbacks of attaching a data partition in previous versions of DB2 is that the execution of the ALTER...ATTACH statement required a Z (super-exclusive) lock on the target table; in this example, that's the SALES table. This means that the ALTER...ATTACH statement needed to wait until all queries against the table were drained before it could perform the ATTACH operation. This left DBAs with quite the conundrum: do you force all running queries off the system and potentially impact your users, or do you wait for the queries to end and block new queries from entering the system until ATTACH processing is complete?

In DB2 10, the DBA's "to force or not to force" soliloquy disappears, because ALTER...ATTACH no longer needs the ever-blocking Z lock. This means that ATTACH processing can run at the same time as *most* queries without impeding their progress. Did you notice that we said "most" and not "all"? As you might expect, there are certain restrictions. For example, queries that are designed to run with the repeatable read (RR) isolation level must be guaranteed to get the same results if they run twice in the same transaction;

naturally, ALTER...ATTACH must block any query that's running with the RR isolation level. In our experience, warehouse queries are usually characterized by dynamic SQL with isolation levels other than RR, so, for the most part, warehouse queries aren't going to run into this restriction and will run online concurrently with ALTER...ATTACH.

Faster Data Roll-in Through SET INTEGRITY... IMMEDIATE UNCHECKED

Before newly attached data is visible to queries, you have to run a SET INTEGRITY operation. In a nutshell, SET INTEGRITY performs any required data validation, and other maintenance operations, before allowing access to the newly attached data in a partitioned table. With this in mind, let's return to our ALTER...ATTACH example and add the SET INTEGRITY step:

```
LOAD FROM lastmonthsales.del OF DEL REPLACE INTO stagingtable;
ALTER TABLE sales ATTACH PARTITION sales_2012_07
   STARTING('2012-07-01') ENDING('2012-07-31')
   FROM stagingtable;
COMMIT;
SET INTEGRITY FOR sales ALLOW WRITE ACCESS
    IMMEDIATE CHECKED FOR EXCEPTION IN sales
      USE sales_exceptions;
COMMIT;
```

In this example, SET INTEGRITY validates that the newly attached data is in the correct date range (July 2012) and also performs any required index maintenance, such as adding keys for each new record. Any rows with exceptions are placed in the specified exception table (SALES_EXCEPTIONS).

As you've likely imagined, a SET INTEGRITY operation has the potential to take a significant amount of time and resources for its data validation and maintenance mandate. Of course, this is going to beg the question, How is DB2 10 going to help me here? The answer is quite simple really: DB2 10 enables you to bypass this processing if you're sure it's not needed. For example, your existing extract, transform, and load (ETL) procedures might have already cleansed the sales data and validated its date range *before* it was loaded into the staging table. In this case, instead of running SET INTEGRITY...CHECKED, you can simply issue the following statement:

```
SET INTEGRITY FOR sales ALLOW WRITE ACCESS IMMEDIATE UNCHECKED;
COMMIT;
```

The `ALLOW WRITE ACESS IMMEDIATE UNCHECKED` option tells DB2 that you've already performed data validation, so the `SET INTEGRITY` operation doesn't have to. So our advice is this: If you're going to use this feature—and we certainly want you to use it if it applies to your situation—be sure that when you tell DB2 that "it's been taken care of," *it really has been taken care of!*

We should also note that `SET INTEGRITY` is already smart enough to avoid index maintenance wherever possible. For example, if you create staging table indexes corresponding to all of the partitioned indexes on the `SALES` table *before* issuing the `ATTACH` statement, the `SET INTEGRITY` operation can just install those already-created indexes as new partitions of the partitioned `SALES` indexes, without having to re-create them. Of course, if you have any nonpartitioned indexes on the `SALES` table, `SET INTEGRITY` will need to add entries to these indexes for all attached records.

All in all, DB2 10 is much faster at `SET INTEGRITY` processing that any version before it; and, specifically, it's much faster at data roll-in, particularly when a partitioned table has only partitioned indexes on it. Figure 5-3 shows an example of the performance improvements that we've seen in our data roll-in tests (and once again, those lawyers require us to tell you that "your results are going to vary"). In this example, we're attaching data partitions

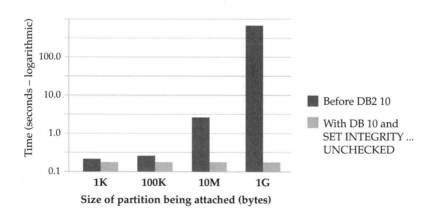

Figure 5-3 *A comparison of SET INTEGRITY...CHECKED and SET INTEGRITY... UNCHECKED from a performance perspective*

of various sizes; there are no nonpartitioned indexes, and all partitioned indexes already exist.

In Figure 5-3, the deeply shaded bars show `SET INTEGRITY...CHECKED` processing times, and the lightly shaded bars show the DB2 10 `SET INTEGRITY...UNCHECKED` processing times. As you can see, this is an enhancement that you can't ignore if you're using a rolling range schema to support your applications.

Performance Assurance: Using the DB2 Workload Management Dispatcher for SLA Attainment

Another exciting new capability in DB2 10 is the new DB2 Workload Management Dispatcher (WLM Dispatcher), which provides DBAs with a fine-grained control mechanism to govern the assignment of CPU resources to the various classes of work in your database system. The WLM Dispatcher is deeply integrated deep within the DB2 engine and is available on the entire platform spectrum where DB2 10 for Linux, UNIX, and Windows runs. We think that this feature will become a "go-to" tool for DBAs because it provides the following benefits:

- Ensures that mission-critical OLTP workloads get the CPU cycles that they need to meet their governing Service Level Agreements (SLAs); during this optimization, the policy can let resource-competing lower priority workloads (such as an ad hoc reporting) consume residual CPU cycles after "critical" workload demands have been satisfied.

- Allocates CPU resources to different workloads in a way that matches the relative importance of those workloads.

- Limits CPU consumption to specific workloads that are accessing your databases.

CPU Shares and Limits

To appreciate just how powerful DB2's WLM Dispatcher is, you should understand two key concepts known as *CPU shares* and *limits*. (We'll show you how those concepts apply to managing SLAs effectively in this chapter.)

CPU Shares

The WLM Dispatcher enables you to assign CPU shares (ranging from 1 to 65535) to a WLM service class. The number of CPU shares that are assigned to a service class reflects the relative proportion of CPU resources that the DB2 database manager will use as a target allocation for the specified service class. For example, let's assume that service class MANAGER is assigned 1000 shares and that service class EXECUTIVE is assigned 2000 shares; these allocations indicate that any workload running under the MANAGER service class should be given approximately one-third of the available CPU resources, and that EXECUTIVE workloads should be given about two-thirds of the computer resources that are available to DB2 (1000 + 2000 = 3000 total CPU shares).

It's important to note that the *actual* (not targeted) amount of CPU resources that are allocated to an operational service class can depend on several other factors. For example, when overall CPU resources are not constrained, the actual CPU that is consumed by the MANAGER and the EXECUTIVE service classes might differ significantly from their defined targets. Indeed, if there is very little workload directed to the EXECUTIVE service class, it might consume only a very small fraction of the CPU resources that are available to it. Another key factor that can influence the amount of CPU that's actually consumed by a service class is the *type* of CPU share it has been assigned.

> **NOTE**   *The WLM Dispatcher adds to the already rich set of capabilities in DB2 WLM to manage your workloads. We're going to assume that you know how DB2 WLM works, because it's been around for a couple of point releases. You'll get a lot more out of this section if you understand DB2 WLM concepts such as service class, subclass, and so on. If you need a refresher, or an introduction, check out the "DB2 Workload Manager for Linux, UNIX, and Windows" Redbook (http://tinyurl.com/7tgxcrn) for more details.*

Hard Versus Soft CPU Shares

In the previous section, we introduced you to a new DB2 10 concept known as "CPU shares" as a relative CPU resource assignment. CPU shares come in two types: hard and soft. With hard shares, DB2 will always respect the relative share assignment. That is, when a service class is assigned hard CPU shares, the WLM Dispatcher prevents that service class from consuming more than its share of CPU resources (when there is work in other service classes running on the system). In contrast, when a service class is assigned soft CPU shares, the service class is able to consume more than its share of CPU resources if spare CPU resources become available on the system. If you're familiar with the industry leading IBM POWER7 virtualization capabilities and its associated static and dynamic logical partitioning (LPAR) capabilities, it's pretty much the same thing: A static LPAR is like a hard CPU share, whereas a dynamic LPAR (DLPAR) is like a soft CPU share.

> **NOTE**   *For the remainder of this chapter, you can assume that when we refer to "host computer," we're referring to any environment that provides you with compute services, including a VMware session, an LPAR, a DLPAR, Resource Partitions, or any DB2-supported virtualization technology.*

We recommend that you become very familiar with soft CPU shares, because we've found them very useful when it comes to assigning preferential treatment to more important work. For example, when used in conjunction with other service classes that are bound by hard CPU shares, a service class that is assigned soft CPU shares is allowed to consume CPU resources beyond its share, assuming that spare CPU resources become available.

A CPU Shares Example: Mission-Critical Workload with Occasional Ad Hoc Reporting   Let's look at a scenario that will help you to grasp the potential of CPU shares in DB2 10. Let's assume that you're a DBA who owns the SLAs for an online auction web site. Clearly, the transaction processing that is associated with bidding and listing is mission critical compared to other workloads on the database server (for example, getting a run rate report of the number of expired auctions that didn't spawn a single bid).

Your capacity planning calculations indicate that the Bid and List application typically requires 40 percent of the database server's CPU resources, and that during peak auction times, the requirement peaks at around 70 percent. The only other workload on this server is an occasional query reporting job that looks for listings with no bids. Although the reporting job is important because it helps to filter out "low-quality" listings, it isn't as important as processing bids and new listings. To manage these workloads, you could create two service classes: one for the OLTPBIDANDLIST workload and one for the ZEROBIDREPORT workload, as follows:

```
CREATE SERVICE CLASS oltpbidandlist SOFT CPU SHARES 7000;
CREATE SERVICE CLASS zerobidreport HARD CPU SHARES 3000;
```

When the associated service classes for your applications have been defined, define the DB2 workload objects that correspond to your OLTPBIDANDLIST and ZEROBIDREPORT workloads and map them to their respective service classes as follows:

```
CREATE WORKLOAD oltp APPLNAME('oltp') SERVICE CLASS oltpbidandlist;
CREATE WORKLOAD reporting APPLNAME('reports')
   SERVICE CLASS zerobidreport;
GRANT USAGE ON WORKLOAD oltp TO PUBLIC;
GRANT USAGE ON WORKLOAD reporting TO PUBLIC;
```

Notice that we're using the application's executable name (APPLNAME) to identify the OLTP and REPORTING workloads that are mapped to the previously defined service classes. DB2 WLM is very flexible, and you can identify a workload through a myriad of identifiers such as user ID, role, group, and group name, among several others. You may also need to grant usage privileges for these workloads, as we've shown.

Let's examine the behavior of this WLM Dispatcher configuration using the timeline that is shown in Figure 5-4. In the figure, you can see that at 1:00 p.m., the OLTP application that handles bids and listings is running as expected, consuming 40 percent of the CPU resources. At 3:00 p.m., a quality manager asks her assistant for a set of zero-bid reports, and her assistant submits all of these reports at the same time. These reports are large, complex queries because they don't just look for zero-bid activity; they classify attributes that are related to the listings (product, seller location, and so on) and could consume upwards of 100 percent of the CPU (assuming that the reporting queries are not managed through allocated CPU shares). However, recall that we defined the ZEROBIDREPORT service class with a hard limit of 3000 CPU shares, giving 7000 CPU soft shares to the OLTPBIDANDLIST application, and this empowers the DB2 WLM Dispatcher to prevent the reporting workload from consuming more than 30 percent [3000/(3000+7000)] of the system's CPU resources.

Now we turn our attention to the latter part of the auction day (when the real activity starts to happen—after work); a spike in bidding and listing activity causes the OLTP component of the solution to demand 65 percent of the CPU. In this case, because the reporting workload is limited to 30 percent

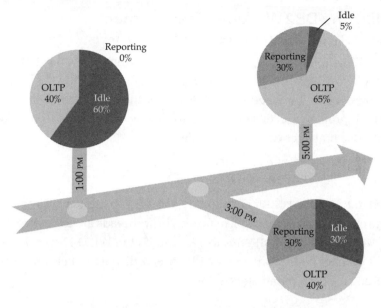

Figure 5-4 *Ensuring that a reporting job doesn't impact a mission-critical transactional workload on your database*

CPU consumption, the increased CPU requirements for the OLTP workload can be accommodated from spare CPU cycles on the system.

As you'd expect, DB2 provides a comprehensive set of interfaces for monitoring the operation of the WLM Dispatcher—for example, the `MON_SAMPLE_SERVICE_CLASS_METRICS()` table function reports on service class metrics over a specified sampling interval. What follows is an example of what you might see if it was run at around 5:00 p.m.:

```
SELECT SERVICE_SUPERCLASS_NAME AS sc,
   DECIMAL(ESTIMATE_CPU_ENTITLEMENT,5,2) AS entitlement,
   DECIMAL(CPU_UTILIZATION,5,2) AS cpu
 FROM TABLE
   (MON_SAMPLE_SERVICE_CLASS_METRICS(NULL,NULL,NULL,NULL,10,-1))


SC                                       ENTITLEMENT CPU
---------------------------------------- ----------- ---
OLTPBIDANDLIST                              70.00     64.33
ZEROBIDREPORT                               30.00     29.43
```

Enabling the DB2 Workload Management Dispatcher for Operational Control

Before DB2 can enforce the policies that are defined for the DB2 WLM Dispatcher, you have to enable the dispatcher feature along with its CPU shares component. To enable DB2 10 to target the service level that is outlined in the previous section, enter the following commands to update the DB2 database manager configuration file:

```
UPDATE DBM CFG USING WLM_DISPATCHER YES;
UPDATE DBM CFG USING WLM_DISP_CPU_SHARES YES;
```

When `WLM_DISPATCHER` is set to YES, the WLM Dispatcher is active and can control the decision that DB2 makes on how threads are to be dispatched. Setting `WLM_DISP_CPU_SHARES` to YES causes the WLM Dispatcher to include CPU share allocations in its CPU thread dispatch decisions. The default setting for both parameters is NO.

CPU Limits

CPU limits represent another powerful WLM Dispatcher control unit. Service classes can be assigned a CPU limit ranging from 1 to 100. The CPU limit for a service class is an upper limit on the *percentage of CPU work* that the associated service class can consume; this percentage is relative to the host computer (or virtualization session, such as an LPAR) on which the service class is running.

You might be wondering, Why are there CPU limits in addition to CPU shares, because it seems that shares alone could get the job done? CPU shares provide the ability to control the CPU resource consumption of service classes when the overall workload of the host computer is heavy, while not wasting CPU resources when the overall workload is light.

However, there might be other scenarios in which it is desirable to limit the CPU resource consumption of a service class, even when the overall workload on the host or LPAR is light. For example, let's assume that our online auction site is trying to control sprawling capital and operational expenditures (CAPEX and OPEX) and wants to implement services in an elastic, Cloud-like manner. The server administration team might consider a hosting environment in which two different end users have purchased database services, thereby creating a multi-tenancy operational environment.

Let's assume that Operations internally allocates $1,000 of hosting services for user MROPS, while the marketing team contracts $2,000 for MRSBID. In this case, the hosting provider might want to create a service class for MROPS with a CPU limit of 33 and another service class for MRSBID with a CPU limit of 66. This ensures that each end user gets no more than the CPU resources that they've paid for, which might be desirable for a multi-tenancy hosting provider, despite the possibility that the selected configuration could result in underutilization of the CPU resources of the supporting computing environment. CPU shares just don't give you this kind of control, but CPU limits do!

A CPU Limits Example: Keeping CPU in Reserve for Other Needs   Let's walk through a simple example that illustrates how a CPU limit can be used: You're the DBA, and it's your job to make everyone happy. (Is this hitting too close to home yet?) Although you feel that you have some control over the workloads that run on the database, the server also consumes CPU resources for other jobs outside of the database. For example, the operations team has to make daily system-level copies of the environment to satisfy its disaster recovery requirements. To ensure that these jobs get some cycles to do their work, you would like to reserve 20 percent of the system's CPU for them and therefore you'd start by defining a CPU limit for the SYSDEFAULTUSERCLASS, as shown next. (For this example, we figure you might was well just rely on this built-in service class; in DB2, by default, all database work that your users submit will map to the SYSUSERDEFAULTWORKLOAD workload, which maps to the SYSDEFAULTUSERCLASS service class.)

```
ALTER SERVICE CLASS SYSDEFAULTUSERCLASS CPU LIMIT 80;
```

Let's assume the start of a day is typical; at around 8:00 a.m. the server experiences a light database workload that requires 20 percent of the server's CPU. As the day progresses, the database load steadily increases with a run rate of 10 percent per hour; but remember, we created a policy that limits this growth to 80 percent of the system's CPU resources. At 8:00 p.m., the administration team has a key automated cron job that requires 10 percent of the system's CPU resources. This job is able to run and progress through its list of programmed activities, because 20 percent of the system's CPU resources was left in reserve by DB2. This scenario is illustrated in Figure 5-5.

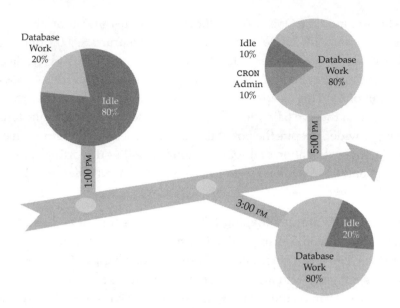

Figure 5-5 *Ensuring that a reserve of CPU cycles is maintained to support scheduled maintenance operations on the database server*

A CPU Limits Example: Maintaining Production and Development Databases in Separate Instances on a Single Host Computer In this section, we'll look at a more complex example. Let's assume that you're running two databases in separate instances on a single database server: one database is for production and the other one is for development.

The production database has two mission-critical workloads running on it: a trading workload that runs during the day, and a batch workload that runs at night. Capacity planning indicates that the trading workload typically requires 25 percent of the database server's CPU resources and can peak at approximately 45 percent of this server's CPU resources. The batch workload shares very similar characteristics with the production workload, because it acts as a replay agent for the transactions that occurred during the day: typical requirements are 25 percent of the CPU with a peak of 45 percent. Finally, some reporting is done directly on the production database; although not mission critical, these reporting jobs should get enough resources to complete within a reasonable amount of time, because they help predict inventory requirements for the day's promotions.

The development database resides in another instance on the same server, and it's used for application development purposes. This database usually has a small CPU consumption requirement, but on occasion, it can introduce significant CPU load onto the database server; for example, when new queries are developed and run before they are fully optimized. (If you're a DBA, you've seen queries that made you shake your head upon discovery—unfortunately, you find such queries after they've caused problems, not before.) Other than those workloads that are associated with the production and development databases, no other workloads are running on this server.

In order for your IT department to satisfy the SLA, you are asked to ensure that the following policies are enforced:

1. Trading and batch workloads get the CPU resources that they need when running during prescribed hours; your boss thinks that allocating "a little extra" above the predicted peaks of 45 percent is a good idea.

2. If exceptional circumstances cause the trading and batch workloads to run simultaneously, they should be given at least two-thirds of their combined peak CPU demand (45 percent for trading + 45 percent for batch = 90 percent; two-thirds of 90 percent is 60 percent).

3. The development workload always gets the CPU resources it needs, up to a maximum of 10 percent of the host's CPU resources.

4. The reporting workload receives leftover CPU resources after all other needs are met.

To implement these targets, the DBA can define a single superclass with a CPU limit of 10 percent on the development database to contain all development work:

```
CREATE SERVICE CLASS dev CPU LIMIT 10;
```

On the production database, the DBA defines a superclass that contains the trading, batch, and reporting workloads, and that has a CPU limit of 90 percent:

```
CREATE SERVICE CLASS prod CPU LIMIT 90;
```

To differentiate the CPU amounts allocated to the different workloads associated with the production database, the DBA has to define subclasses for the trading, batch, and reporting workloads and associate them with a superclass using the following DDL:

```
CREATE SERVICE CLASS trading UNDER prod SOFT CPU SHARES 10000;
CREATE SERVICE CLASS batch UNDER prod SOFT CPU SHARES 10000;
CREATE SERVICE CLASS reports UNDER prod SOFT CPU SHARES 100 CPU LIMIT 30;
```

Finally, on both databases, the DBA needs to define associated workloads and map them to these service classes, as well as grant appropriate usage privileges (you can use the same method that we've outlined in previous examples).

Now, consider how these settings implement the four required policies:

- **Policy element 1**   The CPU limit of 10 percent for the dev superclass leaves 90 percent CPU for the prod superclass if it's needed. When either the trading or batch workload is running, but not both, that single workload is guaranteed to get up to 60 percent of the server's available CPU, well above the estimated 45 percent peak. (This is calculated as 90 percent CPU for the superclass minus the 30 percent CPU limit for the REPORTS subclass.)

- **Policy element 2**   If the trading, batch, and reporting workloads are running simultaneously (and close to their peak workload demands), the soft share settings for these subclasses will cause the WLM Dispatcher to try to allocate CPU such that close to 45 percent is given to each of the trading and batch workloads, and <1 percent is given to the reporting workload. (The ≈45 percent is calculated as: $10000/20100 \times$ 90 percent, and the <1 percent is calculated as $100/20100 \times 90$ percent.) The CPU limit of 30 percent for the REPORTS subclass is a further measure to protect the environment from a scenario in which a set of large reports is running and one (or both) of the trading and batch workloads aren't running when the reports start. In such a case, the reports workload could consume up to 90 percent of the available CPU, and that could potentially prevent the batch or trading workloads from quickly getting the CPU that they need when they start. The 30 percent limit therefore ensures that the batch and trading workloads can quickly reach a combined 60 percent CPU if they run simultaneously (calculated as the 90 percent allocation for the PROD superclass minus 30 percent limit for the REPORTS subclass).

- **Policy element 3** The CPU limit of 90 percent for the PROD superclass means that the DEV superclass will be given 10 percent of CPU if needed.
- **Policy element 4** The soft CPU share setting for the reporting workload gives it the flexibility to consume any available CPU *after* the other service classes consume their allocations (up to the maximum of 30 percent).

Frequently Asked Questions

We close this section with a few FAQs:

Q: Can CPU shares be used with both service superclasses and service subclasses?

A: Yes. The WLM Dispatcher calculates CPU allocation as follows:

```
percent CPU allocated to superclass A =
( Number of superclass A shares /
  Total number of shares of all active superclasses )
    X 100 percent
percent CPU allocated to subclass B =
( Number of subclass B shares /
  Total # of shares of all active subclasses in the same superclass )
    X  percent CPU allocated to the superclass
```

Q: Can CPU shares and CPU limits be used simultaneously in the same service class?

A: Yes. When this is done, the most restrictive condition is honored.

Q: Can CPU shares be used across databases in the same DB2 instance?

A: Yes. The WLM Dispatcher operates at the instance level, which means that when CPU allocations are calculated for a superclass, it uses the sum of all shares for all superclasses in all databases in the instance as the basis for that calculation.

Q: Can CPU shares be used across different DB2 instances?

A: No. CPU shares are not meaningful across different DB2 instances.

Q: Can CPU limits be used across databases in the same DB2 instance? What about using CPU limits across databases in different DB2 instances in the same host or logical partition?

A: Yes to both! Why? Because CPU limits are expressed as a percentage of the overall CPU resources that are available in the host or logical partition.

Finding Another Gear: Continuous, Online, High-Speed Data Ingest

Every DBA who's behind a data warehouse has undoubtedly spent some time thinking about the fastest way to ingest data continuously into the warehouse while honoring the underlying environment's 24×7 availability requirements. To address this challenge, DB2 10 introduces the high-speed INGEST utility.

The INGEST command is a high-speed client-side utility that streams data from files or pipes into a target table. Think of the INGEST command as a cross between the IMPORT and LOAD commands, with the goal of taking the best of these utilities and adding some brand new capabilities. You could summarize the INGEST value proposition as *fast, available, continuous,* and *robust.*

INGEST is *fast* because it's been optimized from the ground up to use a multithreaded design to process data in parallel; it can even ingest data into multiple database partitions in parallel. It's got great table *availability* characteristics because it uses row-level locking, allowing normal read and write access to the target table while the utility is running. Although data population utilities typically ingest preprocessed data directly from files created by extract, transform, and load (ETL) jobs or other tools, INGEST can run in a *continuous* manner by reading a data stream through a pipe. INGEST is also *robust* in that it's designed from the inside out to be tolerant of unexpected failure conditions. For example, if INGEST fails for any reason (such as a system power failure), it can be restarted from the last commit point. A dump file and an exception table provide a comprehensive set of error-handling capabilities.

INGEST is flexible, with native support for common positional and delimited input formats. It comes with a rich set of data-manipulation capabilities and, unlike some batch loaders that support only a few basic SQL statements, it includes SQL-like interfaces for INSERT, UPDATE, MERGE, REPLACE, and DELETE, and the ability to apply SQL expressions to input data. In addition, INGEST can use SQL expressions to build individual column values from more than one data field, making it one of the most flexible data population utilities we know of.

We think that the best way to show the value proposition of continuous data ingest (CDI) is by example, so we've created a couple examples that relate to some typical use-case scenarios.

How Continuous Data Ingest Looks on the Inside

CDI's architecture is depicted in Figure 5-6. You can see in Figure 5-6 that INGEST runs in a multithreaded architecture. This is the core foundation behind its high-speed operational capabilities. *Transporter* threads read from a set of input files or pipes in parallel and then send rows to a set of formatter threads (also in parallel). The *formatter* threads format and prepare data for ingest into DB2, and send it to a set of *flusher* threads that finish the job by sending the data to DB2 using SQL. If you're using INGEST to load data into a partitioned database, DB2 will try to associate each flusher thread with a particular database partition to optimize performance further.

Speaking of performance, just how fast is INGEST? In the lab, we compared INGEST against the alternative of loading into a temporary staging table, followed by running SQL INSERTs from there into the target table. This alternative provides the same high availability that INGEST does; however, in our lab measurements we found that INGEST runs approximately 50 percent faster!

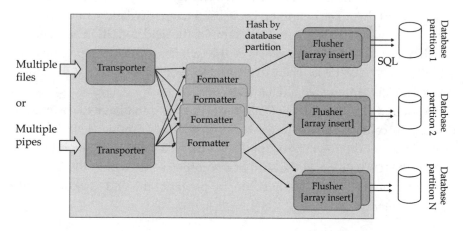

Figure 5-6   *INGEST's multithreaded architecture*

Getting to Know Continuous Data Ingest

A pretty basic requirement in a real-time warehousing environment is to insert rows into a target table from a delimited text file. Let's assume that you have a delimited file (`bids_file.del`) that contains all of the bid information for an expired auction, and you want to ingest this data into the PASTBIDS table. The fields in the `bids_file.del` file directly correspond to the columns in the PASTBIDS table, and the file uses the default comma (`,`) delimiter.

```
INGEST FROM FILE bids_file.del FORMAT DELIMITED INSERT INTO pastbids;
```

To perform the same operation, but with a delimited file (called `bids_pipe`) that uses a vertical bar (`|`) as the column delimiter, and that takes input from a pipe, execute the following command:

```
INGEST FROM FILE bids_pipe FORMAT DELIMITED '|' INSERT INTO pastbids;
```

Now let's insert rows from a positional text file (called `bids_text.txt`):

```
INGEST FROM FILE bids_text.txt FORMAT POSITIONAL
   (
     $field1 POSITION(1:12)   INTEGER EXTERNAL,
     $field2 POSITION(13:20)  CHAR(8)
   )
 INSERT INTO pastbids;
```

This example illustrates the use of an optional *field definition list* that specifies the input data. The definition list is used to specify field name, position, data type, and other options. In this example, the field definition list specifies the character positions and formats of the two fields that are being inserted into the PASTBIDS table. The EXTERNAL keyword indicates that the table's integer data is represented as character data.

We should point out that fields in the input file don't have to correspond directly to columns in the target table. With that in mind, let's take this example to another level by skipping an unused field and generating the TOTAL_PRICE column as the sum of two other fields within the input file (this example really starts to illustrate the power of the INGEST command's SQL-like interface):

```
INGEST FROM FILE bids_file.del FORMAT DELIMITED
  (
      $prod_ID INTEGER EXTERNAL,
      $prod_name CHAR(8),
      $unused_field CHAR(1),
      $base_price DECIMAL(7,2) EXTERNAL,
      $shipping_cost DECIMAL(7,2) EXTERNAL
  )
 INSERT INTO pastbids(prod_ID, prod_name, total_price)
   VALUES($prod_ID, $prod_name, $base_price + $shipping_cost);
```

The INGEST command has the ability to read from multiple input sources, as shown in the following example, which also constructs a DATE column from the file's MONTH, DAY, and YEAR fields:

```
INGEST FROM FILE bids_file1.del, my_file2.del FORMAT DELIMITED
  (
      $month CHAR(2),
      $day CHAR(2),
      $year CHAR(2)
  )
 INSERT INTO pastbids(date_column) VALUES
   (DATE('20' || $year || '-' || $month || '-' || $day));
```

As we suggested earlier, INGEST can do a lot more than just insert data into a table. The following example shows how to use the table's primary key to update rows that already exist in the target table:

```
INGEST FROM FILE bids_file.del FORMAT DELIMITED
  (
      $key_fld1 INTEGER EXTERNAL,
      $key_fld2 INTEGER EXTERNAL,
      $data_fld1 CHAR(8),
      $data_fld2 CHAR(8),
      $data_fld3 CHAR(8)
  )

 UPDATE pastbids SET (data1_col, data2_col, data3_col) =
   ($data_fld1, $data_fld2, $data_fld3)
   WHERE (key_col1 = $key_fld1) AND (key_col2 = $key_fld2);
```

So far, we've seen examples that *either* insert or update data; however, what if your application has to do both? DB2 has long supported merge operations, and you can use the MERGE command with the INGEST command to update any row whose key already exists in the target table, or insert the data if it doesn't. For example,

```
INGEST FROM FILE bids_file.del FORMAT DELIMITED
  (
    $key_fld1 INTEGER EXTERNAL,
    $key_fld2 INTEGER EXTERNAL,
    $data_fld1 CHAR(8),
    $data_fld2 CHAR(8),
    $data_fld3 CHAR(8)
  )
 MERGE INTO pastbids ON (key_col1 = $key_fld1)
     AND (key_col2 = $key_fld2)
    WHEN NOT MATCHED THEN
      INSERT INTO pastbids
    WHEN MATCHED
      THEN UPDATE pastbids SET (data1_col, data2_col, data3_col) =
      ($data_fld1, $data_fld2, $data_fld3);
```

Managing the Not So Easy: Error-Handling Options and More

There will always be times when things don't go as planned. If you encounter problems that are associated with CDI, the INGEST utility has options associated with warnings, errors, and exceptions to help you along the way.

Consider the following INGEST operation:

```
INGEST FROM FILE bids_file.del FORMAT DELIMITED
  DUMPFILE bids_reject_file.del
  EXCEPTION TABLE bidsexcept_table
  WARNINGCOUNT 200
  MESSAGES my_msg_file.txt
  INSERT INTO pastbids;
```

In this example, INGEST places any records that it rejects (for example, because of formatting errors in the input file) into the bids_reject_file.del file. Any records that are rejected by DB2 (for example, because of unique key violations) are placed in the BIDSEXCEPT_TABLE. The INGEST operation will stop if 200 or more warnings or errors occur. And, finally, any messages that INGEST generates are written to the my_msg_file.txt file.

INGEST has a rich set of restartability services. Let's assume, for example, that you are running an INGEST operation that fails because of a system power outage in the primary and redundant power supplies. In this scenario, you need to reissue the INGEST command using the RESTART and (optionally) the CONTINUE key words. For example,

```
INGEST FROM FILE bids_file.del FORMAT DELIMITED
   RESTART NEW 'My ingest job'
   INSERT INTO pastbids;
          !! SYSTEM POWER FAILURE !!
        !! SYSTEM IS SUCCESSFULLY RESTARTED   !!

INGEST FROM FILE bids_file.del FORMAT DELIMITED
    RESTART CONTINUE 'My ingest job'
    INSERT INTO pastbids;
```

When INGEST restarts with the CONTINUE option, it continues from the last commit point. In the preceding example, we've also made use of the RESTART NEW option, which gives you the ability to specify a custom job identifier; this makes it easy to identify the interrupted INGEST job if there's a need to restart it later. (If you don't use the RESTART NEW option, INGEST automatically generates a job identifier for you; we recommend that you give each INGEST job a name that you choose.)

Monitoring INGEST

A DBA is going to want to monitor the progress of any INGEST jobs running on the database server. To make things easy, DB2 10 comes with a rich set of built-in table functions that can be used to retrieve information about in-progress INGEST operations. For example,

```
SELECT client_acctng AS "Job ID",
   SUM(rows_modified) AS "Rows changed", SUM(total_app_commits)
      AS "Commits"
   FROM TABLE(MON_GET_CONNECTION(NULL, NULL))
      WHERE application_name = 'DB2_INGEST'
      GROUP BY client_acctng
      ORDER BY 1

Job ID                                           Rows changed Commits
------------------------------------------------ ------------ -------
DB2100100:20101116.123456.234567:34567:45678           12431      52
DB2100100:20101116.987654.234567:34567:45678           17772      84
   2 record(s) selected.
```

INGEST also provides two client-side commands that retrieve additional details about in-progress INGEST operations: INGEST LIST and INGEST GET STATS. Because these are client-side commands, they retrieve information that only pertains to in-progress INGEST commands that *were issued on the same client machine* (unlike the table function in the previous example).

RUNSTATS Performance and Other Enhancements

The RUNSTATS utility collects statistics about tables, indexes, and statistical views. These statistics help DB2's query optimizer build the best access plans for optimal performance. Some of us used to work in support, and we would always ask if the statistics were up-to-date when a client called about a performance issue (and you can guess what the most common answer was). The last couple of DB2 releases have included many RUNSTATS enhancements. Over the last couple of releases, this utility has become more available, faster running and has more options to lessen its impact, increase collection granularity, and provide a broader range of statistics.

The overall speed and efficiency of a statistics operation is typically very important to DBAs; the sooner the operation completes, the sooner the optimizer can use the new statistics for access plan generation. What's more, the fewer resources that RUNSTATS consumes while collecting statistics, the lower its overall impact to the online database workload. This has been a continuing theme of feature enhancements to this utility in every DB2 release, and DB2 10 is no exception. DB2 10 includes several significant RUNSTATS speed and efficiency improvements as well as several other interesting enhancements. In this section, we'll look at some of the more notable ones.

Sampling for Index Statistics

Calculating table statistics on sampled data was first introduced in DB2 8. DB2 10 expands the sampling techniques that are used for table statistics collection by implementing a similar technique for index statistics collection. Although this might seem like a small enhancement, we think it's rather significant, because, when you think about it, a given table might have several indexes, and statistics collection on indexes could represent a significant portion of the overall RUNSTATS execution time.

When you apply the new DB2 10 sampling techniques to index statistics collection, DB2 calculates statistics on a subset of the index leaf pages or a subset of the index records. A simple example of using the new SYSTEM index sampling technique is shown next:

```
RUNSTATS ON TABLE sales AND INDEXES ALL INDEXSAMPLE SYSTEM(2.5);
```

SYSTEM sampling enables the database manager to determine the most efficient way to sample. In most cases, SYSTEM sampling means that each index leaf page is included in the sample with probability P/100 and excluded with probability 1-P/100. With this technique, all rows that are found on the index leaf page qualify for the sample.

In this example, you can see that 2.5 percent of the index leaf pages are physically read from disk (or logically read from the buffer pool) and included in the sample to calculate the index statistics; 97.5 percent of the index leaf pages are not included in the sample.

The alternative, BERNOULLI sampling, is shown in the following example:

```
RUNSTATS ON TABLE sales AND INDEXES ALL
 TABLESAMPLE SYSTEM (2.5)
 INDEXSAMPLE BERNOULLI (5);
```

With BERNOULLI sampling, *all* index leaf pages are read. As index statistics are being collected, each index *record* (*not* page) is either included or not included based on the specified sampling rate (5 percent in this example). Did you notice that in this example, we BERNOULLI sampled the index and SYSTEM sampled the table? The example illustrates that table sampling and index sampling can be specified independently.

As a rule of thumb, SYSTEM sampling of an index executes much faster than BERNOULLI sampling because fewer index pages need to be retrieved; BERNOULLI sampling requires that all pages be read. In rare cases, SYSTEM sampling, which takes a coarser subset of the data (at the index leaf page level rather than at the record level), might collect statistics that are not as representative of the data as a whole.

You might be wondering, with so many options, when should you use index sampling, which type of sampling should you use, and at what sampling rates? If you're completely happy with the way RUNSTATS works now, in terms of performance and resource consumption, you likely don't need to use SYSTEM index sampling ("if it isn't broken, don't fix it").

From a sampling rate perspective, we recommend that you start with 10 percent. If this sampling rate yields accurate statistics and you want additional performance improvements, consider a smaller sampling rate; if it yields inaccurate statistics, consider a larger sampling rate.

Readahead Prefetching During Index Statistics Collection

DB2 10 introduces a new form of prefetching known as *readahead prefetching*. Readahead prefetching enables DB2 to prefetch table or index leaf pages during scans, even when the leaf pages are not clustered and the usual sequential detection mechanisms do not work. The result is that overall table and index scan performance remains more stable as tables and indexes are updated and become disorganized.

General Path Length Reduction

Calculating statistics can consume a significant number of CPU cycles. Consequently, another area of focus during DB2 10 development was reducing the lengths of the paths that are used while calculating statistics. The result of this fine-tuning effort is that DB2 10 RUNSTATS generally consumes less overall CPU; and if RUNSTATS is running on a CPU-constrained system, this can translate into considerably reduced overall execution times!

Grab Bag of Other RUNSTATS Improvements

Here are some additional RUNSTATS improvements that you should know about:

- You no longer have to fully qualify your table with a schema name (if it's absent, DB2 uses the default schema).
- A new VIEW option facilitates more intuitive use of RUNSTATS on statistical views.
- DB2's automatic statistics collection daemon can now operate on statistical views. You can enable this function with the AUTO_STATS_VIEWS database configuration parameter.

Statistical Views

The DB2 system catalog contains critical statistical information about columns, tables, and indexes. Whenever a dynamic SQL statement is issued, the

DB2 optimizer obtains information from the catalog, which helps it to select the best access path for the query. As statement complexity increases, this information becomes even more important. The best performance tip that we can give you is to keep those statistics up-to-date!

Statistical views (often referred to as *statviews*—we use these terms interchangeably in this book) were introduced in DB2 9 to enable the optimizer to compute more accurate cardinality estimates for queries in which the view definition has overlap with the query definition—in other words, when the query accesses data in columns that are also part of the view definition.

DB2 10 includes a number of improvements that give the DB2 optimizer a broader and deeper set of statistics within the statviews, including improved matching (partial statviews matching), column group statistics on statviews, automatic statistics collection for statviews, and expressions on statviews.

Partial Statviews Matching

The best way to illustrate partial statistical views matching is with an example. Consider the set of tables in Figure 5-7, which closely resembles a star-schema design.

In Figure 5-7, the primary keys of dimension tables A, B, and C are all found in the fact table F. This relationship of keys is normally referred to as primary keys in the outer tables (A, B, C) and foreign keys in the inner table (F). Prior to DB2 10, in order to give the DB2 optimizer better information about the relationship between tables such as those shown in Figure 5-7, you were required to have statistical views on each of the join combinations, as shown in Figure 5-8.

The number of statistical views that are required for this star-schema design is directly dependent on the number of dimension tables. The maintenance costs that were associated with statistical views before DB2 10 were not insignificant; in addition, the costs were compounded as the number of dimension tables increased.

With DB2 10, the multiple statistical views shown in Figure 5-8 can be replaced with a single statistical view that encompasses a join across all of the dimension tables and the fact table, as shown in Figure 5-9.

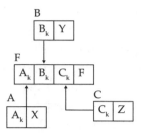

Figure 5-7   *A pseudo–star schema that includes primary and foreign key relationships*

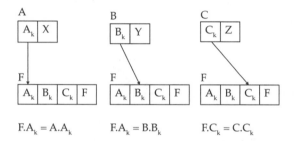

$$F.A_k = A.A_k \qquad F.A_k = B.B_k \qquad F.C_k = C.C_k$$

Figure 5-8   *Statistical views defined on each primary key and foreign key combination prior to DB2 10*

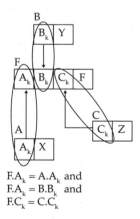

$$F.A_k = A.A_k \text{ and}$$
$$F.A_k = B.B_k \text{ and}$$
$$F.C_k = C.C_k$$

Figure 5-9   *Reducing the administrative burden that is associated with statistical views using new capabilities in DB2 10*

A key requirement for the combined statistical view shown in Figure 5-9 is that referential integrity constraints be defined on the data, thereby enabling the optimizer to derive statistics from this view for any of the joins that might take place, rather than depending on individual join statistics.

Column Group Statistics Gathered on Statistical Views

In prior releases of DB2, you could collect statistics on column groups in addition to individual columns; for example,

```
RUNSTATS ON TABLE employee ON ALL COLUMNS
   AND COLUMNS((salary,bonus)) WITH DISTRIBUTION
```

Before DB2 10, statistical views weren't eligible for column group statistics. The good news is that this restriction has been lifted in DB2 10. Combining column group statistics with statistical views improves access plans, because the optimizer can use the statistics to adjust filter factors and obtain more accurate cardinality estimates.

Automatic Statistics Collection for Statistical Views

DB2 10 introduces a new automatic statistics collection feature for statistical views that you can enable using the AUTO_STATS_VIEWS database configuration parameter. DB2 10 ships with this service disabled by default, so you have to enable it for your database using the following command:

```
UPDATE DB CFG FOR <db-name> USING AUTO_STATS_VIEWS ON
```

The statistics that are collected by the automatic statistics collection service are equivalent to issuing the RUNSTATS ON VIEW <name> WITH DISTRIBUTION command. Did you notice the new VIEW keyword?

Expressions on Statistical Views

Statistical views can contain columns that are the result of expressions or functions that generate a value. Although statistics could be collected for these computed columns, previous versions of DB2 would use only a default value for the selectivity estimate. This meant that, because of poor selectivity estimates, queries with complex expressions might not have benefited from optimal access plans. With DB2 10, the optimizer can use the actual statistics in the statistical view to determine the best access plan for maximum performance.

DB2's automatic statistics collection daemon can now determine an intelligent sampling rate for tables, indexes, and statistical views. You can enable this function with the AUTO_SAMPLING database configuration parameter.

We can't cover all of the details for each of the new DB2 10 RUNSTATS features in this book. We therefore recommend that you visit the DB2 10 Information Center for more complete details and involved examples at http://publib.boulder.ibm.com/infocenter/db2luw/v10r1/index.jsp.

Index Improvements

DB2 10 introduces a number of enhancements regarding how indexes are used within queries. These enhancements can help you in a number of ways, including reducing the need for creating multiple indexes to cover all possible key combinations, and maintaining index access performance even as index entries become fragmented. DB2 10 includes new *jump scan* technology (it's referred to as *multi-range index scan* in the documentation, but we want you to know both terms because the documentation uses the latter) that helps to improve the performance of indexes with gaps in column definitions. The *smart index prefetching* enhancements help indexes that are poorly organized to run faster and reduce the need for index reorganization. DB2 10 also includes index enhancements centered around *smart data prefetching*, which helps to improve the performance of index scans with better data fetch operations for poorly clustered tables, and also reduces the need for table reorganization. (Do you see a trend here?) Finally, DB2 removes the need to evaluate predicates on duplicate keys with its new *predicate evaluation avoidance for duplicate keys* techniques.

Jump Scan (Multi-Range Index Scan) Enhancements

In an ad hoc query environment, it's often difficult to determine which indexes are required to optimize database performance. For example, tuning queries that run against tables with composite (multicolumn) indexes

Transactions

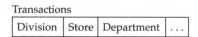

Figure 5-10 *The TRANSACTION table includes three critical index columns.*

is especially difficult. Suppose, for example, that the TRANSACTIONS table includes critical indexes on the columns shown in Figure 5-10.

Let's assume that this is a transaction table for a retail vendor; DIVISION represents sections of a country (EAST, WEST, and so on), STORE represents a unique store identifier within a DIVISION, and DEPARTMENT is a section of the store that sells a particular product line (AUTOMOTIVE, SPORTINGGOODS, and so on). As you can imagine, reporting queries in this scenario could take the form of any combination of these three columns, including queries such as the following:

- *Give me the sales of all Automobile departments by division.* (DIVISION, DEPARTMENT)

- *Give me the sales of Store #24 in the East division.* (DIVISION, STORE)

- *What sales did the Automotive department have in Store #2 in the North division?* (DIVISION, STORE, DEPARTMENT)

To ensure that the performance of these queries is reasonable, a DBA would typically create a minimum of the two following composite indexes: (DIVISION, STORE, DEPARTMENT) and (DIVISION, DEPARTMENT).

Before DB2 10, the DB2 optimizer could take advantage of an index if it was able to match columns contiguously from left to right. In other words, the optimizer could use the (DIVISION, STORE, DEPARTMENT) index to solve queries with the following predicates:

- DIVISION

- DIVISION, STORE

- DIVISION, STORE, DEPARTMENT

Note that the DB2 optimizer can't fully use the (DIVISION, STORE, DEPARTMENT) index to solve a query that involves just the DIVISION and DEPARTMENT columns. In this case, DB2 will have to scan the index and process many unnecessary keys to return the result set. Specifically, the predicates on the non-leading columns of the index would need to be applied individually against each key in the index, and this would slow down the index scan because more rows need to be processed and additional predicates need to be evaluated for each key.

An *index gap* occurs when a query contains predicates that are inconsistent with a composite index such as (DIVISION, DEPARTMENT). Index gaps are a characteristic of queries, not indexes. To optimize a query with just these predicates before DB2 10, another index on DIVISION and DEPARTMENT had to be created; this required more space both for the index itself and for the additional overhead that is associated with maintaining the extra index.

DB2 10 addresses this problem with its new jump scan enablement technology. The DB2 10 query optimizer can create additional access plans that might be more efficient for queries with index gaps by using a jump scan operation. Jump scans eliminate the need for index gap avoidance techniques, such as the creation of additional indexes, which results in fewer indexes, reduced space requirements, and less index maintenance.

Readahead Data and Index Prefetching

When an index is created, the index pages are typically well ordered, as shown in Figure 5-11. In the figure, the pages within the triangle are referred to as *non-leaf pages*, and the pages below the triangle are the *leaf pages* (which ultimately point to the data pages that the database manager is trying to

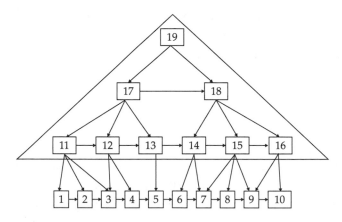

Figure 5-11 *A well-ordered index*

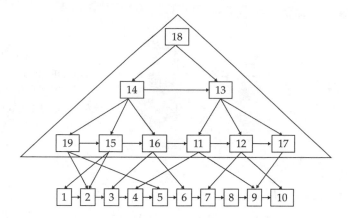

Figure 5-12   *Over time, an index degrades and becomes poorly clustered.*

access by using this index). DB2 takes advantage of this index ordering by enabling the sequential prefetching of these pages with the intent to populate the DB2 heaps with these index pages as quickly as possible, so that an index scan does not need to wait for I/O to complete.

Let's assume that over time a lot of changes are made to a table's data or its indexes, and the data pages have become badly clustered, or the index pages contain very few rows because of deletions. The once well-ordered index that we had in Figure 5-11 might now look very different, perhaps like the index shown in Figure 5-12.

When an index becomes poorly clustered, sequential detection prefetching becomes less efficient, because pages are read out of sequence, which ultimately results in degraded query performance. DBAs would address this problem by running a REORG command against the poorly performing index.

DB2 10 introduces a new prefetching technique called *readahead prefetching*. Readahead prefetching is used to prefetch badly clustered data pages and low-density index pages. Readahead prefetching looks ahead in the index to determine the exact data pages or index leaf pages that an index scan operation will access, and then prefetches them.

DB2 10 uses sequential detection and readahead prefetching techniques together to provide smart data and index prefetching. In most cases, the DB2 10 optimizer will choose sequential detection prefetching but will switch to

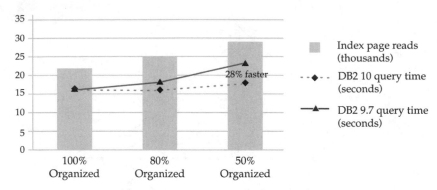

Figure 5-13 *Query performance using smart index prefetching*

readahead prefetching when sequential detection prefetching is not working well enough. Smart data and index prefetching enables the database system to capitalize on the performance benefits of data stored in sequential pages, and it also enables the efficient retrieval of badly clustered data. Badly clustered data won't impact query times as it could have before DB2 10, as shown in Figure 5-13.

Zigzag Joins

Using standard join techniques to combine multiple tables in a star schema doesn't always result in optimal query performance. For example, suppose that a retail system contains the following four tables:

- DAILY_SALES stores transaction records across all stores in the company.
- PRODUCT stores product information.
- PROMOTION stores promotion and sales information.
- CUSTOMER stores customer information.

A typical business question involving this data might be, "How much of a specific product was sold to customers micro-segmented to a specific income range and age category using the given promotion?" Converting this question into SQL, you could end up constructing a query that looks like this:

```
SELECT COUNT(quantity_sold)
  FROM daily_sales s, product prod, customer c, promotion promo
WHERE prod.category = 42 AND promo.promotype = 2 AND
```

```
c.age_level = 4 AND c.income_level = 5 AND
prod.prodkey = s.prodkey AND c.custkey = s.custkey AND
promo.promokey = s.promokey;
```

If DB2 chooses to use a nested loop join to process this query, it will consume a considerable amount of compute resources because of the large number of combinations in the CUSTOMER and PRODUCT join operation, as illustrated in Figure 5-14.

In DB2 10, a new join method, called the *Zigzag join* (ZZJOIN), expedites the processing of queries based on a star schema. Specifically, a Zigzag join (sometimes folks call it a Zipper join) is a join method in which a fact table and two or more dimension tables in a star schema are joined in such a way that the fact table is accessed using an index. This join method calculates the Cartesian product of rows from the dimension tables without actually materializing the Cartesian product; then it probes the fact table using a multicolumn index, thereby filtering the fact table along two or more dimension tables simultaneously. The processing of a Zigzag join is illustrated in Figure 5-15.

Two dimension keys (D1 and D2) are involved in the Zigzag join executed in Figure 5-15. The Cartesian product of these two dimension keys is shown

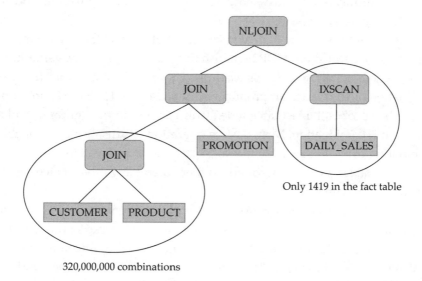

Figure 5-14 *A visual explanation of our sample star schema query using a nested-loop join before DB2 10*

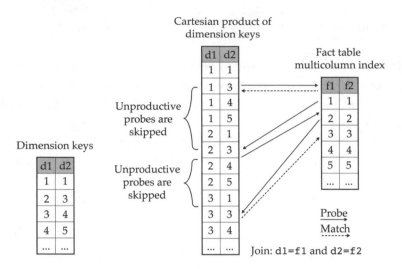

Figure 5-15 *Looking at the operation of a Zigzag join*

in the middle of the figure. (This type of join is simply the D1 dimension joined with every value in the D2 dimension.) It's important that you understand that in the case of a Zigzag join, DB2 won't materialize the entire Cartesian product—we're just showing it for illustration purposes and to clarify Zigzag join processing.

In the far right of Figure 5-15, you can see that the fact table has a multi-column index defined on it. DB2 will use this index to probe for values that match the join predicates. In this example, Zigzag join starts from the first combination of the Cartesian product; in this case, it's [1,1]. The join operation then probes the fact table index (solid arrows in the figure) to find a match to this combination. Next, the join operation returns the next available combination from the fact table index, [2,2] (dotted arrows in the figure). Note that indexes are already sorted, so there aren't any other matching records that start with a 1.

The [2,2] index key is now used to scan the dimensions keys. The value 2 is available for D1, but a 2 is not available in D2. The next available slot has a 3 for D2, so the join looks for a [2,3] key in the multicolumn index. The values [1,3], [1,4],... [2,1] are known as *unproductive probes* and are skipped when doing a Zigzag join. The Zigzag process continues, skipping the unproductive rows, until the end.

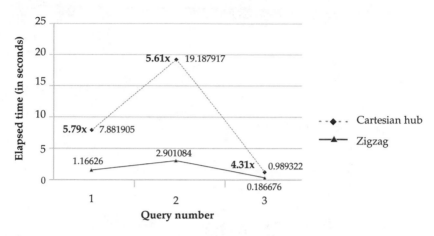

Figure 5-16   *Looking at the operation of a Zigzag join*

Our tests have shown that the use of the Zigzag join technique can deliver substantial compute resource savings and returns queries four to five times faster than traditional join techniques. An example of one of the tests we ran is shown in Figure 5-16.

Miscellaneous Internal Optimization Improvements

DB2 10 includes internal optimizations that improve the run-time performance for many workloads with minimal tuning. By improving run-time performance without the need for excessive tuning, DB2 helps to reduce the cost of ownership of your database solution. Although these changes are transparent to the user and don't require any settings to be changed in DB2, we didn't delve into them in this book; that said, these enhancements are significant enough to list them here:

- Improved access path quality and run-time for key operations

- Optimizer focus on complex queries that are typical of data warehouses

- Greater "out-of-the-box" performance through improvements in the accuracy of cardinality estimates, memory management, hash join performance, aggregations and sorts, star schema optimization, and more!

6

The Even More
Available DB2

It's funny, but whenever discussions arise around database availability, people focus on whether the database is responding, as though your business runs on a single `ping` or `connect` command. Let's step back for a moment and consider that database availability is really a measure of how successful user applications are at performing their required database tasks. If user applications can't connect to the database, or if their transactions fail because of a time-out condition that was spawned by a heavy load on the server, that database solution isn't considered very available. So although we serve up a hearty bowl of high availability acronym soup in this chapter—measures such as recovery point objective (RPO), recovery time objective (RTO), mean time to repair (MTTR), mean time between failure (MTBF), and more—we want you to remember that *only if* user applications are successfully performing their intended work can you consider your database solution to be highly available.

Designing a highly available database solution, or increasing the availability of an existing solution, requires a thorough understanding of the applications that are accessing the database. In this chapter, we focus on the traditional meaning of high availability; for example, we discuss the "drop-dead-simple turnkey" high availability and disaster recovery (HADR) enhancements in DB2 10 and much more. But as you read through the rest of this book, stop to consider all the features that we talk about and how they appear within the scope of high availability. For example, the performance enhancements that are detailed in Chapter 5 include all sorts of features that can affect the overall availability of the database server: from multicore parallelism enhancements, to the integration of the highly available and scalable DB2 pureScale technology into the DB2 code base, to workload classifications that ensure your server doesn't get overloaded, DB2 10 is a release that is steeped in high availability.

In this chapter, we cover the DB2 10 enhancements that minimize both planned and unplanned outages. We discuss other availability topics, such as table space–level recovery in DB2 pureScale and multiple standbys for an HADR cluster, and we also offer some "from the field" advice along the way.

Before We Begin: Be Careful for the Things You Plan and Don't Plan

We've all heard some wild stories about *unplanned outages*. The unplanned system failures that can affect database availability include power interruptions, network outages, hardware failures, operating system or other software errors and, of course, complete system failure in the event of a disaster. If failures occur at a time when users expect to be able to work with the database, a highly available database solution must be able to handle the following problems with minimal impact on solution availability to user applications:

- *It must shield user applications from the failure.* A failure and its recovery should be transparent, so that application end users aren't even aware that a failure has occurred. For example, the DB2 Automatic Client Reroute (ACR) services can reroute database client connections to alternative database servers if a database server fails, and in some cases, they can even restart the transaction (this is referred to as a *seamless* failover). A lot of retry logic is built into DB2 for first failure encounter scenarios, and most availability errors can be returned to the application with SQL code that can easily be handled by simple TRY/CATCH logic.

- *It must limit the effect of the failure.* For example, if a failure occurs on one machine in a cluster, DB2's native cluster manager can remove that machine from the cluster, and transactions that were running on this machine are transparently moved to another machine in the cluster using ACR services.

- *It must recover from the failure and return the system to "normal" operations.* For example, if a standby database takes over database operations for a failed primary database, the failed database might need to restart, recover, and resume operations as the primary database.

In a highly available database solution, the impact of maintenance activities on the availability of the database to user applications must also be minimized; we classify such activities as *planned outages*. For example, if you're the DBA supporting a traditional brick and mortar store that's open for business between the hours of 9:00 a.m. and 5:00 p.m., maintenance activities can occur offline, outside of those business hours, without affecting the availability of the database to user applications. (We'd also like you to know that we really envy you; if you're hiring, let us know.)

Today's world is characterized by a "transaction anywhere and anytime" mentality, and most of us have come to expect that services will be available to us whenever we want them. You'd be surprised how much access to services is directly correlated to consumer vulnerability modeling. Have you ever tried to log onto your loyalty rewards program but the system was down for maintenance? Did you ever check your bank account balance online and notice that certain things didn't add up (we're not taking into consideration your budgeting techniques here): the system was likely under maintenance. If your business is expected to be available to its customers, maintenance activities must run online or be scheduled for off-peak activity periods to have minimal impact on the availability of your services and products.

If you're charged with making business decisions and design choices about the availability of your database solution, we strongly recommend that you weigh the following two factors:

- The cost of database downtime to your business
- The cost of implementing a certain degree of availability

This is a classic conundrum. We can't count the number of times we've heard, "I need the best high availability solution possible, but it can't cost much." Look, as much as we believe that DB2 delivers more value than anything in the marketplace, when it comes to high availability, the more availability you want, the more it costs. Do you need power redundancy? Is the MTTR defined in your Service Level Agreement (SLA) measured in hours, minutes, or seconds? If it's hours, you've got a cheaper set of options.

One real-life example are those "stock ticker" applications that run on various web sites; some are financially related, some are news tickers, some are sport score tickers, and more. Companies that provide these services make a certain amount of revenue every hour ($revenue). One of our clients told us that every second their ticker is down is like driving a brand new Lexus off a cliff. For such a company, a high availability strategy that saves 10 hours of down time per year will earn the business an extra 10 × $revenue per year. Note that we're just talking about the ticker's income stream here; there's a whole other discussion about lost reputations and clientele due to outages.

We recommend that you classify your applications into tiers, such as bronze, silver, gold, and so on. Many vendors will try to sell you the most available and expensive solution for all of your applications. Your objective, however, is to match the right availability solution to the right application requirements. The good news is that DB2 ships with the most comprehensive and tier-oriented high availability solutions in the industry. For example, DB2 comes with a built-in cluster manager (and an SQL interface to manage it) for traditional failover techniques when requirements are measured in double-digit minutes. All DB2 editions include HADR (we don't generally consider DB2 Express-C an edition) for an even higher tier of availability that's typically measured in high seconds to low minutes. Finally, DB2 pureScale is the low double-digit seconds failover technology of choice. Although these failover times are generalizations, you can see how naturally DB2 would fit into a tier classification system for your applications.

DB2 pureScale Availability Enhancements

In Chapter 5, we talked about the merged DB2 pureScale and DB2 10 code bases and the resulting performance enhancements. In this section, we outline the major availability enhancements that DB2 10 delivers to a DB2 pureScale environment. If you need a solid introduction to DB2 pureScale, or simply a refresher, download a free copy of our book entitled *DB2 pureScale: Risk Free Agile Scaling* (www.ibm.com/software/data/education/bookstore).

> **NOTE**   *DB2 9.8 was the initial delivery vehicle for the DB2 pureScale technology; if you weren't using DB2 pureScale, you wouldn't have been*

exposed to this version, because it was solely a DB2 pureScale delivery vehicle.
However, DB2 pureScale is a native part of DB2 10.

Getting to Table Space–Level Granularity for Recovery Operations

DB2 9.8 (DB2 pureScale) databases supported database-level recovery only. For some clients, this was too coarse a recovery level, because they work with very large databases (VLDBs) in transactional environments and logically assign parts of the business to different table spaces. Having to execute backup and recovery (BAR) operations at the database level blunted various opportunities for more efficiency and availability. As of DB2 10, DB2 pureScale supports all of the existing table space–level recovery features in DB2, and you can use the same BAR plans for both single- and multipartition DB2 databases.

DB2 10 preserves most of the existing functionality for table space roll-forward operations, but with additional enhancements, such as the ability to replay merged database log streams and support for DB2 pureScale instances. The real-time merging of DB2 pureScale cluster members that participate in the data sharing group, at the table space level, is the main functional difference when compared with table space roll-forward processing in a DB2 environment. This log merging, which returns log records from multiple members in a well-defined, deterministic order, is fully transparent to the DBA.

By default, table space roll-forward operates in offline mode. It therefore requires a cluster-wide, super-exclusive database connection and holds this lock until processing completes. In other words, it requires that there be *no active connections* to the database and that the database be deactivated to proceed. If the database is activated, the offline request fails and returns a SQL1035N error, which means that the database is currently in use. An offline table space roll-forward operation can't start if the database, or any cluster member, is found to be inconsistent and requires member or group crash recovery. If your cluster is in such a state and you try to perform this activity, DB2 returns a SQL1015N error, informing you that crash recovery needs to be run before this operation can start.

You can also perform an online table space roll-forward operation, which permits concurrent read and write access to all of the data that resides outside of the table spaces that are participating in the roll-forward operation. Online table space roll-forward operations are not affected by, and do not depend on, the state of individual cluster members. More specifically, a member failure does not affect an online table space roll-forward operation that's executing on another member.

An online table space roll-forward operation and member crash recovery can execute independently, because a table space is inaccessible from the time it is restored until completion of the table space roll-forward operation; in most cases, member crash recovery will not have to perform REDO processing on any transactions that affect a table space for which a roll-forward operation is pending or in progress. In those rare cases when the member crash recovery starting point precedes the time at which the table space was restored, and there are log records within the recovery window that require access to the table space, member crash recovery will not process those log records and returns a SQL1271W error to inform you that inaccessible table spaces were encountered during the recovery operation.

We should note that DB2 pureScale allows only a single table space roll-forward operation to run on the cluster at any one time. This policy is enforced through a system-wide lock that's acquired when an online table space roll-forward operation begins (the lock is conditionally acquired in exclusive mode). If the lock is already being held, an attempt to start a new table space roll-forward operation fails with a SQL1269N error.

If you're a DBA with experience in BAR operations, most of what we've mentioned here with respect to online and offline table space roll-forward recovery processing is no different from what you'd expect when working with a "vanilla" DB2 instance.

Odds and Ends that Add Up to Better DB2 pureScale Availability

DB2 10 includes a number of enhancements that give DBAs even more availability for their DB2 pureScale clusters on top of the "big ticket" items that we already covered in this chapter. In this section, we'll briefly describe those enhancements.

The db2cluster Command for Instance Domain Repair and Automatic Failback Control

As of DB2 10, you can use the DB2 pureScale db2cluster command to repair an instance domain. This is a great availability enhancement because certain failure situations can be recovered more quickly by re-creating the cluster manager domain and any associated cluster resources. Moreover, you can use the db2cluster command to control the membership when an automatic failback of a member to its home host occurs. We cover all of this throughout this chapter.

Repairing a Domain   If a failure that requires the cluster manager domain to be re-created occurs within a DB2 pureScale instance, a DBA with the DB2 cluster services administrator role can use the db2cluster command to re-create the domain and the resource models for all instances on the cluster. In this scenario, the cluster manager domain is re-created using the same configuration (tiebreaker and host failure detection time) used in the existing cluster manager domain. For example, to re-create a domain called mypureScaleDomain, you would run the following command:

```
db2cluster -cm -repair -domain mypureScaleDomain
```

To use the db2cluster command to repair the domain of an instance in a DB2 10 pureScale environment, that domain *must* have been previously created using the db2cluster command. Instance domains that are created using the db2haicu command (this utility isn't used in DB2 pureScale environments) can't be repaired with the db2cluster command.

Disabling Automatic Failback   In a DB2 pureScale environment, a reboot or failure of a host computer (or a virtualization session acting as a server) causes its associated member to be automatically moved to a guest host in restart light mode. When the problem on the host computer is fixed and the host becomes available, automatic failback causes the relocated member to be immediately moved back onto its home host. We heard from a number of DBAs that they wanted more explicit control over when automatic failback services would kick in. For example, they might want to verify the health of the restarted home host computer personally *before* the member is automatically moved back and reintegrated into the DB2 pureScale cluster. Without this type of control, a DBA would have to take the home host computer off-line, thereby disrupting transactions for the short period of time that is required to move the member to a guest host and back. DB2 10 gives DBAs the ability to disable automatic failback by running the following command:

```
db2cluster -cm -set -option autofailback -value off
```

As you might imagine, you can also use this command to manually start the automatic failback of a member to its home host computer. For example,

```
db2cluster -cm -set -option autofailback -value on
```

If there's a host failure, and the associated cluster member is ready to fail back to its home host computer automatically, a DBA alert is raised for that specific member if automatic failback has been disabled. You can use the `db2instance -list` command to view such an alert and the `db2cluster -cm -list -alert` command to return detailed information about the surfaced alert with explicit instructions on how to start automatic failback.

DB2 High Availability and Disaster Enhancements

In this section, we explore the exciting new DB2 10 enhancements to high availability disaster recovery (HADR). HADR has been around since DB2 8, so we're going to assume that you know about it. Although we'll cover some of it here, if you need a refresher or an introduction, we recommend checking out "Best Practices: DB2 High Availability Disaster Recovery" (http://tinyurl.com/6m6exm4). HADR provides a turnkey high availability solution for both partial and complete site failures; it protects against data loss by replicating data changes from a primary database source to one or more (the "more" is new in DB2 10) target databases.

Any number of issues related to the hardware, network, or software components that are associated with a database solution can cause a site failure. Without an availability solution such as a shared disk cluster, HADR, or DB2 pureScale, a partial site failure requires restarting the database. HADR technology tries to address the fact that the length of time it takes to restart a database is often unpredictable. For example, because of the logs that need to be processed in a highly loaded transaction environment, it might take several minutes before a database is brought back to a consistent state and made available. With HADR, a standby database assumes control within seconds. When you mix this with the ACR technology that can automatically redirect clients from a failed primary database to a new primary database, you've got a very simple high availability turnkey solution in HADR.

A complete site failure occurs when a disaster, such as fire, causes the entire site to be destroyed. For example, the primary database might be located in the Toronto data center, and the standby database is in Chicago. If a disaster that entirely disables the Toronto site were to occur, data availability is maintained by having Chicago's remote standby database take over as the primary database with full DB2 functionality. After a takeover operation occurs, you can work to fix the original primary database server and return it to its primary database role; this is known as *failback*. A DBA can initiate a failback if the original primary database can be made consistent with the new primary database (and DB2 has a lot of capability in this area, more so than some competing technologies we looked at; if you can't get them consistent, you have to rebuild the clustering pair from scratch). After reintegrating the original primary database into the HADR cluster as a standby database, you simply switch the roles of the databases to enable the original primary database to assume the primary database role once again.

Take Control of Your Availability Needs

HADR is very flexible in that it provides DBAs with a RPO "throttle" (configuration and topology choices that you can make) that gives you a lot of influence over the level of data synchronization between the primary and standby that you need. This is very appealing to DBAs, because different solutions have different RTOs and RPOs, and the flexibility of HADR enables you to tailor the configuration and topology to match those objectives. After all, if you can tolerate data loss, the solution shouldn't be configured in such a way that no data loss can occur, because that can affect the performance of the system. For example, if you didn't pick up the latest NHL hockey game score in your ticker, things are going to be OK; on the other hand, if this is a banking application, you had better not lose that bill payment. These are two examples of solutions that are very well served by HADR technology, but you would leverage its flexibility to configure the HADR services to specific business requirements.

As DBAs, we've been doing this for a long time. For example, if you wanted to favor performance over availability, you'll likely minimize issuing commits and that boosts performance; however, if the amount of time that it takes to recover from a failure is key, you're likely to ensure that you commit frequently to ensure the data is hardened. It's the same with HADR; you can choose various synchronization levels that enable you to favor performance over data synchronization, or vice versa.

Understanding HADR Synchronization Controls

HADR ships primary server–generated log data, at transaction granularity, to its secondary servers, which are continually rolling forward through the logs to keep all of the HADR cluster servers synchronized. Did you notice that we said secondary *servers*? The ability to have more than a single stand-by HADR database is new in DB2 10—more on that in a bit.

HADR provides four different synchronization modes (SYNC, NEARSYNC, ASYNC, and SUPERASYNC) that throttle the degree of data protection against transaction loss that your solution can tolerate. HADR also provides other controls, such as a peer window, which we also discuss in this chapter.

The synchronization mode determines when the primary database server considers a transaction to be complete, based on the state of the logging on the standby database. The stricter the synchronization mode configuration setting, the more protection a database has against transaction data loss. The more protection against transaction loss you want, the bigger the impact on the performance of a typical workload. Figure 6-1 shows the available HADR synchronization modes and indicates when transactions are considered to be committed.

Synchronous Mode (SYNC)

SYNC provides the greatest protection against transaction loss, but as you might expect, it's going to result in the most amount of overheard. Under this mode, log writes are considered successful when the log data is guaranteed to have been stored at both sites—that is, *only when* the log records have been written to physical log files on the primary database *and* when the

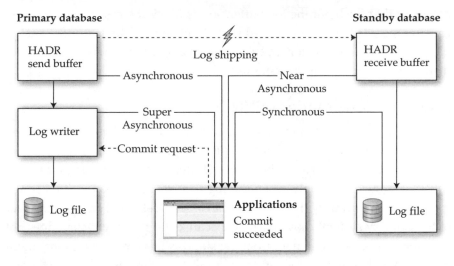

Figure 6-1   *HADR synchronization modes directly affect the amount of data loss that your HADR cluster can tolerate.*

primary database has received acknowledgement from the standby database that the logs have also been written to physical log files on the standby database. In other words, the log data is guaranteed to be stored at both sites before the application's commit is acknowledged.

Near Synchronous Mode (NEARSYNC)

Under NEARSYNC mode, log writes are considered successful only when the log records have been written to log files on the primary database *and* when the primary database has received acknowledgement from the standby database that these log records have also been written to main memory on the standby system. An HADR cluster operating in NEARSYNC mode can lose data only if *both* sites fail simultaneously and the standby has not yet flushed all of the log data that it has received to nonvolatile storage. In our opinion, for most applications (again, depending on the business requirement), this will likely be the most suitable HADR synchronization mode, because it provides a very small window for data loss and has negligible impact on performance. If you think about it, even if there were a failure on both machines, in the same manner that DB2 has very aggressive page cleaners that flush data pages from memory, HADR has very fast and efficient write-ahead logging protocols that flush out the log buffer, so it's likely the case in this scenario that log records have been flushed to disk. Finally, as the log buffer makes its way onto disk, most storage subsystems have cache coherency and other disk write protection mechanisms as well.

Asynchronous Mode (ASYNC)

Compared to the SYNC and NEARSYNC modes, ASYNC has less impact on performance; however, it is also susceptible to a larger window for transaction losses if the primary database fails. Under ASYNC mode, log writes are considered successful only when the log records have been written to the log files on the primary database and have been delivered to the TCP layer of the primary system's host machine. Because the primary system does not wait for an acknowledgement from the standby system, transactions might be considered committed when they are still on their way to the standby database.

Super Asynchronous Mode (SUPERASYNC)

SUPERASYNC, which was introduced in DB2 9.7 Fix Pack 3 (but it's really in place for DB2 10), has the least impact on transaction response but it has the highest probability of transaction losses if the primary system fails. This mode is useful if you can tolerate data loss, but you never want to impede, elongate, or block transactions due to network interruptions or congestion. Under this mode, the HADR pair will *never* be in peer state or disconnected peer state. The log writes are considered successful as soon as the log records have been written to the log files on the primary database (which would be the case if you didn't have an HADR cluster). Because the primary database doesn't wait for any kind of acknowledgement (be it from the communication stack or the standby database), transactions are considered committed regardless of their replication state.

In SUPERASYNC mode, transaction commit operations on the primary database aren't correlated with the speed of the network or the standby database, and therefore the log gap between the primary and standby databases has the potential to increase over time. For this reason, if you're using this mode, we strongly recommend that you monitor the log gap (use the HADR_LOG_GAP monitor element), because it's an indirect measure of the potential amount of data that could be lost if a true outage were to occur on the primary system. Notice we didn't say number of transactions? This gap shows the potential data loss regardless of the number of transactions. For example, in a disaster recovery scenario, any transactions that are committed during the log gap wouldn't be available on the standby database. If the log gap widens to the point where the potential data loss is unacceptable, we recommend that you investigate network interruptions or the relative speed of the standby database server node and take corrective measures to reduce the log gap.

The HADR Peer Window

The HADR peer window feature (introduced in DB2 9.5) specifies that the primary and standby databases are to behave as though they are still in peer state for a configured amount of time if the primary loses the HADR connection in peer state. If the primary fails in peer or this "disconnected peer" state, the failover to principal standby will have zero data loss. Using this feature in your HADR environment provides the greatest data loss protection possible. Note that the HADR peer window is effective only when the primary and standby are configured in SYNC or NEARSYNC modes and as such is effective only between the primary and principal standby (more details follow later in this chapter).

HADR Standby Databases

Note the plurality in this title. DB2 10 adds the ability to associate *multiple* HADR standby databases with a single primary server in an HADR cluster. This is a key DB2 10 enhancement, because in the past you implemented either HA *or* DR with HADR as you were limited to a single standby database. If you wanted to deliver a highly available nonpartitioned database and provide disaster recovery, you typically implemented the HADR cluster for high availability and leveraged Q Replication to create the disaster recovery site. With the new support for multiple standby databases, DB2 makes it possible to achieve both HA and DR objectives with a single technology.

Standby databases can be used in a number of ways. When HADR first appeared in DB2 8.2, you could access only the primary database; the secondary database was busy rolling through logs and data. DB2 9.71 added *reads on standby (RoS)* capabilities that enabled you to offload query workloads from the primary workstation and run report-type workloads on a standby database. For example, in DB2 10, you can use the RoS capability to support read-only workloads on one or more standby databases without affecting the HA or DR responsibility of the standby. Offloading report-type workloads from the primary server that's meant to process transactions within a governed SLA helps to reduce workloads on the primary server without affecting the main responsibility of the standby. (Of course, if you use RoS, the standby becomes a full-fledged active DB2 server and must be fully licensed, in contrast to the partial licensing that's needed when the standby database operates as a warm standby, rolling through the logs to maintain high availability for the cluster.)

DB2 10 also introduces the concept of *delayed replay* for certain standby servers. You can use this feature to create a business policy that keeps a standby database at a predefined lag to the current point in time (PiT) in terms of log replay. This is a very helpful feature, because it can be used to create a buffer zone for those treacherous ("ooops!") errors, or an application that has generated some "crazy" SQL. For example, perhaps an application has started corrupting some data fields. If data is lost or corrupted on the primary server, it can be recovered from the time-delayed standby; without this feature, the corruption gets propagated to the standby. Indeed, ironically, the speed and elegance of HADR can sometimes be too much of a good thing. In a multiple standby HADR environment, you might want to designate one standby to delay the log replay by 60 minutes and allow reporting, another to delay replay by 30 minutes and not allow reporting, and a third with no delay at all, thereby creating a flexible data protection and reporting environment through a management-by-intent business policy.

Finally, HADR provides *rolling DB2 Fix Pack updates* and upgrades to operating systems and hardware (since our first release of HADR). The new DB2 10 support for multiple standbys empowers you to apply maintenance in a way that still protects the primary server through a standby HADR database. We discuss all of these features, functions, and benefits in more detail throughout the remainder of this chapter.

The Specifics: Supporting Multiple HADR Standbys

In DB2 10, you can have a maximum of three HADR standby databases: one standby is designated as the *principal* HADR standby database and the others as *auxiliary* HADR standby databases. All types of HADR standby servers are synchronized with the HADR primary database through a direct TCP/IP connection, all support reads on standby, and all can perform a forced or nonforced takeover from the current cluster's primary server. Finally, all standbys are fed from the currently active primary database.

An auxiliary standby can be configured for time-delayed log replay, which provides more data protection schemes for your environment. Auxiliary standby servers must be configured with the SUPERASYNC mode, but the principal standby server can use any of the supported HADR synchronization modes (because it's really the same standby that you've known from a previous release of DB2).

Finally, DB2 can natively automate failover in an HADR environment through the built-in IBM Tivoli System Automation for Multiplatform (SA MP) services, and in DB2 10, this is supported for the principal standby server *only*. If you want to make one of the auxiliary standby servers the new HADR primary, you have to issue the takeover manually on one of the auxiliary standbys to make one of them the primary.

As we mentioned earlier, there are a number of benefits to using multiple standbys in your HADR cluster. One of the biggest benefits is that you now have the ability to use HADR to achieve *both* your high availability and disaster recovery objectives. For example, you might choose to deploy your principal standby in the same location as the primary, thereby providing high availability for the solution. If an outage occurs on the primary, the principal standby can very quickly take over the primary role within your SLA-bound RTOs. For protection against a widespread disaster affecting both the primary and principal standby servers, you're likely to deploy auxiliary standbys in one or more remote locations in relation to the primary server. In this scenario, the distance between the primary and auxiliaries and the potential for network delays between them have *no negative effect* on the primary server's ability to host transactions, because auxiliaries use the SUPERASYNC mode. If a disaster were to affect both the primary and principal standby servers, a DBA could initiate a takeover on either of the auxiliaries. (You can configure one of the auxiliary standby databases to become the new principal standby using the HADR_TARGET_LIST database configuration parameter—db cfg.)

From a monitoring perspective each standby knows only about the primary and has no knowledge of other standbys in the HADR cluster. This means that if you turn on monitoring for any standby, it will report only its own status and information about the primary.

The primary is aware of all standbys. Old interfaces, such as snapshot, will report on the principal standby only. New interfaces, such as table functions, will report on all standbys. If a configured standby (appearing in a target list) is not connected, it is still displayed as a reminder that multiple standbys are configured.

An auxiliary standby can take over as the primary even if that auxiliary doesn't have an available principal standby server. For example, if you experience an outage on the primary and principal standby, one auxiliary can take over as the primary. However, if you were to stop the database after it becomes the new primary, it can't start again as an HADR primary unless its principal standby is started.

You don't have to maintain the same synchronization modes on the primary and its associated standbys. When you configure the primary's synchronization mode by using the HADR_SYNCMODE db cfg, that setting is considered to be the cluster's *configured synchronization mode*, which defines a policy for a standby server's *effective synchronization mode*; this parameter explicitly sets the synchronization mode for the principal standby as well.

A standby's effective synchronization mode is the value that is displayed by any monitoring interface. As you've likely deduced, the auxiliary's effective synchronization mode is always SUPERASYNC, because that's the only supported synchronization mode for this kind of standby. This setting is used to handle cases in which any standby takes over the primary role, and it governs the synchronization protocol that is used in such cases. For example, suppose that the HADR cluster is operating in NEARSYNC mode when a disaster occurs at the data center where both the primary and the principal standby reside. When a remote auxiliary is promoted to the primary role, the defined synchronization mode will take effect with the currently defined principal standby.

Only the settings of the current primary's HADR_SYNCMODE and HADR_PEER_WINDOW configuration parameters are relevant (and they don't have to match the settings for these parameters on any of the standbys). In fact, any setting for HADR_PEER_WINDOW on an auxiliary standby is ignored, because, as previously mentioned, peer window functionality is incompatible with the SUPERASYNC mode. The principal standby uses the peer window setting of the primary, which is applicable only if the standby is using the

SYNC or NEARSYNC synchronization mode. In short, the standbys have their settings for these parameters defined either by the primary (in the case of the principal standby) or by their role as an auxiliary standby.

Getting to Multiple Standbys from an Existing HADR Cluster

Initializing an HADR system to support multiple standbys is pretty similar to how you would set up your HADR cluster when it supports only a single standby; the main difference is that you have to enable HADR for multiple standbys by setting the HADR_TARGET_LIST db cfg parameter for all servers that are participating in the HADR cluster.

The HADR_TARGET_LIST parameter is required on all members of the HADR cluster (even on auxiliary standbys); it defines what the HADR cluster will look like under the scenario in which the database becomes a primary. You don't have to include all of the HADR cluster's participants in this configuration setting (except on the primary—any datbase that's not defined in the primary's target list is not part of the HADR cluster). Moreover, the HADR_TARGET_LIST doesn't require symmetry or reciprocity if more than one standby exists. Even if you configured the cluster such that databaseA is databaseB's principal standby, databaseB doesn't have to designate databaseA as its principal standby. Each standby that's specified in the target list for databaseA must also have databaseA in its target list. This can get a little confusing, so spend some time on it, because working out the target list for each database is an important step. Essentially the HADR_TARGET_LIST allows you to define the topology of the HADR cluster on each node and will be effective when that particular node is promoted to the primary.

One nice thing about DB2 10's multiple HADR standby support is that you can dynamically add (or remove) standby auxiliaries without taking any sort of outage. Therefore, if you want the flexibility or plan to add other standbys to the cluster in the future, you can enable the HADR cluster for multiple standbys and configure it for only a single principal standby; in other words, we recommend you set yourself up to leverage the new DB2 10 multiple standby support and then operate with a single standby, as was the case before DB2 10. This recommendation gives you maximum flexibility should you require an immediate need for multiple standby servers, but more or less maintain the current environment.

Altering an Existing HADR Multiple Standby Cluster

If you've got an up-and-running HADR multiple standby cluster, you might want to make additional changes to it, such as adding or removing auxiliary standbys or even changing the role of an auxiliary standby to a principal standby. Because HADR is all about availability, it's only natural to ensure that this kind of process can be done online without any downtime on your production system.

To add an auxiliary standby to your HADR deployment, update the primary's HADR_TARGET_LIST db cfg parameter with the host (HADR_LOCAL_HOST) and port (HADR_LOCAL_SVC) information for the standby that you want to add. Don't forget that you also have to add host and port information for the primary to the target list of the new standby—it's that whole mutual inclusion thing we talked about earlier. To add this kind of standby to your HADR cluster, the HADR_TARGET_LIST db cfg parameter must already be set to at least one standby; in other words, you can add a standby to your HADR cluster only if the cluster is already running in multiple standby mode.

Only auxiliary standbys can be dynamically removed from a cluster, and such removal has *no effect* on HADR operations running on the primary and the principal standby. You can remove an auxiliary standby from an HADR cluster by stopping HADR on it (issue the STOP HADR command) and then subsequently removing it from the target lists of the primary and any other standbys.

You might want to change the server that has the principal standby role assigned to it. Such a change requires that you stop HADR processing on the primary; however, this doesn't cause an outage, because the DBA doesn't have to deactivate the primary to perform this operation. After the primary is stopped, you can simply update its target list so that the new principal standby appears first. If the new principal standby is not already an auxiliary standby, you'll need to add the address of the primary database to its target list, too, and then configure the other aforementioned HADR parameters and activate the standby. If the new principal standby is already an auxiliary standby, no further action is needed.

Log Spooling on the Standby

DB2 10 also delivers a new log spooling service for HADR clusters that operate in the new multiple standby topologies or in the traditional single standby framework. This feature enables transactions on the primary to make progress without having to wait for the log replay or actions that are associated with the HADR synchronization setting on the standby. If the standby falls behind the primary while replaying transactions, the primary will continue to send data to the standby, which will continue to write (or spool) the lagging log data to the standby's disk, thereby giving the standby an opportunity to play "catch-up" and read the log data from disk at a later time. Standby log spooling enables an HADR cluster to better tolerate spikes in transaction volume on the primary or a slowdown of log replay on the standby.

If you're planning to use this feature, we recommend that you allocate adequate disk space to the active log path of the standby database, so that it can hold the spooled log data in addition to the disk space that's required for active logs. (Log space is determined by the LOGPRIMARY, LOGSECOND, and LOGFILSIZ db cfg parameters.)

You can enable log spooling by using the HADR_SPOOL_LIMIT db cfg parameter to specify the upper limit on how much data is written, or spooled, to disk if the log receive buffer fills up. By default, this parameter is set to 0, which means that log spooling is not enabled. Setting HADR_SPOOL_LIMIT=-1 puts DB2 into unlimited spooling mode, in which it can use any amount of disk space available to the standby's active log path to write out the spooled log data.

Another thing to consider when enabling log spooling is the possibility of a larger gap between the log position on the primary and the log replay on the standby; this could lead to longer takeover times, because the standby cannot assume the role of the new primary until the replay of the spooled logs finishes.

We want to emphasize that the use of log spooling with HADR doesn't in any way compromise the protection that's provided by this feature. Data from the primary is still replicated in log form to the principal standby using the specified synchronization mode; it just injects a purposed delay to replay the logs.

For-Purpose Standby Time Delays

Typically, when we hear the words "time delay" and "standby," one of us is sitting in a middle seat in coach and arriving five hours late. DB2 10 adds a positive spin to these words with new log delay replay services that help to prevent data loss or corruption due to errant transactions. This feature is supported only on standbys that are configured to run in SUPERASYNC mode, because if log replay is delayed on the standby, there could be a lot of log data awaiting replay (either filling up the HADR receive buffer or, if configured, the log spool). In any other HADR synchronization mode, such a condition would block the primary from executing transactions.

You can create a time delay policy for your HADR cluster by setting the HADR_REPLAY_DELAY db cfg on the HADR standby database. A delayed replay policy instructs the HADR service to intentionally keep a standby database at a point in time that's earlier than that of the primary database by introducing a delay to that standby's log replay processing. When delayed replay is enabled, if an errant transaction is executed on the primary, you've got a "buffer zone" (equal to the amount of delay you've configured for the cluster) to prevent the errant transaction from being replayed on the standby. If you have to recover lost data, just copy this delayed data back to the primary or let one of the standbys with a time delay take over as the new primary database.

Delayed replay works using a timestamp comparison algorithm that compares timestamps in the primary's log stream with the current time of the standby. For this reason, it's vital that you synchronize the clocks of the primary and standby databases.

Transaction commits are replayed on the standby according to the following equation:

> (current time on standby – value of HADR_REPLAY_DELAY
> database configuration parameter) ≥ timestamp of the
> committed log record

You need to ensure that the HADR_REPLAY_DELAY setting implements a large enough delay to let your quality assurance process detect and react to errant transactions on the primary; if you don't do this, you might find that by the time you figure out the problem, your buffer zone has been breached.

Standby time delays can be used regardless of the number of standbys you've configured for your HADR cluster. In an HADR environment running in multiple standby mode, we recommend that you consider having two standbys that stay current with the primary for high availability and disaster recovery purposes, and a third that is configured with delayed replay for protection against errant transactions.

In the event of a failover, any TAKEOVER command that's applied to a standby running with delayed log replay will fail. You need to turn off the delay explicitly by setting HADR_REPLAY_DELAY=0, deactivate and reactivate the standby to pick up the new value, and then issue the TAKEOVER command.

We *strongly* recommend that if you use these new delay services, you also enable log spooling. We're recommending this because when you introduce an intentional delay for a standby, the replay position can get far behind the standby's log receive position. If you're using this feature without spooling, log receive can delay the replay only by the amount of space that it can hold in the HADR receive buffer. If you follow our recommendation, the standby can receive *many* more logs beyond the replay position, providing you with the opportunity for a larger "buffer" zone against data loss. Note that in either case, because of the mandatory SUPERASYNC mode requirement to use this new feature, the primary will *never* be blocked by enabling delayed replay.

Log Archive Management in an HADR Environment

In an HADR environment, any of the nodes may be promoted to become the primary, and as such we recommend that you configure the primary and all standbys to be able to archive log files. Regardless of the setting on a standby, only the current primary database can perform log archiving. If the primary and standby databases are set up with separate archiving locations, logs are archived only to the primary database's archiving location.

In the event of a takeover, when a standby becomes the new primary, any logs that are archived from that point on are saved to the newly promoted standby's archiving location. In such a configuration, logs are archived to one location or the other, but not both. The exception is that following a takeover, the new primary database might archive a few logs that the original primary database had already archived.

What you'll find in a multiple standby system is that the archived log files can be scattered across all of the HADR cluster's archive devices. For this reason, we recommend implementing a shared archive, because this ensures that all files are stored in a single location. A number of operations need to retrieve archived log files, including database roll-forward, a primary re-trieving log files to send to a standby in remote catch-up, and replication programs (such as Q Replication) reading logs. A shared HADR cluster ar-chive avoids distributing these files on multiple archive devices, and DBA intervention will not be necessary to locate the files when they are needed.

If archiving to an archive device isn't feasible, copy the logs into the over-flow log path. We generally don't recommend this, but as a last resort, you can copy these files into the active log path (be really careful, because you risk damaging the active log files). DB2 doesn't auto delete user-copied files in the overflow and active log paths, so you're going to have to make provi-sions to remove these files explicitly when they are no longer needed by any HADR standby (or application).

Log File Management on a Standby

A standby automatically manages log files in its log path, but it won't delete a log file from its local log path unless it has been notified by the primary database that the primary database has archived it. This behavior provides added protection against the loss of log files. If the primary database fails be-fore the log file is safely stored in the archive, the standby database ensures that the log file is archived. If both the LOGARCHMETH1 and LOGARCHMETH2 configuration parameters have been set, the standby doesn't recycle a log file until the primary has archived it using both methods.

Semi-dynamic HADR Configuration Parameters

More and more database and database manager configuration parameters are becoming AUTOMATIC or can accommodate dynamic changes. DB2 10 supports changing any of the HADR configuration parameters without the need for shutting down the primary database. (HADR configuration chang-es take effect only after the STOP HADR and START HADR AS PRIMARY com-mands are invoked, so there is still a disruption to the shipping of logs to the standbys. However, the database availability is not affected.)

Automatic Reconfiguration of HADR Parameters

In multiple standby mode, if the HADR_REMOTE_HOST, HADR_REMOTE_INST, and HADR_REMOTE_SVC configuration parameters (used to identify the primary database for the standbys and identify the principal standby for the primary) aren't properly set, DB2 automatically resets them when HADR starts.

Despite DB2's automatic reconfiguration keeping an eye out for you, we always recommend that you try to set these values correctly the first time, because reconfiguration might not take effect until a connection is made between a standby and its primary. In some HADR deployments, those initial values might be needed. For example, if you're using the built-in server Tivoli SA MP services to automate failovers, the value for HADR_REMOTE_INST is needed to construct a resource name. Note that if the DB2_HADR_NO_IP_CHECK registry variable is set to ON, the HADR_REMOTE_HOST and HADR_REMOTE_SVC values are not updated automatically.

Reconfiguration During and After a Takeover

In a *graceful takeover* operation, the values for the HADR_REMOTE_HOST, HADR_REMOTE_INST, and HADR_REMOTE_SVC configuration parameters on the new primary are automatically updated to its principal standby. The same parameters on the standbys that are listed in the new primary's HADR_TARGET_LIST are automatically updated to point to the new primary, which is a nice piece of maintenance automation that's in the DB2 10 code. Any standby that's not listed in the HADR_TARGET_LIST isn't updated, which is why we recommend listing them all. If a standby isn't listed, it keeps trying to connect to the old primary and gets rejected, because the old primary has now become a standby. The old primary is guaranteed to be in the new primary's target list because of the target list's mutual inclusion requirement.

In a *forced takeover*, automatic updates on the new primary and its standbys (excluding the old primary) work the same way as during a graceful takeover. However, automatic updates on the old primary won't happen until the primary is shut down and restarted for reintegration as a standby.

Any standby that's not online during a takeover (forced or graceful) operation will be reconfigured automatically after it starts. Automatic reconfiguration might not take effect immediately on startup, because it needs the new primary to contact the standby. On startup, a standby might attempt to connect to the old primary and follow the log stream of the old primary.

This causes it to diverge from the new primary's log stream and make that standby unable to pair with the new primary. You must manually shut down the old primary before takeover to avoid this kind of *split brain* scenario.

The All New MON_GET_HADR Table Function

The MON_GET_HADR table function is an SQL-based function that can be queried from any SQL client, and the output can be further processed by SQL filter, join, aggregate, and other functions to provide a user-defined format. This function makes it easy to get status information about the HADR cluster. For example, MON_GET_HADR returns information in a table-like fashion, so that you can dump monitoring information into a spreadsheet or your favorite visualization tool.

Moreover, because DBAs are in love with the db2pd tool, the HADR profile that's associated with this utility (db2pd -hadr) now returns the same fields as the HADR table function; its format has changed to one field per line, similar to that of the current database snapshot output.

Availability Odds and Ends

In this section, we outline some of the other features that make DB2 more available or easier to manage from an availability perspective. We don't cover the finer details of the features that we outline in this section, but we definitely want you to know about them. We left out some high availability features in this section because they are covered elsewhere in this book. For example, DB2 10 adds to availability with new table partitioning enhancements for availability as well as enhancements to the INGEST utility (we cover both in Chapter 5) as well as log compression (covered in Chapter 2), and more.

InfoSphere Replication Server Enhancements

Starting in DB2 10, replication is supported at the schema level. This means that any new table within a configured schema is automatically set up for replication. Before DB2 10, a DBA had to enable replication on a table-by-table basis. In DB2 10, by using the DATA CAPTURE clause on the CREATE SCHEMA statement (or by setting DFT_SCEHMAS_DCC=ON in the db cfg), you can create a management-by-intent policy specifying that new tables are to inherit the DATA CAPTURE CHANGES property.

Roving HA for the Database Partitioning Feature

Since DB2 9.5 Fix Pack 7, DBAs can reduce the amount of time that data is unavailable by enabling automatic roving HA failover in databases partitioned using DPF and configured for high availability. For example, in N+M clustered environments (with N active nodes and a single standby node), a failover operation occurs when one of the active nodes fails. At this point in time, the standby node begins hosting the resources of the failed node. When the failed node comes back online, the clustered environment automatically turns itself offline, so that the node that was originally chosen as the standby node becomes the standby node again. With roving HA failover, the last failed node in the cluster becomes the standby node without the need for additional failback operations.

7

A Big Data World: The Even More Extensible DB2

"May you live in interesting times" is often referred to as the *Chinese curse*. DB2 10 enters the world at a time that's indeed very interesting—some call it an information management inflection point. Looking back, we can't seem to recall a time when such a significant shift in how we collect, process, and make sense of data was at hand.

The subject of this chapter is *Big Data* and the ways that DB2 is evolving and carving out a space for itself in this new world. It's important that you understand the industry trends that are driving the Big Data craze. When you hear the term "Big Data," you think volume, but chances are that even the most seasoned DBAs aren't used to the Big Data volumes that are out there and available. Now consider how fast that data arrives at your organization's doorstep (velocity) and how many different kinds of data there are (variety), not just structured data. Perhaps Richard Saul Wurman, creator and chair of the popular TED (Technology/Entertainment/Design) conferences, defines Big Data in the most poetic way:

> There is a tsunami of data that is crashing onto the beaches of the civilized world. This is a tidal wave of unrelated, growing data formed in bits and bytes, coming in an unorganized, un-controlled, incoherent cacophony of foam. It's filled with flotsam and jetsam. It's filled with the sticks and bones and shells of in-animate and animate life. None of it is easily related; none of it comes with any organizational methodology....The tsunami is a

wall of data—data produced at greater and greater speed, greater and greater amounts to store in memory, amounts that double, it seems, with each sunset. On tape, on disks, on paper, sent by streams of light. Faster and faster, more and more and more.

The fact that the world is drowning in data has been dominating the headlines for years. Indeed, this represents a problem for IT shops around the world, which haven't been able to control or manage it. We find that IT is in a conundrum: as the amount of data that is available to an organization increases, the percentage of that data that the organization can understand is actually decreasing!

Why and how has Big Data become such an epidemic challenge and unprecedented opportunity? The catalyst for this accelerated data growth is an increasingly instrumented and interconnected world that generates data at machine and social speeds. Several factors are driving this hyper-growth, but none has had as much impact as the Internet and its resulting consumerization of IT.

The Internet has made enormous volumes of data readily accessible, and it's easy to find unlimited sources of data (of varying quality) at the end point of every URL. The Internet has become the greatest generator of data the world has ever known. For example, social networks are great at enabling interactions, but each and every interaction we engage in generates a treasure trove of data with the potential to deliver business insight.

It's estimated that Facebook will impact one out of every seven inhabitants of our planet by August 2012. And while we share our children's achievements and successes with friends and family, Facebook is generating double-digit TBs of log data per day alone, and that doesn't even include uploaded pictures. This data holds the type of insight that we're not able to derive from traditional transactional data sources.

Think about it: are you able to determine influencers of your customer's buying decisions from cash register receipts? Social graphs are key to this kind of insight. A social graph is a representation of our personal relationships. For example, Leon is related to and friends with a large number of people, each one of these friends is related to and is friends with even more people, and they have friends, and so on. All of these relationships represent Leon's social graph, and in a socially intelligent, interconnected, and instrumented world, the social graph is key to understanding monetization, and more. If a web site such as Facebook holds the social graph for one-seventh of the world's population, we're quite certain that the businesses of the world (and venture capitalists) are eager to benefit from this data opportunity.

Google+ is another social network, and it's expected to reach more than 400 million members by the end of 2012. LinkedIn holds profiles for 130 million professionals and has already parlayed itself into a very successful job search and recruitment business. Imagine if you could capture the conversations of 100 million people and were able to analyze these conversations and extract the content that is of interest to you? This is exactly what Twitter has done. Twitter captures multiple terabytes of tweet data per day and makes it available for analysis. For people with the skill and the tools, there has never been a greater opportunity to make a difference.

It's certainly not hard to see the proliferation of intelligent, interconnected, and instrumented devices. Sure, there are smart bridges that can evaluate their own structural health by measuring the integrity of the cement and rail cars that can identify parts in need of repair before they fail. But just take a look around at all of the young people with their fancy intelligent devices such as iPhones, Android phones, BlackBerries, and tablets. We're willing to bet that most of these folks have location awareness services enabled, thereby adding a spatial element to the massive amounts of temporal and sentiment data that they continuously generate. Indeed, these data dimensions synergize to make the information that is gleaned from them more contextually relevant, identifying, and revealing.

Without question, IT departments find themselves under a great deal of pressure to support the professional use of every gadget that people find under their Christmas tree and believe will make them more productive at work. At the risk of stating the obvious, there's been a change in the way that we interact with the world: the PC is no longer the dominant application delivery platform, and mobility is here to stay.

The volume of data that's generated by humans pales in comparison to the data volumes being generated by the recent proliferation of electronic sensors. Many of us became aware of radio-frequency identification (RFID) tags because Walmart drove the initial technology into skid-level supply chain management. As the cost of RFID tags has decreased during the last five years, their proliferation has risen sharply. RFID tags are now used at the individual item level; they are sewn into clothing, appear on milk containers (to monitor temperature safety thresholds during shipping), are implanted in cattle, and much more. The number of these tiny data generators in use rose from 1.3 billion in 2005, to 30 billion in 2011, and by all accounts this growth is accelerating. (We should note here that the moment we saved our files, these numbers are out of date, so don't focus on the actuals, just that they are big and growing.)

Although the Internet, mobile devices, and sensor networks might have solved the problem of data generation and collection, they've overwhelmed the data storage and analysis capabilities of existing systems and technologies and have become a tipping point in the Big Data epidemic. Indeed, IT has never seen such opportunities or faced such challenges as it does today.

Looking Forward: How DB2 Helps Tame the Big Data Problem

At its core, DB2, and Netezza for that matter, have long had database engines optimized for Big Data, and this is why they are key technologies in the IBM Big Data platform. Most of you aren't new to DB2, so you're likely very familiar with the DB2 database partitioning feature (DB2 DPF). Although the ship vehicle of this technology has changed names a number of times during the last two decades (DB2 PE, DB2 EEE, ICE, Balanced Warehouse, Smart Analytics System, and so on), it's still the same functionality: a shared-nothing massively parallel processing (MPP) as close to linear as you can get scalability engine. As you get to know the ubiquitous Hadoop Big Data engine, you'll quickly realize that IBM has had this same approach for decades: it brings processing to the data (or as the Hadoop people say, "ships function to data") as DB2 DPF uses clusters of servers, with each server in the cluster having its own independent compute resources, and uses a "divide-and-conquer" methodology for scale. (The IBM Hadoop offering is called InfoSphere BigInsights.)

The function-to-data approach is unlike the approach of traditional systems, in which data is fetched from disk and brought to the central CPU location where the algorithm executes. (Popular grid web sites that use your laptop's CPU to process data use this approach, often referred to as the "data-to-function" approach.) In fact, it's because of Big Data that the data-to-function approach started to break down. Nevertheless, DB2 DPF, Netezza, and Hadoop split work into chunks that can be executed on the subset of data and bring this unit of processing to a node in the cluster where data resides.

In fact, the *entire* IBM Big Data platform (more on that in a bit) is MPP-enabled, and we've got more than two decades of experience optimizing workloads to run on MPP run times. Quite simply, the very core of DB2 has been a ready participant in part of the Big Data world for quite some time.

When you look across all of the key features in DB2 10, you see many that were designed to tackle Big Data problems. From new automatic algorithms that yield even higher compression ratios, to DB2 pureXML, to enhancements that enable the INGEST utility to perform even more efficiently when bringing data from files and pipes into DB2 tables, DB2 10 has a number of features that address the volume, variety, and velocity characteristics that are associated with Big Data.

The most direct Big Data enhancements in DB2 10 are associated with the variety characteristic. As mentioned earlier, the Big Data world is filled with unstructured data, the kind of data that most relational DBAs are not used to. This means that data types such as text, XML, image, and audio play a much more important role, and DB2 10 brings important enhancements in the areas that deal with these data types. We'll cover them in the sections that follow.

Faster XML Processing

The ability to deal with XML data natively is a hallmark of the DB2 pureXML technology that's freely available in every DB2 edition. The prefix *pure* represents the core differentiating technologies that DB2 provides for handling XML data.

DB2 pureXML made its debut in the DB2 9 release and provides innovative storage management, indexing, and optimization services for XML data. DB2's XML data type enables you to store well-formed XML documents in their native hierarchical form within the column of a table, without altering the fidelity of the XML document. This XML data is stored on disk in a rich, Document Object Model (DOM)–like parsed tree representation, which translates into high performance and flexibility (other methods force a trade-off between the two). DB2 pureXML services never treat XML data as though it isn't XML data by stuffing it into a large object or shredding it into relational tables. We strongly recommend looking into the DB2 pureXML technology for any XML-related Big Data problem that you might encounter.

At this point, you're thinking that all of the major database players claim to provide native XML support, but in every other implementation that we've examined, there seems to be some trade-off. Either you store your XML in a large object (LOB), which comes with all sorts of consequences (such as having to parse the data each time you want to read it), or you shred it into relational tables, which greatly inhibits the schema flexibility that XML promises or you have to chose from a dizzying array of options. We recommend that when you investigate "native" XML support in a database, you *always* look behind the data type and programming API. When we dug beneath the marketing veneer of some of the better-known databases in the marketplace, we found the pureXML technology in DB2 to be truly unique.

DB2 10 adds some performance fine-tuning techniques to its DB2 pureXML services that are very well suited to Big Data XML.

First, there are improvements in the XML engine for processing several popular types of queries. These include queries that use the XMLTABLE function, nonlinear XQuery queries, queries with early-out join predicates, and queries with a parent axis. If you solve business problems by using these types of queries, you can expect improved performance by simply upgrading to DB2 10.

Second, you can define some new index types on data that's stored using DB2 pureXML services. DB2 10 introduces new formats for indexes on XML data based on the DECIMAL and INTEGER data types. Before DB2 10, you were limited to indexes of type DOUBLE, which didn't provide the native DB2 XML engine with all of the opportunities to achieve the highest performance possible. DB2 10 also enables you to define indexes over FN:UPPER_CASE XML functions, resulting in fast case-insensitive searches of your XML data. Indexes can also be defined over FN:EXISTS functions, thereby speeding up queries that search for a particular element in an XML column.

Finally, Java programmers can now take advantage of the more compact binary XML (XDBX) format to speed up the transfer of XML data between a Java application and the DB2 10 server.

Efficient Text Search

Computer-generated logs, business correspondence, text documents, and other forms of text are ubiquitous in a Big Data world. Dealing with text data that's stored in DB2 gets a boost of simplicity in DB2 10.

In DB2, creating and maintaining text search indexes is the job of the Text Search service, which, at times, can be a resource-consuming task that has the potential to interfere with other operations on the database server. You could schedule this service around peak workloads, but that involves work to tune those schedules. DB2 10 enables you to host the Text Search service on a separate server that gets dedicated resources and doesn't interfere with other DB2 work. This option is especially useful in partitioned database environments; not only does it alleviate resource contention, but it also facilitates the distribution of text queries across a DB2 cluster.

DB2 10 now supports *fuzzy* searches. Google is a great example of the power of the fuzzy search. Google uses its stored searches with fuzzy search techniques to suggest what you might be looking for, even when you mistype. This is exactly what the fuzzy search capability in DB2 10 does: it suggests words whose spelling is similar to the search term.

Proximity search is another neat new DB2 10 feature. It returns documents with target strings that are located within a specified distance of one other.

For example, perhaps you're trying to locate the loyalty ID within a web form–submitted comment that's part of a sentence describing a missing air miles request. For those who need to search text in the Japanese, Korean, and Chinese languages, DB2 10 now comes with specific dictionaries that are used to parse words within a sequence of characters.

The DB2 10 Resource Description Framework: A Good Thing that Comes in Threes

The explosion of the Internet's popularity and the proliferation of web resources have caused many people to recognize the need for a cohesive framework for managing metadata in such a vast sea of resources. For example, a simple web page might have a title, an author, creation and modification dates, and attribution information, all of which can be of significant value if machines could be enabled to search for and discover resources on the web. The ability of computers to use such metadata to understand information about web resources is the idea behind the *Semantic Web*. The Resource Description Framework (RDF) is a W3C standard for describing web resources. RDF describes web resources in the form of *subject-predicate-object*. Consider, for example, "Leon Katsnelson is Canadian" or "Leon Katsnelson knows Paul Zikopoulos." These types of data entities expressed in the form of subject-predicate-object are called *triples*, and they are stored in specialized *triplestore* databases.

DB2 10 can function as a native triplestore database, providing the ability to store and query RDF data. The triplestore itself is implemented as a set of five DB2 tables and includes an access API that's entirely client-based and provide commands and Java interfaces for working with RDF data. DB2 RDF support is shipped as part of a set of Java client-side libraries. Specifically, DB2 RDF is implemented in the `rdfstore.jar` file and a couple of other `jar` files containing its dependencies. Before a Java application can start exploiting the new DB2 RDF functionality, the JENA and ARQ `jar` files need to be downloaded from their open source repositories and all `jar` files are placed in the CLASSPATH. Because the implementation is entirely client-based, DB2 RDF support can be used with older versions of DB2 as well as with DB2 for z/OS servers.

Creating an RDF store in DB2 is a simple matter of executing the CreateRDFStore command from a machine that has DB2 client software:

```
java com.ibm.db2.rdf.store.cmd.CreateRDFStore STORENAME
-db DB2_DBNAME -user DB2User
-password DB2Pass [-host DB2Server] [-port DB2Port] [-schema DB2Schema]
```

Alternatively, if you have existing RDF data, you can use CreateRDFStoreAndLoader to create an RDF store and a special loader file that you can run to actually load the data:

```
java com.ibm.db2.rdf.store.cmd.CreateRDFStoreAndLoader STORENAME
-db DB2_DBNAME … -rdfdata NQUAD_Datafile -storeloadfile STORE_LOADFILE.SQL
```

Make It SPARQL: Getting Data from an RDF Data Store

Let's assume that you've got an RDF data store with some RDF documents in it; now what? Of course, you will want to query the RDF store. The RDF query language is called *SPARQL*. SPARQL is a standard that was devised by the W3C, the same people who developed many of the other standards on which the Web is based. SPARQL is a query language much like SQL, and it's not tied to any particular RDF data store. To use SPARQL, you typically write a Java application and leverage the Jena API. Jena's support for SPARQL is contained in a module called ARQ. And there you have it: These are all of the pieces that you need to work with an RDF data store in DB2. The rest is up to your Java coding skills and imagination.

To get started with RDF and SPARQL, we recommend that you take a look at the "Search RDF data with SPARQL" tutorial (http://tinyurl .com/4stuch) on developerWorks. We are also planning to host free classes on BigDataUniversity.com, so be sure to check there too!

DB2 and the IBM Big Data Platform

As advanced as DB2 is, it doesn't address every need you'll encounter in a Big Data world—for that you need a Big Data platform. We figured it would be worthwhile to spend a little time giving you a look at the IBM Big Data platform so you can see the breadth and depth of IBM's approach to Big Data and why so many analysts comment on IBM having a complete vision.

Earlier in this chapter, we defined Big Data using three key characteristics: *volume, variety*, and *velocity*. As a relational database management system, DB2's ability to handle XML data is unmatched in the industry. Its ability to search text fields is also very advanced. These qualities have enabled DB2 customers to extend the function of DB2 well beyond traditional transaction processing and data warehousing tasks.

There's no question that DB2 can process tremendous volumes of data, and that it's especially adept at dealing with data that we would term *value rich*. Transaction records from a point-of-sale (POS) system, in which every recent record holds information that is critical to the business, are an example of value-rich data.

Perhaps the largest subset of Big Data, however, has a much lower concentration of value (at least initially)—for example, logs containing routing information for every session, or ten years' worth of POS data, or terabytes of Twitter posts. This type of data has discovery potential and might contain some amazing new insights. One challenge in the Big Data world is the need to process a lot more data to get to value; hundreds of TBs instead of GBs, PBs instead of TBs. Is DB2 the best tool for processing huge volumes of data that is sparse in value and largely unstructured? We think that there are better tools for this kind of job and that they complement one another; in the future, the IT landscape will be characterized by a mixture of different database engines, each optimized for specific kinds of data or tasks.

You might have heard of *Apache Hadoop*. This is a good example of such a tool. A popular use of Apache Hadoop is processing very large data sets with the goal of enriching information content and loading it into a traditional data warehousing system (often called *dynamic extract, transform, and load* [ETL]). Other uses include sessionization of clickstreams and online database archives. In the end, the most successful, agile, and impactful organizations are going to deploy a platform for Big Data, not a product. Within that platform will be multiple tools, and picking the right tool for the job is going to yield the best results.

Many people explicitly associate Big Data with the Apache Hadoop project and its ecosystem, which contains what's referred to as "NoSQL databases." (NoSQL doesn't mean "no SQL"; it means "not only SQL.") What's more, there are some that believe that Big Data means the end of SQL-based relational database systems—that newer technologies (such as *NoSQL* databases) will somehow replace the need for traditional databases engines. We're not going to dwell on why we think that this is impossible. Just ask yourself, "What are we trying to accomplish?" and "What kind of data do we need to address the business problem that we are trying to solve?" What you're going to find is that your business problem involves a mixture of data, and you'll end up combining a number of different approaches to tackle it.

In the SQL world, consistency is of utmost importance, and it's baked into relational databases; for this reason, we sometimes nickname relational databases *schema first*. NoSQL databases worry about consistency after that fact; they don't subscribe to all of the ACID (atomic, consistent, isolated, and durable) properties of the relational world. NoSQL databases are sometimes referred to as *schema later*. It's a great example of why both technologies are needed and why neither is going away. If it's a transaction order, statement, or record, we're quite certain that consistency matters. But if you're trolling through log data and applying sessionization techniques to discover why someone abandoned her online shopping cart, or loading tweets, we're sure that consistency isn't as important.

The IBM Big Data Platform

IBM's approach to Big Data is very different; it's based on a more comprehensive and holistic view of the Big Data challenges and opportunities that your organization is facing today. IBM's approach is also based on the need to integrate Big Data technologies rather than rip and replace the entire IT infrastructure of the enterprise. To achieve that, IBM has developed a platform with the following offerings:

- InfoSphere Streams to process data in motion
- InfoSphere BigInsights (an embraced open source Apache Hadoop implementation that's extended to make it more enterprise-ready) to process data at rest
- Data warehousing technologies such as IBM Smart Analytics System and Netezza to process data at rest
- Services to integrate various data domains and the Information Management infrastructure

Figure 7-1 gives you a bird's eye view of the IBM Big Data platform, showing both its comprehensiveness and reach.

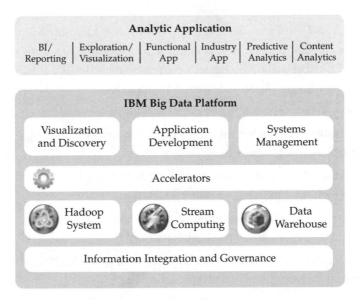

Figure 7-1   *The IBM Big Data platform*

Because the Hadoop world is not built on ease-of-use, accelerators are wrapped around the IBM Big Data platform so that you can get going faster. There are toolkits (either planned or available) that put you in the driver's seat for text extraction, call detail record (CDR) accelerators for in-motion data, and much more. It's a powerful platform, and analysts have taken notice.

Hadoop for the "DB2 Person"

Because Apache Hadoop carries such a strong association with Big Data, and *Hadoop* might even be a new term for you, we think that a brief overview is in order. Although entire books are dedicated to the Hadoop technology, we want to introduce this new world in a way that makes sense to a DB2 person. If you want to learn more than what we cover in this section, check out www.BigDataUniversity.com; this is the best *free* "at your place, at your pace" learning resource on this topic around. Most of the instruction is done through easy-to-follow videos, and you can practice the skills that you have learned using the free products that are provided.

Hadoop is an open source project managed by the Apache Software Foundation. Describing Hadoop as a project is a little misleading. In reality, it is a collection of very complex projects and related subprojects that create a comprehensive ecosystem for processing very large data sets. At Hadoop's core is *Hadoop Distributed File System* (HDFS) and Hadoop MapReduce (a framework for distributing and executing processing tasks over clusters of servers). The rich Hadoop ecosystem currently includes the following components (according to Apache Software Foundation):

- **Avro**   A data serialization system (avro.apache.org/)
- **Cassandra**   A scalable multimaster database with no single points of failure (cassandra.apache.org/)
- **Chukwa**   A data collection system for managing large distributed systems (incubator.apache.org/chukwa/)
- **HBase**   A scalable, distributed database that supports structured data storage for large tables (hbase.apache.org/)
- **Hive**   A data warehouse infrastructure that provides data summarization and ad hoc querying (hive.apache.org/)
- **Mahout**   A scalable machine learning and data mining library (mahout .apache.org/)

- **Pig**   A high-level data-flow language and execution framework for parallel computation (pig.apache.org/)
- **ZooKeeper**   A high-performance coordination service for distributed applications (zookeeper.apache.org/)

HDFS is quite different from traditional file systems. Like any other file system, it manages the storage and retrieval of files. However, unlike traditional file systems that store entire files on a single computer, files stored in HDFS are distributed across a cluster of computers. A Hadoop computer cluster consists of a *NameNode* that's responsible for managing the Hadoop cluster's metadata and one or more *DataNodes* that hold the data itself. HDFS is not a replacement for (but sits on top of) OS-level file systems.

A typical data file is composed of multiple data blocks, and these blocks are distributed among the data nodes of the cluster. This means that any one file can span the limitations of the space that is available on a single disk drive or server. In other words, HDFS is designed to handle very large files—the larger the better. Because large-scale cluster environments are more prone to failures involving individual components, HDFS is designed to tolerate such failures by replicating blocks throughout the cluster. (You can configure the extent of this replication, but the default behavior is to create three replicas for each file block.) HDFS is fairly easy to expand when more storage is needed; you just add new data nodes to the cluster and rebalance existing data to take advantage of the new data node, a process that is familiar to people using DB2 databases partitioned using DPF.

MapReduce is the framework for performing computations on a Hadoop cluster. We specifically refer to MapReduce processing as "computations" to draw the distinction between distributed query processing in the relational database world and parallelized program execution with MapReduce.

The name "MapReduce" describes the way in which jobs are processed. Each job begins with a set of map tasks that are executed in parallel. Map task outputs are sorted and passed to a set of reduce tasks that are also executed in parallel. The entire process is managed and monitored by the framework, which not only schedules the execution of tasks, but is also able to restart failed tasks. The really interesting part about the MapReduce framework and HDFS is that the execution takes place on DataNodes. This enables the MapReduce framework to schedule execution on those nodes that house the target data, resulting in minimal movement of data across a cluster. This is a key point when you think about how much data is involved.

MapReduce programs are typically written in Java. However, by using Hadoop Streaming (not to be confused with IBM InfoSphere Streams), other programming languages can be used. Building Java MapReduce programs can be quite challenging for many data professionals, especially those in the database world; indeed, it's the Java professional who initially feels most at home in the Hadoop world. Hive provides an SQL-like language, called *HiveQL*, which helps get around the Java domain requirement. You can use HiveQL to query data that is stored in HDFS. When you run HiveQL queries, you're actually creating MapReduce jobs on your Hadoop cluster under the covers.

Before you can use HiveQL, you have to run the corresponding data definition language (DDL) to create tables and the rest of the Hive infrastructure, just as you would in DB2 if you were creating a brand new database. IBM InfoSphere BigInsights offers additional options for leveraging the power of Hadoop without writing Java MapReduce programs. For example, BigInsights offers Jaql, a high-level query language that is designed for processing large data sets. When you execute a Jaql query, it is rewritten as a series of MapReduce jobs for parallelized execution across a BigInsights Hadoop cluster. BigInsights includes an end user spreadsheet-style Big Data visualization toolset called BigSheets. When business analysts perform discovery using BigSheets, it's generating jobs using the Pig language under the covers for you, which in turn execute as MapReduce jobs on the underlying Hadoop cluster.

We've mentioned BigInsights several times. In a nutshell, BigInsights is an enterprise-ready distribution of Apache Hadoop from IBM. IBM has taken the best of the open source Hadoop function and delivered it in a way that is easy to consume and to deploy within the constraints of an enterprise IT environment. We often refer to BigInsights as "embraced and extended" Hadoop. For example, the IBM Hadoop distribution isn't forked, and we maintain Hadoop committers in our lab, but we extend this core functionality with services that IBM knows really well: availability, scalability, security, compression, a rich management toolset, and more.

Moving Data Between Hadoop and DB2

There are a number of integration points between DB2 and BigInsights. For example, there's often a need to bring data residing in a Hadoop cluster into a DB2 warehouse, because, although the warehouse is often a better place for operational reporting, unstructured data in Hadoop can be used to supplement the warehouse data. You can get the data out of a BigInsights cluster into DB2 in two ways: you can have Hadoop efficiently push the data into a data warehouse, or you can have DB2 read data from HDFS.

Pushing data into DB2 is accomplished by using a Jaql job to read data from HDFS and then using JDBC to write the data to a DB2 table. To avoid complications associated with restarting failed tasks, we recommend that you write to a temporary table first, and then copy the temporary table's contents to the target DB2 table.

Pulling data from HDFS into DB2 is accomplished by using a Big Data extension to the DB2 SQL API: the `HdfsRead` and `JaqlSubmit` user-defined functions (UDFs). These UDFs, as their names suggest, read data from files in HDFS and invoke Jaql jobs.

Moving data from DB2 into HDFS is accomplished by using a Jaql job that reads data in DB2 tables through Java Database Connectivity (JDBC). This Jaql job can use multiple JDBC connections to parallelize the read operation. This is especially handy in partitioned database environments; the Jaql job can operate on multiple database partitions in parallel and uses multiple mapper tasks to write to HDFS.

These integration points are very useful, because today's IT budgets don't have the resources or risk tolerance to tear down existing processes just to try something new.

Wrapping It Up

Big Data is a vast new subject that is experiencing a great deal of interest and growth. People with skills in this area are in high demand, and there is a severe shortage of skilled people. To help address this shortage, IBM is sponsoring BigDataUniversity.com, a vendor-independent online education community. We've mentioned it a number of times in this chapter, but we can't stress enough how important it is to understand Big Data, and this is the best place we can think of to start. You can learn more about BigInsights and Streams by reading "Understanding Big Data: Analytics for Enterprise Class Hadoop and Streaming Data" at http://tinyurl.com/88auawg.

8

Ease of Use: The Even More Manageable DB2

It's ironic that in a world where so much press coverage centers around the outsourcing of IT jobs to lower-cost labor centers (such as those found in the BRIC countries—Brazil, Russia, India, and China), the cost of human capital shows nearly double-digit compound annual growth rates (CAGR) when viewed as a percentage of overall IT budgets. In other words, in a world where the cost of folks like us is supposed to be going down, IT is spending more and more money on personnel. And, although we're not complaining, we don't see IT salaries growing year-over-year at double-digit rates, so this must mean that the cost is coming from more and more IT staff required to manage more complex systems.

DB2 has a rich ease-of-use pedigree whose inflection point was DB2 8.2; from that point on, our features really started to turn the industry on its head. From the conversion of many configuration parameters to automatic control, to the self-tuning memory manager (STMM), to a turnkey high availability disaster recovery (HADR) feature, DB2 is one of the easiest databases to use.

We admit that it hasn't always been that way, and this is to your credit. How so? We can remember manually configuring Advanced Program-to-Program Communications (APPC) or Internet Packet Exchange/Sequenced Packet Exchange (IPX/SPX) protocol connections to get a DB2 5 client to talk to a DB2 5 server; it was painful. But back in those days, DB2 was perfecting its core capabilities from an enterprise performance and security perspective. Sure, there were lots of knobs and controls, but what an engine! In DB2

8.2, with the introduction of HADR, the Database Configuration Advisor, Design Advisor, and much more, things really changed. While some vendors had to move from core competencies around ease-of-use to find a way into enterprise-grade database computing, DB2 was moving the other way: no one could question its enterprise-worthiness, but everyone wanted it to be easier to use, and DB2 8.2 was where it really started to shine. For quite some time now, new features that make their way into DB2 have to go through rigorous consumability reviews. In fact, you'll find DB2 at the core of the IBM PureSystems that combine IBM hardware and software with patterns of expertise for a simplified experience. Often referred to as expert integrated systems, it is the consumability and autonomic sensory mechanisms that make it all possible. For example, DB2 has a tuning knob that has it run in SAP mode, WebSphere mode, Cognos mode, and more!.

Today, if you're supporting performance-sensitive systems, you can choose to "drive" DB2 in automatic mode and then quickly shift into manual mode on the fly—just as in today's advanced cars—to take advantage of a lot of fine-tuning opportunities for the task at hand.

Let DB2 tune your system to the best of its abilities; it will look for the optimal database memory heap allocations, set up a backup policy, compress multiple objects, define the aggressiveness and the number of page cleaners and writers, configure the fast communication manager (FCM), automatically manage storage, set up a cluster, and so much more, all on it's own. If you're an expert DBA and "can do all this in your sleep,"…well, sleep a little longer! Let DB2 do most of the work for you and apply your expertise to solving business problems as opposed to administrative ones. If you're relatively new to DB2, this is a great opportunity to gain insight into how DB2 operates, because all of the algorithms behind the ease-of-use features are just expert codified approaches that DB2 experts use.

By reducing administrative overhead, DB2 helps you to focus on solving business problems, instead of managing statistics collection tasks or pruning recovery artifacts from disk.

In this chapter, we outline some of the more important ease-of-use features that are part of DB2 10. Most of these features are covered in detail elsewhere in this book; for example, the suite of DB2 compression technologies, which showcases ease-of-use in every new capability that has been added across releases, is covered in Chapter 2.

The Top Ten: DB2 10 Ease-of-Use Enhancements

Although we don't expect to get a shot at David Letterman's Top Ten List, we do think that listing DB2 10's top ten ease-of-use features (in no particular order) is a good way to give you a quick rundown of those enhancements.

Number 1: Compression Adapts to the Data

In DB2 10, table data can be compressed with *page-level compression dictionaries* in addition to the table-level compression dictionary used in prior DB2 releases; this new feature is referred to as *adaptive compression*. Under this compression scheme, each page of table data has a page-level compression dictionary that takes into account all of the data that exists within the page. Page-level compression dictionaries are automatically maintained as the data changes. This means that DBAs don't need to perform a table reorganization to compress the data on these pages; what's more, if a DBA uses the management-by-intent framework in DB2 to declare that a table is to be optimized for storage, DB2 compresses related objects (such as indexes, XML data, large objects [LOBs], and temporary table spaces) automatically. Details in Chapter 2.

Number 2: Time Travel Query and Temporal Tables

To comply with government regulations and industry standards, many businesses need to preserve the history of data changes. Other businesses need to track the time period during which certain data is considered to be valid from a business perspective.

Before DB2 10, developing your own temporal table support infrastructure was an expensive proposition; it involved technically complex and time-consuming efforts around the coordination of additional tables, triggers, and application logic. Of course, adding more objects to your schema can add complexity and risk to recovery policies as well. By using the DB2 10 temporal table framework, you can enable your business to store and retrieve time-based data without having to build, maintain, and administer a complex temporal infrastructure. Details in Chapter 4.

Number 3: Temperature-Driven Data Placement

In today's database systems, there is a strong tendency for a relatively small proportion of data to be "hot data" and the majority of the data to be "warm or cold data." Current data is often considered to be hot data, but it typically cools with age. *Multi-temperature storage management* represents a considerable challenge to DBAs who want to avoid storing cold data on fast storage. As a data warehouse consumes more storage, optimizing the use of fast storage becomes increasingly important.

DB2 10 empowers you to manage your IT budget more efficiently by configuring your database such that only frequently accessed data (*hot data*) is stored on expensive fast storage, such as solid-state drives (SSDs), and infrequently accessed data (*cold data*) is stored on slower, less expensive storage, such as low-RPM hard disk drives. As hot data "cools down" and is accessed less frequently, you can dynamically and easily move it to slower storage. What's more, there's tooling that allows you to set a business policy to dynamically move data among storage tiers based on age and enhancements to the DB2 Workload Manager to allocate compute resources to queries that are hitting different storage tiers. Details in Chapter 2.

Number 4: Row and Column Access Control

To comply with various government regulations and industry standards from around the world, organizations need to implement procedures and methods to ensure that information is adequately protected. These regulations and standards stipulate that an individual is allowed to access only the subset of information that is needed to perform a specific job. For example, according to the US Health Insurance Portability and Accountability Act (HIPAA), doctors are authorized to view only the medical records of their own patients, not the records of other patients. For information that is stored in relational databases, such requirements put the onus on security administrators to control access to data at the row and column level.

Traditional methods for controlling access to data at the row and column level have relied primarily on building security logic into the applications and burdening the DBA with the task of managing a complex array of views that could reach into the hundreds. In addition to the many security concerns that are inherent to this approach, developing and maintaining security policies in this manner has proven to be a huge burden for administrators and application developers alike. For example, whenever a security policy needs to change, so does the application. DB2 10 introduces a new row and column access control service that helps organizations significantly reduce the cost of developing and maintaining security policies. Details in Chapter 3.

Number 5: Built-in SQL Global Variables

DB2 10 introduces a whack of new SQL global variables to give you more flexibility. For example, you can use one or more of these global variables to express a security rule, such as giving access to a row or a column only when the user connection originates from a specific IP address or host name. We don't cover these in this book, but here is a list of the built-in global variables that have been added in DB2 10:

- **CLIENT_HOST**   Contains the host name of the current client, as returned by the operating system (OS)
- **CLIENT_IPADDR**   Contains the IP address of the current client, as returned by the OS
- **PACKAGE_NAME**   Contains the name of the currently executing package
- **PACKAGE_SCHEMA**   Contains the schema name of the currently executing package
- **PACKAGE_VERSION**   Contains the version identifier of the currently executing package
- **ROUTINE_MODULE**   Contains the module name of the currently executing routine
- **ROUTINE_SCHEMA**   Contains the schema name of the currently executing routine
- **ROUTINE_SPECIFIC_NAME**   Contains the specific name of the currently executing routine
- **ROUTINE_TYPE**   Contains the data type of the currently executing routine
- **TRUSTED_CONTEXT**   Contains the name of the trusted context that was used to establish the current trusted connection

Number 6: Built-in SQL Functions

New DB2 10 SQL functions also give you more flexibility. For example, you can use one or more of these functions to express a security rule, such as giving access to a row or column only when the user is a member of a particular role or group. We list these built-in functions here; they aren't covered elsewhere:

- **VERIFY_ROLE_FOR_USER**   Checks whether a given user is a member of a specific role. It returns 1 when this is true, and 0 otherwise.

- **VERIFY_GROUP_FOR_USER**   Checks whether a given user is a member of a specific group. It returns 1 when this is true, and 0 otherwise.

- **VERIFY_TRUSTED_CONTEXT_ROLE_FOR_USER**   Checks whether a given user has acquired a specific trusted context role. It returns 1 when this is true, and 0 otherwise.

Number 7: Performance

From new kinds of joins, to better multicore parallelism, to better concurrency and availability of range partitioned tables, to data ingest, DB2 10 offers many performance enhancers for your database system. Some require adding a new parameter to your favorite command, and others will get the job done for you in the background, without any effort on your part. Details in Chapter 5.

Number 8: Managing Database Configurations and Recovery

The InfoSphere Optim family of tools is continuously being enhanced to improve your overall database management experience. For example, tooling support has been provided for all of the new capabilities described so far in this chapter. The DB2 10 release includes a new tool called *IBM InfoSphere Optim Configuration Manager*. This tool provides centralized management of database client and server configurations, which enhances audit readiness and helps administrators to manage change, solve problems, and plan for database maintenance. Here are some of its key features:

- Discovering and tracking changes to connection or driver properties, host name, IP address, user ID, and client version information

- Discovering and tracking changes to configuration parameters and database objects, security, and storage

- Tracking client access to data servers, including enforcing and redirecting database connections for migrations, load balancing, and problem isolation

Although the feature is not new in DB2 10, it's worth noting that the DB2 Advanced Recovery Solutions toolkit contains a rich suite of products that DBAs are going to love when the pressure is on to adhere to SLA-governed recovery point and recovery time objectives. The DB2 Advanced Recovery Solutions toolkit includes the following tools:

- **DB2 Merge Backup**   Improves the speed of your backup and recovery processes and minimizes application impact.

- **DB2 Recovery Expert**   Enables faster recovery with finer granularity, while protecting your critical business data. It empowers DBAs to eliminate data errors before they compound into costly business mistakes, and to track and report data changes in response to auditing requests.

- **Optim High Performance Unload**   Quickly extracts large amounts of data with minimal impact on system productivity. It can be used for full data and system migrations from one DB2 instance to another.

In short, the DB2 Advanced Recovery Solutions toolkit enhances your existing disaster recovery strategy and increases the availability of your database. It enables DBAs to perform targeted analyses and streamlines recovery operations. It helps to answer questions like these: What happened? Who did it? When did it happen? It enriches native DB2 recovery capabilities with the ability to recover individual database objects, potentially avoiding the need to perform full-scale disaster recovery.

The DB2 Merge Backup toolset is a relatively new offering (to the DB2-supported distributed platforms) that enables you to speed up DB2 backups on your production servers and to have full current backups available with much shorter restore times. DB2 Merge Backup combines incremental and delta backups with the latest full backup to create a new full and current backup without actually taking a new full backup and slowing down your production system. All of this processing runs outside and independently of the current DB2 process. If a restore operation is required later, DB2 Merge Backup can help to speed up the recovery process. Details are on the Web at http://tinyurl.com/cdjfxkb.

Number 9: Tools Unite!

As part of the ongoing effort to simplify the overall user experience and deliver more value to our Optim customers, the latest release of the no-charge Data Studio product that shipped in October 2011 combines all of the features and functions of four different tools into one comprehensive product. Data Studio 3.1 combines the latest features and functions of Optim Database Administrator (ODA), Optim Development Studio (ODS), Optim Data Studio, and Data Studio Health Monitor. The result is a powerful, integrated product for application development and database administration that's available at *no charge* for all users of DB2 for Linux, UNIX, and Windows. Learn about this by reading the free Getting Started with IBM Data Studio for DB2 ebook (http://tinyurl.com/2782g76).

Number 10: HADR Delay and Log Spool Are Cool

We *love* these features; well, to be honest, we love a lot of what DB2 10 brings to HADR. They enable you to create a time delay for log replay on a standby (of which there can be more than one in DB2 10), thereby creating a "buffer" to avert human error or data corruptions. For example, suppose you have a production system with HADR and you add another standby to the cluster; this new standby is always 30 minutes behind the primary with respect to data flow. If an errant application starts to change everyone's pay to zero (don't laugh; we've seen it happen), you've got time to prevent the errant transaction from being replayed on the standby. Details in Chapter 6.

9

The Ultimate Elastic Operating Model: DB2 in the Cloud

Judging by the amount of ink that has been dedicated to the topic, we can safely assume that there's no hotter area of IT right now than Cloud computing (perhaps Big Data, and it's fair to say they are related). Spurred by the well-documented successes of large-scale Internet companies and tens of thousands of startups, both large and small organizations want to take advantage of the same technology and operating models. In a world of severely constrained capital spending and ever-increasing demands to "do more with less," no IT leader can afford to ignore the Cloud promise of the *Pay-As-You-Go* and *Pay-Only-for-What-You-Use* models.

The move to Cloud computing is a major transitional undertaking that's often driven by an organization's CFO or CIO. After all, Cloud computing is a pervasive and fundamental shift in the way an organization's IT capabilities are delivered.

In a traditional IT scenario, systems are provisioned to meet the needs of a specific project, but under the Cloud computing paradigm, a *shared* pool of resources is built in the anticipation of future workloads and their dynamic needs. These resources are subsequently allocated to projects "on demand." The infrastructure is agile, because computer resource delivery matches the task at hand.

At first look, this might not sound like anything new or different from what would be good practice in any organization. What makes Cloud computing

189

so different is the degree of sharing and the level of automation that enables an almost immediate allocation of resources. For example, let's assume that you have to test an emergency fix for a production-level application that runs on DB2 and WebSphere. This application is a third-party product that was dropped into your production environment just over a month ago and has recently started causing problems. How long would it take you to get three servers up-and-running with this stack? Let's assume that you've got Linux already running on these servers. When were they last patched? How long would it take to get them physically moved to your approved security zone? Cabled up? And so on. In many cases, just filling out the request forms and locating the servers can gobble up days, weeks, or more.

Try to imagine the amount of hands-on and administrative work that would go into setting up this test environment, remembering that you're going to need this environment only for the few hours that it takes to run the necessary QA tests.

Now step back and imagine that you've got an environment in which you can provision the compute services that you need in 20 minutes—*without* the paperwork, meetings, approvals, and so on. No, you're not dreaming; this is a reality that leading organizations are enjoying today by applying a Cloud computing approach to many of their IT needs.

We've seen enough Cloud initiatives to be able to tell you that, although your company is likely to benefit from the Cloud because of the huge potential for cost savings, the *biggest* benefit you'll discover along the way is *business agility*.

Getting to Know Cloud Computing

The National Institute of Standards and Technology (NIST) identified five characteristics that define Cloud computing:

- On-demand self service
- Broad network access
- Resource pooling
- Rapid elasticity
- Measured service

Did you notice that none of these characteristics is technology related? That's by design. Cloud computing *is not* about technology as much as it's about the *delivery and deployment of* technologies that we already use. Cloud computing is not a single deployment methodology either: it's a synergistic combination of several models that provides an agile and efficient framework for how to deploy services in your organization.

You will often hear different adjectives to describe the Cloud. For example, a *public Cloud* is built and operated by a *Cloud service provider (CSP)* that takes on the responsibility to build the data center, stock it with equipment, and operate the entire infrastructure while offering a service to the public on some sort of metered basis (for example, on an hourly basis). Examples of CSPs include Amazon Web Services, IBM Smart Cloud Enterprise, and Rackspace Cloud.

The hallmark value proposition of a CSP is that your organization can transfer the entire cost model to the operational expense (OPEX) side of the ledger by paying only for the infrastructure that you use, and only when you use it.

Let's look at another example that demonstrates the elasticity of the Cloud approach. Assume for a moment that you have a new version of an application that you must put into production, and that this process requires some stress testing to make sure that the application can handle the estimated peak load. Expanding on the earlier example, let's assume that you need a DB2 server, five WebSphere Application Servers, and ten servers to drive a workload pattern that realistically approximates your company's time-of-day usage characteristics. You're expecting this test to last for a week.

Building an environment like this is no small feat. Considering that it will be needed for only a week, the economics of repurposing equipment that you might already have, or purchasing new equipment, makes such a project unpalatable. If you had to purchase this equipment, a budget of $100,000 wouldn't be unreasonable. Of course, the timeline for approvals, purchasing delivery, and setup would likely be weeks, if not months. The alternative? The Cloud! It's a solution with which you can define and power-up such an environment in less than an hour.

In this example, quantifying the associated cost curve might look something like this:

Load Test: Equipment Cost Estimates

	Server description memory, CPU, storage	Servers	Hours	Cost server/ hour	Total
DB2	68.4GB, 8 cores, 1.7TB	1	168	$1.80	$302.40
WebSphere	7.5GB, 2 cores, 850GB	5	168	$0.32	$268.80
Load balancer	1.7GB, 1 core, 160GB	1	168	$0.09	$14.28
Workload driver	1.7GB, 1 core, 160GB	10	168	$0.09	$142.80
Total cost for the week					$728.28

Now consider taking advantage of the Cloud's elastic nature to approximate your daily use patterns with a variance in the number of workload drivers you have at a particular point-in-time in the day. For example, if you're a wealth management business, the IT demands placed on you by your clientele may be such that you need to have all ten servers at the open and close of the stock market (2 hours × 5 days a week), five servers during the business day (5 hours × 5 days a week), and only one server driving workload between market close and the next day open and on weekends to settle the day's trades and final book of business calculations.

Load Test: Equipment Cost Estimates

	Server description memory, CPU, storage	Servers	Hours	Cost server/ hour	Total
DB2	68.4GB, 8 cores, 1.7TB	1	168	$1.80	$302.40
WebSphere	7.5GB, 2 cores, 850GB	5	168	$0.32	$268.80
Load balancer	1.7GB, 1 core, 160GB	1	168	$0.09	$14.28
Workload driver, night/weekend	1.7GB, 1 core, 160GB	1	168	$0.09	$14.28
Workload driver, midday	1.7GB, 1 core, 160GB	4	25	$0.09	$8.50
Workload driver, peak	1.7GB, 1 core, 160GB	9	10	$0.09	$7.65
Total cost for the week					$615.91

Obviously, the same logic and calculations can be applied to the WebSphere servers to reduce costs even further. Notice that these costs are inclusive of all OPEX costs such as power, cooling, depreciation, and so on. This simple example should make it quite clear that the Cloud can offer significant cost savings for projects with short-term requirements or significant variations in workload. It's not unreasonable to replace hundreds of thousands of dollars in CAPEX costs with a few hundred dollars of OPEX costs. However, we've found in our experiences that customers embarking on a Cloud journey for license costs savings end up finding the biggest benefit is reducing the elapsed time associated with getting their projects going from weeks or even months to a couple of hours.

At the same time, you might have also deduced that the Cloud may not be an effective cost-containment option for steady workloads running around the clock—and indeed that can be the case. In such environments, the Cloud really shines for its flexibility and agility; as we previously mentioned, for many organizations, the Cloud's flexibility and agility virtues become the driving agents and a more cherished benefit than cost savings alone.

The other popular Cloud deployment model is called *private Cloud*. Simply put, a private Cloud is IT infrastructure built according to the same principles as a public Cloud but is intended exclusively for the benefit of the enterprise or the organization that is building it. Public Clouds are built by third parties, but private Clouds are built by the organizations that own the IT infrastructure's capital and operating budgets.

A common question that we get is, "How is private Cloud computing any different from what we do in our IT environments today?" Traditionally, IT infrastructure has been sized, procured, and provisioned for the needs of individual projects. Project needs are carefully analyzed. After supporting budgets are approved, vendors are selected, and (eventually) equipment is purchased and deployed. This is often a frustrating process that can take months or even years to complete. That said, the result is a highly optimized environment that represents an excellent fit for the needs of the project.

When building a private Cloud, the needs of any one project are rarely taken into consideration. Instead, pools of generic compute, storage, and networking resources are created in anticipation of future workloads. Resources are virtualized so that they can be assigned on a granular basis, and the operation of these resource pools is highly automated to provide a self-service environment where resources can be rapidly provisioned or deprovisioned without the need for IT involvement.

The result is a highly agile environment that can be used to provide resources in minutes instead of months but that isn't optimized for any particular workload (more on that in a bit). The Cloud might not be the perfect solution in every case, but we recommend that it become one of the tools that you can use to solve the right problem. Mission-critical applications that require a great deal of customization and that have very specific needs might not be a good match for the Cloud. On the other hand, the Cloud approach can be ideal for development and test environments, departmental systems, or any other project for which speed and simplicity of deployment are key.

The DB2 CloudReady Computing Strategy

If and when the decision to embrace Cloud computing is made, database professionals need to understand which of their systems, if any, can be moved to the Cloud and how their operating procedures will change if this were to happen.

The IBM Information Management strategy for DB2 in the Cloud is to make it "ready when you are" if and when a Cloud opportunity presents itself in your enterprise. We collectively refer to all of this work as *DB2 CloudReady*. You can see the four key pillars of DB2 CloudReady in Figure 9-1.

A number of DB2 technologies make it a tremendous fit for the Cloud computing model. Although an in-depth description of these features is well beyond the scope of this book, we're sure that you will find a brief overview helpful.

Virtualization Is Key

Virtualization is at the core of Cloud computing, and DB2 has a long, solid history of supporting virtualization. For many years, virtualization has been synonymous with VMWare; in fact, virtualization first gained widespread use with Intel x86 architectures and VMWare became a very popular virtualization technology for this architecture.

The IBM DB2 development and engineering teams have worked hand-in-hand with VMware experts for years to ensure that when you're running DB2 on this platform, you not only get the top-notch performance and

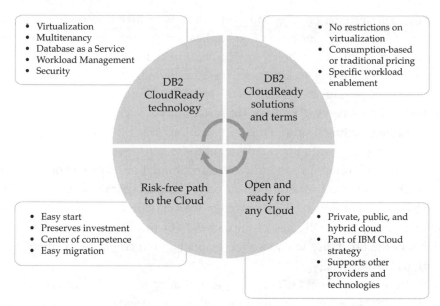

Figure 9-1 *DB2 CloudReady pillars to accelerate Cloud adoption*

reliability you'd expect from DB2, but the opportunity to exploit key features as well, such as the self tuning memory manager (STMM).

If you're considering DB2 in a VMware environment, we recommend that you search the Internet to find a treasure trove of best practices papers, case studies, and other widely available materials. What you'll find is that DB2 virtualized environments are appropriate for demanding production applications, including those of the mission-critical variety, such as SAP systems and more.

Although VMware continues to dominate virtualization within the enterprise, public Clouds are relying more and more on open source hypervisors, such as Xen or KVM, and PowerVM. DB2 is fully supported when running in these virtualized environments.

Database Room to Let: Multitenancy

Multitenancy is a concept that's often mentioned in the context of the Cloud, especially when discussing *Software as a Service (SaaS)*. Multitenancy is a way to deliver services to multiple customers from a single shared instance of an application. Why is multitenancy important? The shared nature of multitenant systems enables SaaS providers to realize economies of scale by operating a single instance of an application to serve an entire customer population. Think about the alternative: having a dedicated application system for each customer would make the SaaS model cost prohibitive. Some enterprise IT organizations deliver their services in a similar fashion and benefit by implementing multitenant systems.

If you're building a multitenant application, *Separation of Concerns (SoC)* is an important consideration. You want to be sure that there's no way for one tenant to monopolize the resources and hinder another customer from achieving committed service levels. And, of course, there's no quicker way to undermine confidence in your system than having one tenant access another tenant's data. DB2 has multiple levels of multitenancy services that give you the flexibility to choose the manner in which you implement this kind of sharing.

Multiple instances of DB2 on a single operating system image is one way in which DB2 helps with multitenancy while assuring SoC. (The number of DB2 instances that you can create, in practice, is limited only by the available computer resources.) In such environments, each instance provides *complete* SoC, both from security and resources points of view. Each DB2 instance operates independently from other instances on the same operating system image, and resource allocation can be fine-tuned and easily managed.

Another SoC tier occurs *within* each DB2 instance, which can have 256 independent databases, thereby providing complete isolation from accidental (or intentional) cross-tenant data access. You should be aware, however, that with this kind of service, when it comes to resource management, the ability to assign resources to a particular database in the instance is not as easy to achieve.

DB2 schemas represent an even more granular level of SoC in DB2's multitenancy repertoire. DB2 schemas provide a great way to separate the name spaces of individual tenants who are sharing a single database. You can create up to 32,000 individual schemas within up to 256 databases, which equates to more than 8 million schemas in a single instance. In other words, if you want to dedicate a separate schema for each customer, you can have as many as 32,000 customers sharing a single database.

Marrying schema-based multitenancy with the ability to tie individual table spaces to the schema makes managing all of the objects and resources of each tenant very easy. For example, you can use table space–level backup to protect data belonging to a particular customer. Or you can easily move

all of the data for a customer from one database to another by using the
db2move command.

Finally, the new DB2 10 row and column access control (RCAC)—covered
in Chapter 3—makes it easier to build applications with an even higher degree of multitenancy. RCAC gives DBAs the ability to segregate data access
by individual rows in a table (and mask it), making it possible to hold data
for multiple tenants in the same table, yet provide sufficient protection from
inadvertent or malicious access to the data by other tenants.

Figure 9-2 summarizes these multitenancy capabilities in DB2 10. If you
want to learn more about DB2 and multitenancy, Raoul Chong's article

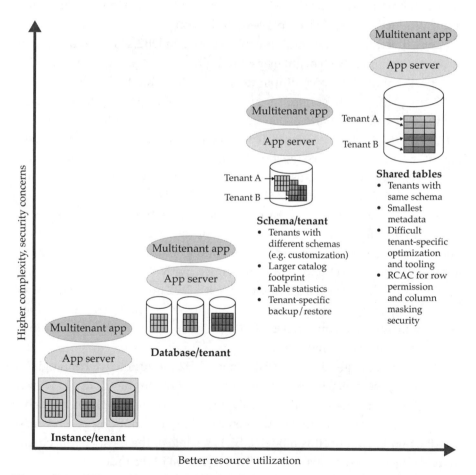

Figure 9-2 *DB2 provides the capability and granularity to address any separation of
concerns issue in a multitenant environment.*

"Designing a Database for Multi-tenancy on the Cloud" (http://tinyurl.com/72xkg9k) is a great place to start.

Application Customization

When discussing multitenancy and SoCs, security is always a key focus. Another critical consideration is the ability to customize the application for each tenant. In some cases, this customization can be limited to the user interface and accomplished through simple things, such as the customization of cascading style sheets (CSS). However, serious SaaS offerings invariably have to allow for schema customization, too. After all, you can almost guarantee that no two companies will have exactly the same way of describing their products, customers, employees, and so on.

Let's illustrate another multitenancy service in DB2, a shared table, with a simple example. We'll begin by assuming that you want to store a number of employee records for multiple tenants in the same table. This is where DB2 pureXML really shines. In such a scenario, a great approach would be to place common parts of the schema into relational columns and all of the attributes that are customizable into a pureXML column. As we talked about in Chapter 7, unlike most other RDBMSs that we know of in the marketplace, DB2 allows the use of different schemas for different XML documents stored in the same XML column. This DB2 multitenancy feature means that you no longer have to create sparse relational records to accommodate customization (this is how some of the largest SaaS vendors do it today). For example, you could have Tenant A defined with 20 attributes for their employee object and Tenant B defined with 50, yet the data for both can reside in the same EMPLOYEE table, with DB2 providing data validation services against each tenant's unique employee schema. And as we have already mentioned, you can use RCAC to ensure security of access for individual rows in the shared table.

We've outlined just a couple of the many DB2 CloudReady technologies—the truth is, we could have written an entire book on the Cloud. However, technology alone doesn't make DB2 the great choice for the Cloud that it has become. As mentioned, first and foremost, Cloud computing is a business model, and to support this model, DB2 has some of the most advanced and liberal CloudReady terms and conditions (T&Cs) in the industry.

Cloud Is a Business Model, so Licensing Matters

Consumption-based pricing is undoubtedly one of the big attractions of Cloud computing: paying only for the resources that you use, and only when you use them. On the other hand, many customers have already procured their own software licenses and would like to bring them into the Cloud. DB2 licensing T&Cs support both models, giving you the ultimate flexibility for Cloud operations. You can pay by the hour for DB2 as part of both the IBM SmartCloud Enterprise and Amazon Web Services offerings, or you can bring your own licenses to the Cloud. This really underscores one of the key values that DB2 delivers to its customer base: its licensing is future-proof.

This is a really important point that we don't want you to miss. When you purchase a DB2 license, you might not know exactly how you will be deploying it. For example, you might decide to change the underlying OS or hardware platform, deploy it in a virtualized environment in your own data center, or run it on a public Cloud. No matter where and how you decide to deploy, you can use your license without having to go back and renegotiate the terms. This is great for smaller shops all the way to companies with large-scale enterprise licensing agreements (ELAs). The renegotiation of terms is a business risk that many customers for a different database technology know all too well. With DB2, if you decide to move from a Windows platform to a Linux platform, and then move from an Intel-powered platform to a Power system, or slip into a VMware environment and then decide to take it to the public Cloud, you can bring along your existing entitlements if you choose to do so.

DB2 can be deployed on a variety of Clouds. IBM SmartCloud Enterprise is a natural choice for customers with established relationships with IBM and DB2, and the Amazon Cloud is well-known in today's marketplace; both of these Clouds support DB2 in *Pay-As-You-Go* or *Bring Your Own License* model.

Some of you might be concerned about being locked into the Cloud. You might be worried that there's no standardization, and that after you place your data behind the API of a particular provider, you'll be at the mercy of that CSP. A number of solutions have emerged to address this issue of Cloud lock-in, most notably, RightScale.com, which delivers a multiple-Cloud management platform. It provides IT organizations with the ability to treat multiple Cloud providers as resource pools and to move processing freely between those pools. For example, you can shift your processing between multiple Amazon Web Services (AWS) regions, or data centers that are run by Rackspace, SoftLayer, Datapipe, or several other vendors.

Hosting a private Cloud as just another resource pool creates the opportunity to implement a hybrid Cloud infrastructure in which the private Cloud is used for steady state workloads, and additional capacity can be procured from a public Cloud during times of peak usage. For example, retailers are going to experience significant increases in compute demands during Black Friday, and both US and Canadian wealth management companies will see peak demands when people rush to maximize their 401K or Registered Retirement Savings Plan (RRSP) contributions.

We've made DB2 available in the RightScale Catalog (http://bit.ly/IBMonRightScale), which hosts a number of multiple Cloud images (images deployable to several different clouds) and system templates that can be deployed through RightScale. All of these templates are easily customizable and contain helper scripts that can be used while operating your DB2 environment. For example, we've created scripts that perform DB2 backup and recovery operations for DB2 Cloud servers. We've also provided scripts and templates that establish HADR clusters for high availability and have experience putting these to good use ourselves on the BigDataUniversity.com web site. RightScale also enables the creation of *deployments*, a collection of systems that operate in concert to implement a particular application. Moreover, some systems, such as application and web servers or load balancers, can be placed into sophisticated scaling arrays that grow and shrink in size based on the workload.

In summary, if you're interested in deploying DB2 in a Cloud environment, you will find a great deal of choice when it comes to both private and public Clouds. A comprehensive collection of templates and scripts on RightScale.com gives you flexible options for deploying and operating complex application environments. RightScale offers a free developer account, and if you're going to participate in the Cloud at your place of work, this is a great way to learn and to understand the system. If you're a DB2 client who's embracing the Cloud, we recommend that you check out RightScale.

IBM Workload Deployer and DB2 in a Private Cloud

In the previous section, we talk about leveraging RightScale to allocate resources transparently on public and private Clouds. Although RightScale is a very popular choice with startups and Internet companies alike, other options are also available for enterprise customers. IBM Workload Deployer (IWD) is of particular interest to customers who need to provision environments that are based on the IBM middleware stack, such as DB2 or WebSphere.

We've learned that some people make the mistake of assuming that IWD is a "Cloud in a box" type system, so we want to tell you that IWD *doesn't* provide a Cloud infrastructure. Rather, as its name suggests, it deploys workloads and systems into a private Cloud infrastructure that has been put in place previously. In other words, your IT team has to build the server, storage, and network infrastructure for a private Cloud, and then IWD can deploy middleware onto this infrastructure.

IWD can deploy two types of environments: *virtual system patterns* and *virtual application patterns*.

Virtual System Patterns

Virtual system pattern are basically collections of virtual servers that closely resemble a similar collection of physical servers that you might be using in your current environment to deliver a particular application. For example, you might have a cluster of five WebSphere servers connected to a two-server DB2 HADR cluster. In this case, IWD could be used to define all of the systems and "wire" them together into what it calls a *system pattern*, which can be used to deliver on the application's requirements.

Such a system pattern is deployed as a collection of virtual machines, each one representing a server in the pattern. IWD makes this a very simple, and, more important, a repeatable process. Each server is created from a server image that represents an expertly configured, tuned, tested, and approved state of the system. Systems are subsequently wired together using script packages. IBM ships several DB2 images as part of the IWD catalog. These images represent a good starting point for creating DB2 images that are appropriate for your organization. If you don't find a DB2 image that fits your needs in the IWD catalog, check out the "DB2 Images for IWD" web site for additional images at http://tinyurl.com/bsafjf8. If you're still not able to find the image that you need, you can send a request to the IBM IM Cloud Computing Center of Competence at imcloud@ca.ibm.com.

The best way to start creating DB2 images that satisfy the requirements of your organization is to clone images in the IWD catalog or those that already exist on the "DB2 Images for IWD" web site. You can then power up an instance of the DB2 server using this cloned image, log in, and configure it just the way you need it. When you're ready, you can save it back to the catalog as your own private image. You can optionally make this new image available to other teams that might need the server characteristics that you have defined. For example, perhaps you created three images and classified them according to their availability characteristics: bronze, silver, and gold. You could repeat this process, creating configurations that satisfy the needs of the teams that will be using DB2 servers on the private Cloud; and since you've got a turnkey deployment infrastructure, you can quickly adapt and match database services on demand to business availability needs.

IBM also ships several predefined topology patterns. These patterns include simple one-server patterns as well as complex environments with multiple WebSphere servers and DB2 HADR cluster configurations. We recommend that you use the system cloning approach to work with these patterns as well.

We started our discussion on DB2 and Cloud computing by emphasizing the fact that Cloud computing is first and foremost a deployment and business model. DB2 images are a good example; these images are not sold as yet another DB2 edition—they represent the same DB2 that you purchase and deploy on bare metal hardware, on virtualized systems, and on public and private Clouds through IWD. It's hard for us to overstate the benefits of this model: It allows DB2 customers to purchase DB2 capacity and to deploy it in whatever way they see fit, and to change the deployment as their needs and the technology evolve, all without any renegotiating contracts or having to initiate any procurement processes.

Virtual Application Patterns

Virtual application patterns are also a higher level of abstraction that represents a collection of components, and these components are virtual middleware services. In the case of a virtual application pattern, you're deploying DB2 as a service (DBaaS), and this capability requires the purchase of some supporting products.

For workloads that are characterized as traditional transactional applications, IBM offers the Transactional Database Pattern, and for applications that need more of a data warehousing flavor, there's the IBM Data Mart Pattern. In both cases, deployment is incredibly simple. All you have to do is specify the name of the database, provide a description, specify whether you intend to use it in a production or preproduction environment, specify the maximum size of the database (the default is 10 GB), and indicate whether or not you want to enable Oracle compatibility. That's it!

At this point, IWD will deploy the DB2 service and configure it to fit your intended use. If you're an experienced DBA, we're willing to bet that you're cringing right now and asking yourself, "How can IWD properly configure DB2 services with so few parameters?" It's important to point out that, although it's certainly possible to use IWD to deploy standalone database services, the most likely use of the DBaaS model is as a persistent store that is part of the overall virtual application pattern. In other words, this capability is designed for rapid development and deployment of database services to developers. Agility and speed of provisioning are the goals, not achieving highly optimized and tuned environments. Those of you who need highly customizable environments that fit into established processes are likely to select DB2 images and virtual system patterns to deliver DB2 servers.

We already mentioned that one of the common misconceptions about IWD is that it's a "Cloud in a box." IWD is best described as a Bring Your Own Hardware (BYOH) Cloud solution where IWD itself is used to provision and manage the IBM middleware in the Cloud environment. At the time this book was written, IBM announced its expert integrated PureSystems platform: a new line of systems that combine hardware and software. The first offering in this platform is the IBM PureApplication System, a platform that integrates several hardware architectures, high-speed networking, and IWD-based software provisioning and management services. What completes these systems (and sets them apart from others) is the extent to which they are customized for particular application workloads. IBM worked with hundreds of enterprise applications and clients to derive optimal highly tailored configurations. You may be asking yourself, "What is the difference between IWD and an IBM PureApplication System?" Both systems deliver the benefits of Cloud-style computing. IWD helps with the provisioning and management of supported software on a customer's prebuilt computer infrastructure. On the other hand, IBM PureApplication Systems reduce the cost and complexities of building such infrastructure by delivering an expertly designed, built, and tested infrastructure based on extensive experience gained from thousands of client engagements.

Wrapping It Up

Choice is a wonderful thing, and DB2 CloudReady capabilities provide many choices. You can choose to deploy DB2 on a number of public Cloud providers; you have multiple choices for deploying DB2 on private Clouds; you have a choice between consumption-based and traditional pricing; and you have a plethora of options for multitenancy. But with choice comes the challenge of matching the available options to your needs. IBM doesn't sell "DB2 for the Cloud." Instead, DB2 is built to be CloudReady. That means that this new version of DB2 is ready to go on the Cloud if you are ready. If you want to go, we'll be there, making DB2 an excellent choice today, regardless of what your future use for Cloud computing might be.

10

DB2 Compatibility for Easy Migration

Although a single SQL language standard defines the core functionality for relational databases, many database products have proprietary language extensions that are not part of the ANSI/ISO SQL standard. They also have custom features and functions that aren't even governed by the SQL standard. As a result, you often find that database products differ in the supported SQL syntax, data types, stored procedural language, concurrency control mechanisms, application interfaces, and other features. Therefore, you can't easily transfer database and application development skills from one database system to another.

The key question is this: Why are certain levels of expertise from the business and development side tied to a single database technology? Don't you want to move your smartest people freely to the most important projects at hand? Shouldn't the underlying technology for those projects be chosen on the basis of "technological fit" rather than "these are the skills I have on deck"? What happens if you want to use a better database technology for the job? What if the ever-increasing burden of service and support from an aggressive vendor makes you want to pursue other avenues? The skills vacuum can present a big obstacle when you try to replatform an existing application from one database product to another.

This landscape changed significantly with DB2 9.7, which introduced a wide range of compatibility features that substantially reduced the time and complexity of replatforming database applications from Oracle to DB2. In fact, we don't even call it "porting" anymore; we call it *enabling*. DB2 9.7 enabled Oracle business logic and schemas to run with a native optimizer (it's not emulation!). This development took the industry by storm, with many customers and analysts claiming that the DB2 Oracle compatibility layer handled around 98 percent of their Oracle code natively.

Even if you don't have Oracle in your "shop," you should take the time to get acquainted with the compatibility features in DB2 9.7 and the extensions in DB2 10. For example, there are new functions and utilities that will make your life easier even if you've never touched an Oracle database; you can call these functions using either the DB2 or the Oracle nomenclature.

DB2 9.7 enabled you to break free from high-cost support contracts associated with many of your Oracle-based applications by including the following extensions to the database engine and utilities that simplify the porting process:

- **Currently committed**   This (now default) locking mechanism keeps applications that are updating data from blocking other applications that are reading data. In addition, any application that is reading data doesn't prevent another application from updating that data. Implementation isn't as "troublesome" from an administrative perspective as what you may be used to with Oracle's Multiversion Read Consistency (MVRC), but you get all of the benefits that are implied by their catchphrase, "Readers don't block writers; writers don't block readers."

- **New data types**   The compatibility of DB2 with other database systems was greatly increased by its support for nonstandard data types, such as NUMBER, VARCHAR2, BOOLEAN, NCHAR, and NVARCHAR2. DB2 9.7 also supports the TIMESTAMP(n) data type, which lets you specify a precision of n (between 0 and 12) for fractions of a second. For example, using TIMESTAMP(12), you can manage timestamps with picosecond precision. DB2 9.7 also offers support for VARRAY types, associative arrays, record types, and constants.

- **Various time, math, and string functions**   Many databases have proprietary functions to manipulate data values in SQL statements. DB2 supports many of these nonstandard functions so that you can more easily move SQL from other database systems to DB2. For example, DB2 9.7 also supports string functions such as LPAD, RPAD, SUBSTR2,

INITCAP, and others, as well as conversion functions such as TO_DATE, TO_NUMBER, TO_CHAR, and TO_TIMESTAMP. Useful functions such as NVL, NVL2, RATIO_TO_REPORT, NEXT_DAY, and others also became available. In short, a long list of functions (string manipulation, date/ time, and more) was added to the set of DB2 functions that you can call through either its DB2 name or the native Oracle name.

- **Nonstandard SQL**   Most database products also have their own SQL dialect with proprietary keywords, operators, and even entire statements. DB2 is compatible with such SQL differences, because it understands and supports features such as the following: the TRUNCATE statement to remove all rows from a table, the ROWNUM and ROWID pseudo-columns, CREATE OR REPLACE statements to replace database objects that already exist, a CONNECT BY syntax to formulate hierarchical and recursive queries, the DUAL dummy table, joins using the plus (+) operator, implicit casting of data types in expressions, and much more.

- **PL/SQL (Procedural Language extensions to Structured Query Language)**   Support for a subset of the Oracle database procedural language (PL/SQL) in procedures, functions, triggers, and as stand-alone statements was added, giving DB2 a native PL/SQL compiler that converts PL/SQL directly into executable instructions for the DB2 runtime engine. Therefore, the procedures, functions, triggers, packages, and other objects that you hand coded in PL/SQL can now run in DB2 with no (or minimal) changes.

- **Package support**   A *PL/SQL package* is a collection of database objects, such as procedures, functions, variables, and data types. A PL/SQL package enables you to define objects that are externally visible, as well as "local" objects that are visible only within the package. Many Oracle applications have an extensive set of PL/SQL packages, and the ability to run these packages natively in DB2 is a cornerstone of DB2's compatibility. DB2 9.7 enabled you to create PL/SQL packages when support for the PACKAGE statement (MODULE is the keyword used for these objects in DB2) was added.

- **Package libraries in DB2**   Several popular package libraries have been ported to DB2. These libraries add functionality to SQL, including capabilities for communicating through messages and alerts; creating, scheduling, and managing jobs; operating on large objects; executing dynamic SQL; working with files on the database server file system; sending e-mail; and more. For example, DB2 provides built-in packages that implement a range of helpful utilities, including the `UTL_FILE` package, which has functions for file manipulation on the database server; the `UTL_MAIL` package, which enables you to send e-mail from SQL statements; and many more.

- **CLP Plus**   If you have worked with Oracle in the past, chances are you've written SQL and command scripts in the SQL*Plus command line processor. Luckily, you can use your existing scripts and skills seamlessly with DB2 through the compatible CLP Plus command line processing tool. CLP Plus supports the same command options, column formatting, variable substitutions, and so on, supported by the SQL*Plus command line processor.

- **And more**   DB2 9.7 provides support for the Oracle Call Interface (OCI) and other features, including a rich set of tools that reduce or eliminate the amount of work that you need to do to re-platform your database.

Our clients' well-publicized Oracle-to-DB2 enablement experiences have been simply amazing! It seems like every quarter we find more and more clients have made the switch in a safe, secure, and cost-effective manner using the DB2 Oracle compatibility technology. Findings indicate that on average, 98 percent of their SQL and PL/SQL code ran natively on DB2 without changes! This high degree of compatibility reduces the full burden of the cost of choosing a new database platform like DB2 (if you're hosting an Oracle application) to a fraction of what it once was. This is good news for you, because you're no longer locked into a single database vendor. Instead, you can move from one database system to another when cost, technical merit, or the vendor relationship makes such a change desirable.

The Quest for 100%: New DB2 10 Compatibility Features

DB2 10 takes compatibility with other database systems even further! The new compatibility features in DB2 10 include several trigger enhancements, locally declared data types and procedures, and various new scalar functions. Let's look at each of these new features in turn.

Getting All the Details on DB2-Oracle Compatibility

We're not going to cover the existing DB2-Oracle compatibility features in this chapter, because we just don't have the space. However, if Oracle enablement in DB2 is new to you, you can access some great material that will get you up-to-speed in no time. Just prepare to be amazed! First, get a copy of the book entitled *Break Free with DB2 9.7: A Tour of Cost-Slashing New Features* at http://tinyurl.com/789a2nv (McGraw-Hill, 2009). We detailed this feature in that edition. Even better, remember the name Serge Rielau, because he's the "who's who" of this technology, and he wrote an excellent article entitled "Run Oracle Applications on DB2 9.7 for Linux, UNIX, and Windows," which you can find at the IBM developerWorks site at http://tinyurl.com/y8ehtdc. The DB2 Information Center (http://publib .boulder.ibm.com/infocenter/db2luw/v9r7/index.jsp) is also a good source of information, as is the corresponding IBM redbook, *Oracle to DB2 Conversion Guide: Compatibility Made Easy* (http://tinyurl.com/88poc6v); this redbook dives deep into the DB2 9.7 compatibility features. Finally, a staple bookmark on this topic is the Oracle to DB2 wiki ("Oracle Application Enablement to DB2 for LUW") at www.oracle2db2wiki.com.

More Flexible Triggers

Triggers in DB2 10 are more flexible and more compatible with other databases. DB2 10 enhancements include PL/SQL triggers that fire once per statement, multiple-event triggers that fire in response to any one of several events, and trigger event predicates.

PL/SQL Triggers that Fire Once per Statement

As you're likely aware, triggers can be defined to fire once per affected row or once per statement that fired the trigger. DB2 10 supports statement-level triggers as compiled triggers or PL/SQL triggers, which wasn't possible in DB2 9.7. That means you can use the FOR EACH STATEMENT option in the CREATE TRIGGER statement for PL/SQL triggers. When such a trigger is fired, the trigger body is executed only once, regardless of the number of rows that are affected by the DML statement that fired the trigger.

Multiple-Event Triggers

Before DB2 10, a database trigger was fired by one of three possible triggering events: an INSERT statement, an UPDATE statement, *or* a DELETE statement. This created a certain amount of complexity, because a trigger could respond only to a single triggering event. If you needed a triggered action regardless of whether a row was being inserted, updated, or deleted, you had to create and maintain three separate triggers.

In DB2 10, you can create *multiple-event triggers*. Multiple events are supported for both row-level triggers (FOR EACH ROW) and statement-level triggers (FOR EACH STATEMENT). Multiple-event triggers and event predicates (discussed in the next section) enable you to write more sophisticated trigger logic or to migrate triggers from other database systems to DB2 with no or minimal changes. (For accuracy, we should note that the multi-event trigger capability was quietly added in DB2 9.7 FP5, but its roll-out party is the DB2 10 release.)

The following code snippet shows part of the data definition language (DDL) for a multiple-event trigger in DB2 10 that will fire in response to any INSERT, UPDATE, or DELETE statement against the PRODUCT table:

```
CREATE TRIGGER logdatawrite
  AFTER INSERT OR DELETE OR UPDATE ON product
  FOR EACH STATEMENT
    BEGIN
      . . .
    END#
```

Notice that we're using the "#" sign as the statement termination character for the CREATE TRIGGER statement. We did this because the semicolon was used to terminate statements within the trigger body.

The following code snippet is another example of a multiple-event trigger. In this case, the trigger will fire whenever a row is deleted or the PRICE or STATUS columns are updated.

```
CREATE TRIGGER productchange
    AFTER UPDATE OF price, status OR DELETE ON product
    REFERENCING NEW AS new OLD AS old
    FOR EACH ROW
      BEGIN
        . . .
        END#
```

If you specify multiple events in a CREATE   TRIGGER statement, the triggered action must be a compound SQL (compiled) statement. Consequently, as of the general availability date of DB2 10, multiple-event triggers are not supported in a partitioned database, which doesn't permit compiled triggers.

Trigger Event Predicates

DB2 10 offers new trigger event predicates that you can use in the body of a trigger to identify the event that fired the trigger. This is particularly helpful in multiple-event triggers, which can be activated by multiple types of DML statements. The three supported event predicates are specified by the keywords UPDATING, INSERTING, and DELETING and can be used wherever a Boolean expression is allowed. For example, you can include these predicates in the WHEN clause or in IF statements to specify different actions depending on the event that fired the trigger.

Consider the following trigger that leverages event predicates associated with IF statements such that different actions are performed in response to different triggering events:

```
CREATE TRIGGER tr_product
  AFTER INSERT OR UPDATE OR DELETE ON product
  REFERENCING NEW AS new OLD AS old
   FOR EACH ROW
     BEGIN
      IF INSERTING THEN ...  END IF;
      IF DELETING OR UPDATING  THEN ...  END IF;
     END#
```

In this trigger, one set of actions is performed if an INSERT statement fires the trigger, and another set of actions is executed if the trigger is activated by an UPDATE or DELETE statement. Before DB2 10, you would have had to create three separate triggers to implement this same logic. The new multievent triggers with event predicates enable you to define and maintain all triggered logic for the PRODUCT table in a single place, which lowers the administrative cost associated with such business logic.

Let's look at one more example of a trigger that uses event predicates:

```
CREATE TRIGGER product_upd_del
  AFTER UPDATE OR DELETE ON product
  REFERENCING NEW AS new OLD AS old  FOR EACH ROW
  WHEN (UPDATING AND new.status = 0) OR (DELETING AND old.status > 0)
```

```
BEGIN
  INSERT INTO prod_review
    SELECT * FROM product p
    WHERE (UPDATING AND p.status = new.status)
      OR (DELETED AND p.group = old.group);
END#
```

In this trigger, event predicates in the WHEN clause ensure that the trigger fires only if the status of a product is changed to 0 or when a product with status > 0 is deleted. In these cases, the trigger inserts certain rows from the PRODUCT table into the PROD_REVIEW table by way of an INSERT statement with a subselect that uses event predicates to select the appropriate rows, regardless of whether an update or delete event is being processed. Finally, we'd be remiss if we didn't mention the new ability to perform UPDATE operations in BEFORE triggers, which created headaches for DB2 database developers in the past.

Locally Declared Data Types and Procedures

In DB2 10, you can *declare* user-defined types (UDTs) and stored procedures that are local to a compiled compound SQL statement in both the PL/SQL and SQL procedural language (SQL/PL). Declared data types and declared stored procedures are different from created data types and created stored procedures, because declared objects don't have entries in the database catalog, can't be manipulated with DDL statements (such as DROP or ALTER), and can only be used within the scope in which they are defined.

Declared procedures are defined and invoked much like created procedures, but the most notable difference is the use of the keywords DECLARE PROCEDURE instead of CREATE PROCEDURE. Moreover, declared procedures can't be external procedures written in Java or C; they must be written in SQL PL or PL/SQL. Finally, declared procedures can be *overloaded*, meaning that you can declare multiple procedures with the same name but with different numbers of arguments. Declared procedures can't return result sets, but they can have OUT parameters, including OUT parameters of type CURSOR.

The following SQL PL code snippet shows a locally declared procedure (you can do the same thing in PL/SQL code):

```
BEGIN
    DECLARE PROCEDURE processProd(pid INTEGER)
       BEGIN
          INSERT INTO outofstockproducts
             SELECT * FROM product WHERE product.id = pID;
          DELETE product WHERE product.id = pID;
       END;
    FOR prodcursor AS
       SELECT id FROM product WHERE inventory = 0;
    DO
       CALL processProd(prodcursor.id);
    END FOR;
END#
```

This procedure takes a product identifier (pid) as an input parameter and performs a certain set of actions on the product with that pid. The procedure is called once for every product whose inventory has dropped to zero.

New Scalar Functions

DB2 10 introduces several new scalar functions that increase its compatibility with other database systems.

The new INSTRB function returns the starting position, in bytes, of one string within another string. For example, the expression INSTRB('Database System','base') returns the value 5, because the search string 'base' starts at the fifth byte of the source string 'Database System'. Determining the position in bytes, rather than in characters, can be particularly useful if you work in code pages with multibyte characters.

Another new DB2 10 function is called TO_SINGLE_BYTE; as its name implies, this function takes a string as input and returns another string in which all multibyte characters are replaced by equivalent single-byte characters. If a multibyte character doesn't have a single-byte equivalent, it remains unchanged.

Finally, the LISTAGG function aggregates a set of strings into a single string by concatenating the input values and, optionally, separating them with a delimiter. Because LISTAGG is an aggregation function, it produces one concatenated string for each group that's generated by a GROUP BY clause.

The following example clarifies how that works. The PRODUCTS table contains five product names in two categories. The SELECT statement groups the products by category and combines the product names in each group into a single, comma-delimited string.

```
CREATE TABLE products(category INT, name VARCHAR(20));

INSERT INTO products VALUES (1, 'Snow Shovel'), (1, 'Ice Scraper'),
          (2, 'Beach Ball'), (2, 'Sun Glasses'), (2, 'Sunscreen');

SELECT category, LISTAGG(name, ', ') AS prodlist
FROM products
GROUP BY category;

CATEGORY    PRODLIST
---------- ----------------------------------
         1 Snow Shovel, Ice Scraper
         2 Beach Ball, Sun Glasses, Sunscreen

 2 record(s) selected.
```

Wrapping It Up

DB2 10 makes it easier than ever to move applications from other databases to DB2. More flexible database triggers, new support for declared procedures and data types, and additional scalar functions stretch the DB2 compatibility value proposition so that an even broader spectrum of applications can run on DB2 virtually unchanged.

Additional Skills Resources

Rely on the wide range of IBM experts, programs, and services that are available to help you take your information management skills to the next level. Participate in our online community through developerWorks. Find whitepapers, videos, demos, DB2 Express downloads, and more. Visit ibm.com/developerworks/data/.

IBM Certification Exams

Find industry-leading professional certification exams, including new certifications for DB2 10.1:

- DB2 10.1 Fundamentals (Exam 610)
- DB2 10.1 Database Administrator for LUW (Exam 611)
- DB2 10.1 Advanced Database Administrator for LUW (Exam 614)

Visit ibm.com/certify for more information and exam availability.

IBM Training

Find cost-effective and green online learning options, such as private online training, as well as traditional classroom education, all taught by our experienced world-class instructors. DB2 10 training includes the following:

- DB2 10.1 for Linux, UNIX, and Windows New Features and Database Migration Considerations
- Fast Path to DB2 10.1 for Experienced Relational DBAs
- DB2 10.1 for Linux, UNIX, and Windows Quickstart for Experienced Relational DBAs

Visit ibm.com/software/data/education for details and course availability.

Information Management Bookstore

Find the electronic version of this book, links to the most informative information management books on the market, along with valuable links and offers to save you money and enhance your skills. Visit ibm.com/software/data/education/bookstore.

IBM Support for DB2 10

Access the award-winning IBM Support Portal to find technical support information for DB2 10, including downloads, notifications, technical documents, flashes, alerts, and more. Visit ibm.com/support.

Stay current on the latest DB2 10 support information through our blog, available at ibm.com/developerworks/mydeveloperworks/blogs/IMSupport/.

Data Management Magazine

IBM Data Management magazine delivers interactive, highly dynamic content, including webinars and video about the technical topics of interest to you. Connect with a community of the world's top information management professionals and a broad range of voices from across the industry. Visit ibmdatamag.com.

Big Data University

Learn SQL, DB2, and other hot technologies at your pace and at your place. Big Data University offers helpful online courses with instructional videos and exercises to help you master new concepts. Course completion is marked with a final exam and a certificate. Visit bigdatauniversity.com.

International DB2 User Group (IDUG)

IDUG is all about community. Through education events, technical resources, unique access to fellow users, product developers, and solution providers, IDUG offers an expansive, dynamic technical support community. IDUG delivers quality education, timely information, and peer-driven product training and utilization that enable DB2 users to achieve organizational business objectives and to drive personal career advancement. Visit idug-db2.com and idug.org.

Join the Conversation

Stay current as DB2 10 evolves by using social media sites to connect to experts and to contribute your voice to the conversation. Visit one or more of the following:

- twitter.com/#!/ibm_db2
- facebook.com/DB2community
- youtube.com/channeldb2
- linkedin.com/groups?gid=3006734
- Smarter Questions Blog   smarterquestions.org/
- Thoughts from Information Management Support blog
  ibm.com/developerworks/mydeveloperworks/blogs/IMSupport/